G000045255

THOMAS HARDY'S WOMEN

In Life and Literature

'O faultless is her dainty form,
And luminous her mind;
She is the God-created norm
Of perfect womankind!'

From the poem: 'The Well-Beloved' by Thomas Hardy

Peter Tait

HALSGROVE

In loving memory
of Joyce Tait (1921–2016)
and Calvert Tait (1924–2008)

'Nobody would ever know the truth about him; what it was he had sought that had so eluded, tantalised and escaped him; what it was that had led him such a dance.'

From the novel: *The Well-Beloved* Pt. 3, Ch. 7

Published in 2020

A CIP catalogue record for this book is available from the British Library.

ISBN: 978 0 85704 349 8

Halsgrove
Halsgrove House,
Ryelands Business Park,
Bagley Road, Wellington,
Somerset TA21 9PZ
Tel: 01823 653777
Fax: 01823 216796
email: sales@halsgrove.com

Part of the Halsgrove group of companies
Information on all Halsgrove titles is available at: www.halsgrove.com

Printed and bound in India by Parksons Graphics

CONTENTS

Preface

This is the third book I have written on Thomas Hardy and the first work of non-fiction, following two novels on Hardy's two wives. The first, *Florence: Mistress of Max Gate,* was based on the life of Florence Hardy, in the years up until 1916, and was written to response to a question that had long intrigued me, namely, how did Florence, a newly married woman, thirty-nine years younger than her husband, cope with the publication of the *Poems of 1912–1913* published so soon after their marriage? How did she make sense of the moving and intensely personal elegies that Hardy had written to Emma when Emma and Thomas had been estranged for more than a decade and certainly for longer than Florence had known him?

A second novel *Emma: A Woman Betrayed* * followed in due course, in an effort to provide some redress to Emma by offering a different perspective on Hardy's first marriage and especially on unravelling the years that overlapped with Florence's appearance on the scene.

Although works of fiction, in their plot and narrative, neither novel strayed far from what is commonly known about Hardy and his wives; nor did either book align itself with some of the speculative theories about Hardy that have appeared in a number of the biographical and literary books and articles, theories that include questions of illegitimate children, possible affairs or liaisons or even about his sexuality. Rather I felt that the content of both books gave credence to Anthony Powell's assertion that *'People think that because a novel's invented, it isn't true. Exactly the reverse is the case. Biography and memoirs can never be wholly true, since they cannot include every conceivable circumstance of what happened. The novel can do that.'*

Without ever being able to prove such a contention, I felt that the two novels came as close to a truth as the available facts would allow. Flirting with the known facts was only ever going to produce a version of what may have happened. I was, however, curious as to whether a non-fiction book could get any closer to discovering more about Thomas Hardy than we already knew.

Having delved into the relationships of Hardy and his wives, I was particularly interested to find out more about Hardy's relationships with other women. I wanted to explore the attitudes and behaviours that were evident elsewhere in his life and fiction and find out how representative they were of Hardy, the man and the writer. In attempting to get beneath the skin of Hardy, I wondered whether the picture I would end up with would have any more validity than the fictional versions. On reflection, I think that by joining yet more dots, a clearer picture of Hardy has emerged although it may still prove to be more interpretative than actual. Getting to see the real Thomas Hardy is never easy, because he made it so, but we should not stop trying to understand him, for that way we can better understand his world, real and fictional. That is the premise of this book.

Acknowledgements: first and foremost, I would like to acknowledge my debt to the major biographers of Thomas Hardy along with those many writers and devotees who have provided such invaluable material and insights on his life and works. The bibliography provided is, however, is by no means exhaustive and I apologise for any significant omissions or oversights. I am grateful to the Dorchester Museum for allowing me access to the Thomas Hardy Memorial collection, to the National Trust and their photographic archive and to the Thomas Hardy Society (not least for their excellent journal). Researching and writing about Hardy is similar to attempting to solve a mystery where much of the evidence has been deliberately destroyed, leaving us to find clues from other sources and most importantly from Hardy's own writing: novels, poems and letters.

I would like to pay particular thanks to Halsgrove Publishing for editing the text, assisting with the illustrations and for the excellent cover design. I have enjoyed the journey in exploring the complex triangle created by Hardy, with himself at one vertice and the women in his life and the women he created at the others.

Finally, thank you to my wife Sarah who has had to live with Hardy and his many women, real and fictional, for longer than is any woman's due. She has been encouraging and supportive and has offered practical help in proof-reading and editing the text as well as offering her own woman's perspective on the aberrant author. Unlike Hardy's own experience of married life, which was deeply flawed and unhappy, I have been blessed.

* Previously published as *Emma; West of Wessex Girl*

Introduction

'A Lover of Women'

'He had, surely, a deeply intuitive understanding of female nature ... Hardy's guileless and ecstatic response to women in life irradiated his writing at every level . . . For Hardy really is a lover of women in the fullest physical sense.'[1]

Thomas Hardy's portrayal of women as victims of circumstance and social convention is one of the distinctive features that set him apart from other nineteenth century novelists. In writing, implicitly or explicitly, about lesbianism, rape, illegitimacy, divorce, adultery and incest, all linked to the wider vulnerability of women, trapped by marriage or societal expectations, he helped expose the hypocrisy of society in its attitudes to women the way few others dared. He became, belatedly, an advocate of women's suffrage and supported Emma in her campaign, counting among his closest friends a significant number of women with feminist interests and aspirations. His most intimate female friends were, in the main, independent, modern women, usually well-connected, and with a spirit and interests not unlike his own. Yet, by contrast, his own nature and his relationships with women were ambivalent.

Hardy often seemed to play the role of the perennial wooer or suitor, as reflected in his writing and letters, a perpetual adolescent as Gittings described him, and while he could be persistent, his ardour usually lapsed over time or was doused, as in the instance of Florence Henniker, although in that instance his amour morphed into a life-long friendship. Yet there is more evidence in his writing, his marriages and his relationships that he saw women either in pragmatic terms, as we may see in his marriage with Florence, or in a strictly utilitarian way, as fuel for his writing. That is not to say that the attachments he formed or his two marriages were without emotion or feeling, but that the idea of marriage, perhaps, appealed more than its actuality. He was a romantic, who espoused the idea of love, but seemed unconvinced by its durability, refuting the idea of romantic love transcending marriage. He had a love of women no doubt, and of beauty, in particular, and all his writing is suffused with a repressed sense of desire and longing, but always with an eye to the inevitability of fate, of time passing, however well-dressed it might appear. Moreover, he was mindful of human foibles, many of which he exposed in the person of his heroines. He did so often by attributing specific traits to womankind, which upset many feminists then and now. He never lost his eye for a beautiful woman, from his early dalliance with Rosamund Tomson until well into his eighties as evidenced by his embarrassing flirtations with Gertrude Bugler. He was always inclined to place beautiful women on a pedestal, imbuing them with a dash of romance and mystery, as this remarkably personal reflection in *The Life* showed:

'That girl in the omnibus had one of those faces of marvellous beauty which are seen casually in the streets but never among one's friends. It was perfect in its softened classicality – a Greek

face translated into English. Moreover, she was fair and her hair pale chestnut. Where do these women come from? Who marries them? Who knows them?'[2]

Hardy always seemed to be chasing these elusive women throughout his life and in his writing and yet, when he captured them in his novels or poems, his response was too often to make them tragic figures, against whom the fates had conspired or who were unattainable, usually because they were dead and therefore could not contradict anything he wrote against them. Bathsheba summed up the lot of women, especially attractive women, as seen by Hardy, when she reflected *'Loving is misery for women always . . . dearly am I beginning to pay for the honour of owning a pretty face.' (Ch. 30)*

Confronted by the inevitable, the predestined, Hardy's women often found themselves powerless, defenceless, with no control over the machinations of their own lives or, indeed, their ultimate fate. They were endlessly subject to the caprice of men or, as Tess found out, to the judgement of the President of the Immortals, powerless to act as greater forces sported with their lives. Better it seemed to be unattractive and plain and to be ignored than to be cast as corks upon the sea of human failing as Hardy was wont to do. If we look at survivors in his fiction, they are more than often, the meek and obsequious. Yet through his heroines we can find moments of deep insight, warmth, humanity and pathos. Hardy had the ability to make us feel for his heroines as they underwent the travails of married life and to see the constraints of their world through fresh eyes.

In his first volume of biography on Thomas Hardy, Gittings cited a review of *The Well-Beloved* which described the novel's lead character as *'A man who all his life is in love with love rather than any particular woman'*. It was a view he argued could be *'the verdict on Hardy himself'*.[3] It is a compelling argument. Hardy's penchant for pretty women and his inability to sustain a long and loving relationship (possibly the exception being with Florence Henniker, largely because she kept him at arm's length) had a good deal to do with his upbringing and the exhortations of his mother. Hardy was not unusual for a writer in compartmentalising his life (no doubt why he saw little wrong in publishing his elegies to Emma in the first year of his marriage to Florence), and seeing his writing and his life as two distinct entities. Insensitivity to causing hurt by slighting women in some way was a part of his person, as his sisters and wives found out, yet when made aware, he could choose to show contrition and guilt. He was single-minded in his work as evident from the clues littered about in his novels and poetry. When Jude commented, *'Every successful man is more or less a selfish man'* (Pt. 6, Ch. 4) it was undoubtedly a comment on Hardy's own life. Today, we would describe Hardy as obsessive, compulsive even, conscious of who he was and mindful of what he was capable of giving in time and affection. He was also aware of what was beyond his capabilities or his emotional range. It was as if his life was always measured in some way and that while the heart was occasionally allowed a little flutter, it was the head, and his writer's ambition, that invariably won through.

On the surface, neither of Hardy's marriages appeared happy or fulfilled, although for different reasons. Apart from non-literary failings by both husband and spouse, of which there were doubtless many, Emma was soured by Hardy's prose, particularly by *Jude the Obscure*, which she detested. Florence, later, was similarly scarred by his poetry, and especially his elegiac poems of 1912-1913. There are various times in his fiction when he casts an unfavourable eye on the state of matrimony. In the annotations he made in the margins of a book given to him by Florence Henniker in 1894, in response to the idea of men being devoted to an ideal of womanhood without properly understanding woman's complex nature, Hardy suggested that, perhaps, *'REAL woman is abhorrent to man? Hence the failure of matrimony?'*[4] Even the women he admired or lavished poems upon, never seemed quite as he wrote of them at the outset after the friendships or relationships had evolved. He could be reserved and touchy, preferring his own company and, famously, if apocryphally, he disliked being touched. Seldom do we see the affectionate side of his nature in either of his marriages, despite Florence writing that he craved affection. He was often nervous and once told Florence that *'he thought he had never grown up'*[5] It is clear that emotionally he was immature; it was not that he did not feel love or affection for either Emma and Florence at times in his married life, but that he was unable to sustain any feeling for another, except through his writing. Emma and Florence both felt betrayed by him, each bearing their own crosses. Emma realised the futility in trying to compete with his heroines, once commenting *'Thomas understands only the women he invents – the others not at all'* while poor Florence was never able to escape from the shadow of the rehabilitated Emma, commenting, *'You have to be dead to be acknowledged'*[6]

The final section of the book looks at another subset of Hardy's women, his heroines – a term loosely applied here to include all his major women characters. Hardy is now in control (although never wholly so, one feels) and shows a remarkable acuity of perception of the female psyche and their helplessness in the light of social issues of the day. From the flighty Fancy Day in *Under the Greenwood Tree* to the darker and more complex character of Arabella in *Jude the Obscure*, Hardy explored a range of female types whose daily lives and conversation were often closely linked with such diverse issues as the stigma of illegitimacy, incest and poverty, but whose lives were ultimately ordered for them by the author. Some of the issues he felt strongly about, such as his views on the sanctity of marriage, took time to filter through his fiction, because of the censorship laws of the time or by what his publishers felt was acceptable (or what was palatable to the reading public). By the time Hardy completed *Jude the Obscure*, however, he had dealt with many of the most contentious issues relating to women, and most importantly, had highlighted their lesser status and freedom in the eyes of society and the law.

Individually, his 'creations' could be capricious and headstrong, gentle and loyal and even though they struggled when they found themselves powerless, victims of fate or circumstance, they are invariably women who demand our attention. Powerlessness in the face of adversity was a hallmark of many of Hardy's heroines. So too was their strength of character that often belied their passive role in a hostile world into which they had been cast. In a review published in 1880 on the publication of *The Trumpet Major*, Havelock Ellis wrote, *'Mr Hardy's way of regarding woman is peculiar and difficult to define, not because it is not a perfectly defensible way, but because it is in a great degree, new. It is . . . far removed from a method, adopted by many distinguished novelists, in which woman are considered as moral forces, centripetal tendencies, providentially adapted to balance the centrifugal tendencies of men.'*[7] If there is a criticism that can be levelled at Hardy's womenfolk, it is that they are not free, but, *'mere playthings of an inscrutable fate'*. More pointed, if we are to believe Hubbard, *' . . . Hardy's women are woof and warp of his thought. They are nothing in themselves. They are merely corks on a current.'*[8] There is a sense of the inevitable denouement to many of his novels, yet the argument that

Hardy didn't allow his heroines any slack and allowed them even less autonomy is more than a little unfair. Throughout his novels, Hardy created women that he chose to love or not love, and over the course of his novels, he does both. Some are notional figures, but others are not and offer robust justification for their life's actions and outcomes. A number of his heroines are invariably influenced by women he had known in his own life, but it is also true that many of the women Hardy befriended after 1890 were expressions of a woman type he had imagined and created – that is, first he drew the picture, his ideal, then later went out and found the model. So Rosamund became Eustacia, Gertrude, Tess and so on.

As well as giving us a new type of woman in fiction, we are constantly, drawn to parallels between the characters and the women in Hardy's life, and also to what was happening at the time that he was writing. Tess may have been his ideal, but he also hankered after women who were more akin with Eustacia, flawed women, made interesting by their failings and imperfections. Rather than being nothing in themselves, to Hardy, they were part of his extended family.

As there is a substantial amount of scholarship on almost all of the heroines, it is useful to start with a caveat or two. With so much already written on all the leading characters of Hardy's novels, the focus of this section is on the character of the heroines and who or what they represented. Several of the heroines, for instance, are directly linked with the women in Hardy's early life; others represent viewpoints and attitudes that Hardy felt strongly about; still others tell us something about Hardy's own romantic views and inclinations. In relating the characters to people Hardy knew and looking at the relevance of the words he placed in their mouths, there will inevitably be some overlap, but the crossover between fact and fiction in Hardy is often hard to separate and some quotations naturally exist in both worlds. A vast resource is, of course, his poetry and its representation of real and fictional women, only lightly touched on in the book. In 1919, in a letter transcribed by Florence for Thomas we are told that *'Speaking generally, there is more autobiography in a hundred lines of Mr Hardy's poetry than in all his novels'*.[9] It is, however, likely that this was a deliberate ploy to deflect questions about Jude in particular. Of course, we should be aware of the importance of Hardy's poetry as a source of information about his relationships with women (and it can seem that an attractive woman had only to look at Hardy to have a poem written of her), but it is the novels' heroines that give us a far better insight into Hardy's own emotions and attitudes, indeed, into his soul.

Hardy always enjoyed the company of women and one suspects, he filled many of his waking hours, whether writing or not, thinking about them – which is no doubt why his heroines take centre stage in most of his novels. He was a strange combination: a cynic on love, yet a romantic, albeit one who eschewed commitment; shy and socially self-conscious, yet in his writing, provocative and controversial. His heroines are the hub of much of his fiction just as the women he knew through kin and friendship shaped and moulded his own life and writing.

Of all the influences on his life, however, none surpassed that of his mother, *'our well-beloved'* as he had once called her. And apart from her abiding presence, of all his other womenfolk, it is surely no surprise knowing what we know of Hardy that it was she and Tess that he loved most of all.

Chapter 1

Jemima Hardy

'O my mother, my mother! Would to God that I could live my life again, and endure for you what you endured for me!'
The Return of the Native [1]

'She was, without question, a remarkable woman. In addition to mastering the art of cookery she learned something of glove and dressmaking, and became as well read as her mother. Early experience of adversity fashioned the sternness she had inherited from her Sweetman grandfather and the courage of his mother into a character of great power, so that throughout her life she was able to dominate her household, including her son Thomas – especially including her son Thomas – in almost every aspect of their lives.'
Robert Gittings [2]

It is fitting that any book on Hardy's women begins with Jemima, not only because she was the first woman in his life, but arguably, the most influential. For the first sixty-four years until her death in 1904, Hardy's mother exerted an unshakeable influence upon him; no other woman came close to shaping his opinion. Her homespun philosophy and trenchant views on marriage, on his relationships with women, (none of whom, it seemed, she approved of) and family were suffused with a deep and abiding pessimism that influenced his writing and left an indelible mark on Hardy that continued throughout his life.

At the age of thirty, Thomas jotted in his notebook that *'Mother's notion (and also mine) – that a figure stands in our van with arm uplifted, to knock us back from any pleasant prospect we indulge in as probable'* [3] – a belief so dark and fatalistic that it goes some considerable way to explaining Hardy's pessimistic world-view. But what made her so and why was she so determined to ensure that the grim realities of life (if understandable from her own impoverished upbringing) should be visited upon the son whose intellect and ability she championed?

Jemima Hardy was born in 1813 in Melbury Osmond, a small hamlet north-west of Dorchester. She was, as Hardy describes her in *The Life* apparently a girl *'of unusual ability and judgement, and an energy that might have carried her to incalculable issues,'* but that she suffered from the early loss of her father when she was nine as well as *'some very stressful experiences of which she could never speak in her mature years without pain'* noting that she had *'mollified her troubles by reading every book she could lay hands on.'* [4]

In this respect, she followed her own mother's example. Elizabeth (Betty) Sweetman was a woman who was also reputedly intelligent and well-read, but whose own prospects had been curtailed by marriage followed soon after by the birth of her first-born and then, in 1822, by the early death of her husband leaving her destitute with several children to bring up on her own.

It was this difficult and impoverished childhood that coloured Jemima's life and that of her children. She grew up quickly, helping her mother by taking on manual chores such as tambouring gloves and learning to cook. We cannot be sure of her appearance as a young girl, but in photographs taken in later life, Jemima exhibits the strong physical features of her family, a firm jawline, aquiline nose and short stature. To this rather severe picture, Hardy added some extra detail of his own from his own memory, noting that his mother's hair was chestnut in colour and her eyes, hazel. Like her own mother, Jemima was a voracious reader although there is little evidence that she could write anything more than her own name. Her years in service, working first for the Honourable Reverend Charles Redlynch, an elderly uncle of the third Earl of Ilchester in Maiden Newton, brought her into a new and more exciting world than she had known and gave her a taste of life outside of the Dorset shires. She soon made herself so useful to her employers that she travelled with the family on their regular sojourns to Weymouth. When time permitted, she read widely, gaining an insight into a life markedly different to that she had known as a child. In 1836, after her employer's death, she joined the even more distinguished household of the Reverend Edward Murray, brother in law of the Earl of Ilchester, grandson of the Duke of Atholl and a renowned scholar and author, where she continued to read and absorb the atmosphere and mores of this very literary household. In 1837, the family took Jemima to London for the season, which made a lasting impression upon her, but soon after her employer took up a new appointment in London and this time, they left Jemima behind.

One consequence of Jemima's time at Stinsford House was that she began to attend church in Stinsford, where the Reverend Murray was the Minister. At some stage, she caught the eye of one of the church musicians, Thomas Hardy, a local builder from Upper Bockhampton. With her hopes of a life in London thwarted and her time in the employment of the Fox-Strangways' relatives ended, Jemima seemed to lose her way and, as had been the case with her own mother, before long she found herself at twenty-six years standing at the altar heavily pregnant alongside her handsome, but somewhat reluctant suitor.

With her own prospects undone both by marriage and the birth of Thomas, Jemima harboured even greater ambitions for her first-born whom she recognised early on as being unnaturally gifted. Perhaps to compensate for the fact that Thomas was an enfeebled and weak baby who was slow to develop physically, Jemima lavished her considerable attention on developing his intellect. She taught him to read (by all accounts, he was reading by the age of three) and passed on her great love of literature. Jemima guided his reading judiciously and he learned to trust her judgement as well as her knowledge of local folk lore, superstitions and country ways that was later to be so omnipresent in many of his novels.

At the age of eight, having been well tutored by his mother, Thomas was deemed of an age to attend the recently opened village school in Lower Bockhampton that had been built by the Lady of the Manor, Julia Augusta Martin with encouragement from the Vicar of Stinsford, Mr Shirley.

This was to spark the first significant incident in Thomas's early life. Mrs Martin took a keen interest in the school that had been set up under her patronage and perhaps not surprisingly was soon drawn to Thomas who, even at this young age, was starting to show considerable promise. Her interest in 'Tommy', however, was not welcomed by Jemima and especially not the physical attentiveness that she lavished upon him, that included sitting Thomas on her knee while caressing and kissing him. What probably impelled Jemima to intervene, however, was not just the overly affectionate nature of Mrs Martin, who she knew had no children of her own and, not unsurprisingly, doted upon her charges and especially the promising Thomas, but rather Thomas's reciprocal fondness for her and the emotional hold Mrs Martin appeared to have over him. Perhaps Jemima was right to feel aggrieved when we read in *The Life*, the admission that Thomas had grown fonder of Mrs Martin than he *'cared to own'*, and that his feelings for her were *'almost that of a lover.'*[5]

More than twenty years later, Thomas received a letter from Julia Augusta Martin asking him to call on her. It had quite an effect on Hardy who recalled that *'she revived throbs of tender feeling in him, and brought back to his memory the thrilling "froufrou" of her four grey flounces when she had used to bend over him, and when they brushed against the font as she entered church on Sundays'* – particularly vivid and sensual memories for a young boy of eight years old.[6]

Despite Jemima's justifiable concerns of the effect Julia Augusta Martin was having on Thomas, her decision to intervene was not without consequence. Her family took the slight personally with the result that Mr Martin withdrew all offers of work on the estate, traditionally a regular source of employment, from Thomas's father, a decision that undoubtedly led to words back at the house at Upper Bockhampton for the extra financial burden it placed on the family. Upset at the forced separation, Thomas saw Mrs Martin once more before her family moved to London when he inveigled himself into a harvest supper held on the estate. According to Hardy's own recollection, when she saw Thomas she rebuked him by saying, *'O Tommy, how is this? I thought you had deserted me,'*[7] something he remembered for the rest of his life.

After Jemima took the young Thomas out of the Church of England school at Kingston Maurward, in late November 1849, she decided to take him to stay with his cousin Martha in Hatfield, who lived some 20 miles to the north of London where she was awaiting the birth of her fifth child. They stayed there over the new year, with Thomas attending the local school for a month and not returning until sometime early in 1850, despite his mother having left his younger sister, Mary, behind at Upper Bockhampton. This period allowed Jemima to reclaim Thomas as her own and further strengthened the intense mother - son relationship that was to have such an enduring impact on Thomas. It also provided Jemima with the opportunity to change schools after her return, which she promptly did, although the new school in Dorchester meant a 3-mile walk (and was run by a non-conformist headmaster, another rebuke to the Church school established by Mrs Martin). Despite the time they had shared together as mother and son, it did little to assuage the young Thomas's sense of loss in being taken away from Mrs Martin's bosom. While it is easy to make too much of this episode as a battle for Thomas's affections, such was the heightened emotion that Thomas felt, and painstakingly recorded in *The Life*, it is hard to dispute Tomalin's assessment that *'for her part, she may not have been fully aware of the effect her kisses and caresses produced on the boy, and would have seen her own enjoyment as innocently maternal. In truth she was giving him his first love affair.'*[8]

As he entered his teens, the relationship between Jemima and Thomas remained uncommonly close, and while both shared a love of reading and literature, it was their walks together and their intuitive understanding, one of the other, that bonded them ever more tightly together. Even at a young age, his mother was encouraging his reading, giving him Dryden's *Virgil* and Johnson's *Rasselas* when he was only eight years old.[9] Throughout his childhood, Jemima made time to spend with Thomas, not afforded with either of his sisters or brother. Yet while none of the other three children enjoyed such a close and intimate relationship with their mother, nor were they saddled with the ambitions she had for her first-born. As Gittings noted in *The Young Thomas Hardy*, Jemima concerned herself with all aspects of his upbringing, *'. . . his moral development as much as his intellectual growth'*[10] while in *The Life* we read that *'A member of his family recalled, even after an interval of sixty years, the innocent glee with which the young Thomas and his mother would set off on various expeditions. They were excellent companions, each having a keen sense of humour and a love of adventure.'*[11]

Not unsurprisingly, there has been some attention paid by scholars to the Oedipal in Hardy's life, but without any revelations other than the pair was particularly close. One writer reflecting on Hardy and D H Lawrence made the dubious claim, especially in regard to Hardy, that *'Hugely important as mothers are for Hardy and Lawrence, even more significant for both writers, and much more extensively represented in their works, are their wives.'*[12] While the latter point might be valid, the first in regards the influence brought to bear upon Hardy is most definitely not.

As a young man Jemima continued to be protective of him, especially around his attractive cousins, while always ambitious that he make his mark in the world. Having encouraged him to go to London in 1862, in order to escape Dorset and better himself, (Thomas had secured a position as a draughtsman for a leading ecclesiastical architect, Arthur Blomfield), Jemima was disappointed when he decided to return to the family home in 1867. Back in Upper Bockhampton, he took up employment in Dorchester, first with Cricks and then when his business was taken over, with George Crickmay, an architect based in Weymouth. She may not have been aware that in his spare time, he was busy writing the manuscript *The Poor Man and the Lady.*

At the same time, Thomas had built an uncommonly close friendship with a neighbour Horace Moule and had also begun walking out with his cousin, Tryphena, having previously tried his luck with at least two of her older sisters. These three years were to be a very significant time in his life, although in the eyes of many biographers, they are still shrouded in mystery and obfuscation.

In 1870, Thomas met Emma Gifford during an architectural commission in Cornwall and when Jemima eventually found out about the burgeoning relationship, her over-protectiveness of her son manifested itself again. By this time, however, Jemima's hold had weakened and Thomas took pains to keep Emma from her. When Thomas eventually married Emma four years later, we do not know what her feelings were although it is certain that she felt Emma was not good enough for Thomas, a view no doubt countered by Emma, who felt that on the contrary, her family was socially superior to the Hardys, coming from a professional rather than a working class background. It was not until 1876, when Thomas eventually brought Emma to his family home to meet his parents, almost two years after they were married, that Jemima's self-fulfilling expectations were able to be given voice. By all accounts, it was not a happy meeting and although Thomas never commented on the breach between the two most important women of his life, it was clear that it had considerable ramifications for his marriage.

By the 1880s, Hardy had grown to accept the difficult truth that he had two households to answer to, that of Emma and that of the family home at Upper Bockhampton presided over by the ever-censorious Jemima. The two women were never to see eye to eye and for the remainder of Jemima's life, relations continued to deteriorate. It was a fraught situation, tolerable at least while Emma enjoyed cordial relations with both of Thomas's sisters, although sadly this state of affairs was not to last either. In a letter to a friend about this time, Emma wrote on the subject, a loosely veiled attack on Thomas and Jemima: *'Interference from other is greatly to be feared – members of either family too often are the causes of estrangement – a woman does not object to be ruled by her husband, so much as she does by a relative at his back – a man seldom cares to control such matters, when in his power, and lets things glide, or throws his balance on the wrong side which is simply a terrible state of affairs, and may affect unfavourably himself in the end.'*[13]

The feud became increasingly bitter when Thomas and Emma moved to Max Gate in 1885 (itself, a victory for Jemima in drawing her son closer to his birthplace and family home), and before long, relations broke down altogether. For the last few years of Jemima's life (and thereafter until Emma died) there was almost no contact between the households. Only Thomas managed to bestride both worlds without too much apparent awkwardness or compromise, but it cannot have been easy.

For the thirty years in which Thomas and Emma were married prior to Jemima's death in 1904, Jemima had become increasingly tetchy. She was, as she made clear, THE Mrs Hardy and Emma an imposter, and her curmudgeonly and prickly nature made any lasting relationship impossible. Thomas was frustrated by the situation, increasingly finding himself having to support one against the other, without upsetting either. There was even less chance of any rapprochement after the mid 1890s when a complete breakdown in relations between Thomas's sister Kate, and Emma meant that any hopes of improving relationships between Bockhampton and Max Gate were effectively over. Jemima had proved to be a formidable adversary for Emma and her effect on the marriage is hard to calculate, but she certainly gave them little tangible support as a couple. The fact that Jemima never lost her mental faculties or strength of personality in many ways made the situation worse and while her memory and knowledge of local families and folklore were often mined by Thomas, he struggled to know how to appease her when she was at her most irascible and demanding.

Jemima had been an overpowering presence in Thomas's life. Her influence was considerable from his early childhood and kept Thomas in check although when away from Bockhampton, away from her thrall, he would not countenance any interference in his personal life or in his writing. She was still able to make her feelings known, however, and was bitterly disappointed when Thomas broke ranks by marrying Emma in the face of her exhortation that *'she wanted them (i.e. her four children) never to marry, but to live together in pairs, son and a daughter, and thus maintain throughout life the unity and interdependence of their childhood.'*[14]

Whether it was a consequence of their mother's wishes or not, of the four children of Thomas and Jemima, Thomas was the only one to marry. What's more, the absence of any children from any of the siblings meant that their line of the family died out with Kate's passing in 1940. We cannot be sure that it was her influence alone that led to Mary, Henry and Kate not marrying, for other factors are invariably at play in such matters. However, knowing that they would be going against their mother's express wishes can hardly have added to the lure of any budding romance they might have ever considered entertaining.

We are never quite sure of how Thomas viewed marriage even though he embraced the institution twice, or of any other reason for their childlessness, medical, deliberate or otherwise. Certainly, we know he was sexually active until his eighties, but the lack of children from either marriage (and ignoring the suggestion he had fathered an illegitimate child when a young man), does suggest the fault may well have lain with him. But it is possible that Hardy was careful not to procreate for another reason, that implied in *Jude the Obscure* when he draws a parallel between the Hardy's and the Fawleys:

'The Fawleys were not made for wedlock: it never seemed to sit well upon us. There's sommat in our blood that won't take kindly to the notion of being bound to do what we do readily enough if not bound. . . .' (Pt. 1, Ch. 11)

The question as to whether Jemima had planted something of such kind in his consciousness is not an unreasonable speculation although there is again, no evidence, that he could not have children or any medical reason why he and Emma should not. But even if her wishes about marriage had been disregarded, one senses the brooding presence of Jemima hovering over Thomas and Emma, ever more cantankerous and more resolved not to like Emma, would have made life even more difficult. No doubt she resented Emma's social airs and graces, especially as, in her view, Emma had little by looks or intelligence to enhance her husband's presence or any reason why she should benefit from his success as a writer. Thomas, for his part, struggled throughout her life to keep the two women apart and indeed, in all of Hardy's letters to Emma, Jemima's name is mentioned only once, and that a bland comment about her health in November, 1903, not long before she died.

Other biographers make similar, if disparate points about Jemima's influence, suggesting that at a sub-conscious level in Hardy's writing, she was always at work. Some observations are not always obvious. One of his biographers, Robert Gittings argued that *'He was attracted again and again by the same type of woman, a replica of his own mother, with the striking features of all the women of the Hand family'*,[15] at the first glance, a curious observation considering how different were Emma and Florence, both physically and in temperament from Jemima (to say nothing about his various muses and heroines). Gittings, however, argued that Thomas's fascination with the Sparks cousins, particularly Martha and Tryphena, was indicative of his attraction to a 'family type' and that this was rooted in his Oedipus personality, noting

'More than most mother-fixed youths, Hardy was falling in love with his mother over and over again, in a physical and consistent way that was a typical part of his almost literal-natured nature.'[16]

While Jemima was alive, Thomas always considered the cottage at Upper Bockhampton 'his home', even if Emma never accompanied him on the visits that he undertook each Sunday while his mother was alive. And yet, strangely, Jemima never felt the same sense of belonging, despite living there for fifty-three years. After the death of Thomas senior, (and despite her son often referring to the cottage as his 'mother's house'), Thomas noted in *The Life* that *'my mother says she looks at the furniture and feels she is nothing to it. All those belonging to it, and the place, are gone, and it is left in her hands, a stranger.'*[17]

In looking for references to Jemima in Hardy's writings, the most obvious is in *The Return of the Native* where Clym Yeobright's mother is invariably identified with Jemima. Reading the novel, one is struck by the devotion shown by Clym, describing his mother as, *'a sublime saint whose radiance even his tenderness for Eustacia could not obscure'* (Bk. 6, Ch. 4) a sentiment that Emma would have begrudgingly identified with. Apart from the close mother-son bond, there are also indications that Thomas realises he should have heeded his mother, especially coming back home (a comment on his own return to Bockhampton from London in 1867) in his relationship with Eustacia (Emma), when she admonishes him: *'Why is it a woman can see from a distance what a man cannot see close'*; and that Clym would have done well to look at his cousin, Thomasin instead. (Bk. 3, Ch. 6)

We do not know whether by this Thomas is alluding to Tryphena Sparks, the youngest of the Sparks cousins, with whom he was particularly close for a number of years, although his mother thoroughly disapproved of the liaison between the two cousins and may even have tried to forbid them from meeting at all. There are other allusions in his writing, including his oblique reference to his mother's family name in *The Hand of Ethelberta*. His most wholesome tribute to his mother, however, was not in character, but place with *The Woodlanders* set where she had been born and grew up, in present-day Melbury Osmond. The story was full of her own story and stories and not surprisingly, many years later, he described it as the story he liked best of all.[18]

After Jemima's death, Thomas picked up his pen to try and encapsulate what his mother had meant to him. While he idealised his parents' courtship in 'A Church Romance', the poem that gives the greatest sense of immediacy is 'After the Last Breathe' an elegy written in the weeks after Jemima's death. It is not a particularly joyful or warm poem – quite the opposite and the overriding impression one gains from reading it is a sense of relief, relief for Jemima, that she has escaped her 'wrongers' and escaped the cell of time:

And yet we feel that something savours well;
We note a dumb relief withheld before;
Our well-beloved is prisoner in the cell
Of Time no more;

But it is relief also for those who had to care for her, minister to her and devote themselves to her. Whether intended or not, one cannot escape the feeling that Thomas was relieved that he no longer had to deal with the repercussions of her constant attacks on Emma. It is no coincidence that he and Emma grew closer in the ensuing months, freed from the watchful eye and sharp tongue of his mother, although the respite, such as it was, was short-lived.

Of his mother, Hardy recorded in *The Life*, *'She had been a woman with an extraordinary store of local memories, reaching back to the days when the ancient ballads were everywhere heard at country feasts, in weaving shops, and at spinning wheels; and her good taste in literature was expressed by the books she selected for her children in circumstances in which opportunities for selection were not numerous.'*[19]

While we do not know if he had written more that had been edited out by Florence, the paucity of what was said was not untypical of Hardy. By ignoring the filial affection that he undoubtedly felt for her, and passing over her influence as a mother, he focused instead, on the influence she had on his education and his writing. He loved her, was devoted to her, but was also very aware of the damage she had done to his relationship with Emma. Despite his filial devotion, and his weekly visits to Upper Bockhampton when they lived at Max Gate, there is only one letter to his mother in all his collected letters and that, a short note of two sentences sent from Rome in 1887, telling his mother that he had travelled along the Appian Way, *'the road by which St Paul came into Rome, as described in the last Chapter of Acts.'* It was signed simply 'TH'.[20]

It was Jemima who encouraged him to read and read well; Jemima who filled his head with traditional stories of family and local history, of folklore and superstitions; and Jemima who made herself indispensible to him, in her own none too subtle way, throughout his life. After the Hardy's had moved to Max Gate, Thomas began seeing more of his mother again, calling on her, always alone where they would talk and she would reminisce. When she was nearly eighty years old, Hardy wrote down her description of the three Hardy's – father, uncle and grandfather – recalled from several years before his own birth: *'They were always hurrying, being rather late, their fiddles and violoncello in green-baize bags under their left arms. They wore top hats, stick-up shirt collars, dark blue coats with great collars and gilt buttons, deep cuffs and black silk "stocks"or neckerchiefs. Had curly hair, and carried their heads to one side as they walked. My grandfather wore drab cloth breeches and buckled shoes, but his sons wore trousers and Wellington boot.'*[21]

It was quite extraordinary detail and an example of how her stories and anecdotes enriched Hardy's writing, especially his depiction of the countryside and what was to become Hardy's 'Wessex.' She was a font of knowledge, of plants and flowers, customs and local gossip. At times, even Thomas was sceptical of what she said to him and on one occasion, having been told that his father's great-great Irish grandmother had 'tankard legs' noted in his diary *'though how my mother should know what the legs of her husband's great-great grandmother were like I cannot tell.'*[22]

In examining Hardy's relationships with women, it is to Jemima that we should keep returning, digging into the little we know. She was overly protective, as mothers sometimes are, ambitious for her bright child, interfering in regards his relationships and quite capable of being awkward and manipulative. Gittings described her world as a *'fortress against the vagaries of other women'*,[23] and one to which Thomas often turned for her observations and simple homilies on life, usually in the form of aphorisms on the wiles of women. But she also imbued him with a sense of fatalism, through local folklore, telling of the old traditions coloured by her own experiences growing up as a pauper relying on parish relief.

After his marriage and the publication of his first novel, Hardy's own life took on a trajectory that she could hardly comprehend. His literary success and his popularity were beyond her and while she was proud of his achievements, she was not one to make a fuss. Possibly always taking on the challenge of trying to impress his mother meant that Hardy remained under her influence throughout his life. Her worldview, her homespun philosophy, her vitality and determination, her deep pessimism regarding human nature and the accommodation of her faith with Thomas's rationalism, bound them like no marriage could ever do.

The last word is from a near neighbour and family friend of the Hardy's who observed that Jemima '*. . .never understood the measure of her son's greatness. Possibly there was no reason why she should. In a lonely cottage on one of the mystical and lonely moors of Dorset the beat of the outer world brought to her no stir nor consequence. But the affection between them was as deep-rooted as the great outlying trees and as natural. No worldly happening shaped their affection, and no worldly affection ever spoiled it.*'[24]

Chapter 2

Mary and Kate Hardy

'If there were in my Kalendar No Emma, Florence, Mary,
What would be my existance now -
A hermit's? – wanderer's, weary? –
How should I live, and how
Near would be death, or far?
'Conjecture'

The family of Thomas senior and Jemima Hardy consisted of four children, with a decade separating the second and third born, dividing the siblings conveniently into two pairs, each similar in temperament and character. Thomas (1840) and Mary (1841) were the first born, both quietly spoken and reserved, and often shy and self-conscious in company, traits that described Mary throughout her lifetime although fame wrought a considerable change in Thomas. They were followed by the more confident and sociable Henry (1851) and Kate (1856). Their coupled lives were such that by the time Henry and Kate reached the early adulthood, their horizons had been widened and their lives inevitably affected by association with the success of their brother. Whatever else happened in their lifetime, the bonds between them and the family hearth remained strong, something Emma deeply resented. Despite any differences they had as a family, Emma invariably found that blood was thicker than water and when necessary, they were capable of closing ranks against her. The secrecy that we associate with Thomas was theirs also, as was their often morbid observation of anniversaries, with Katie in particular, never failing to observe the anniversary of her parents' deaths, or later, that of Mary's, but most significantly, despite his often offhand treatment of them, they never let Thomas down.

As a young boy, Thomas was never short of female company. Apart from the all-pervading influence of his mother, his sister Mary, with whom he shared most of his childhood, was an abiding presence. It is to Mary, therefore, a mere eighteen months younger than her brother that the biographer gravitates, to see the fledgling brother-sister relationship and its effect on the young Thomas.

Mary was born on 21 December 1841 at the cottage at Higher Bockhampton and for her early years, shared a bedroom with Thomas. Being so close in age and knowing how much time they had with each other, it is therefore somewhat strange that Thomas describes his early life as one of solitude and yet that is how he remembered it. Certainly, in reading *The Life* it is as if Mary is almost invisible throughout those early years when they would inevitably have spent considerable time together. Only in the occasional poem do we get some indication of their relationship, such as it was, and yet even then, the impression is fleeting. In 'Middle Age Enthusiasms' a poem Thomas later dedicated to Mary, he writes of a 'sweet place' they once found on a walk, ' a secret light of greens', to which they cried *'We'll often come: We'll come more, noon, eve, everywhen!'* before, in anticipation of Frost's own conclusion in 'The Road Not Taken', writing in the very next line, ' – *We doubted we should ever come again.'* It is an extraordinary poem, not for the recording of time shared, but for the rarity, the paucity of it all. It is as if he is straining to make something of their shared youth, by remarking how transitory it all is, that underneath they shared a deep pessimism, so the line, they *'laughed at life and care'* is followed immediately by another, *'Although we knew no laugh lay there.'*[1] Thomas's deep-felt pessimism, an unwelcome gift from his mother, was never far from the surface.

Mary, like her older brother, was subject to Jemima's ambition for her to rise above the life that she herself had endured from the outset. Jemima was determined that the life in service she could see unfolding for the Spark nieces was not going to do for her children and set out to provide Mary with a proper education. For two years, her parents paid for her to go a private school in Dorchester in order to learn some of the refinements of life, including painting and playing the piano.[2] Later, she spent a further two years at the very successful school run in Dorchester by William Barnes and his wife Julia, a time that fed her love of literature and provided the excellent all-round education that in many ways made her her brother's equal.

Her mother's ambition for Mary led her to approach the Diocesan Training College for Schoolmistresses in Salisbury for a place on their course that she was granted, at no small expense to the family. Teaching was still regarded as an *'essentially working class – or, at best, a lower middle-class occupation'* but it was one of the few occupations open to women, even if Mary was not that enamoured of the prospect of spending her life in a classroom.[3] It was Thomas, by now a confident young man who was asked to accompany Mary to Salisbury, which he duly did. He made sure the experience was not wasted, drawing on the memory when writing *Jude the Obscure* some thirty years later. Mary soon vindicated the family's confidence in her ability when she won a Queen's scholarship at the start of her second year that meant all future fees were waived.

After leaving College she was appointed to a teaching post at a village school in Denchworth, near Oxford where she was so lonely that she implored her mother to allow her younger sister, Kate, now aged six years, to come and live with her – to which Jemima agreed, possibly sensing that the young sister would also fulfil the useful purpose of keeping any possible suitors at bay. It was clear that Mary felt a need to be closer to her family, and that this was more important to her than the opportunity for a social life. By ensuring that she was safe from a life in service, Jemima had bound her to her family, in a way that would prove just as restrictive.

Of Thomas and Mary at this stage, we know very little. We are told that Mary visited Thomas in London once or twice during the time he lived there between 1862 and 1867. They wrote, often in the 1860s, probably infrequently thereafter. Occasionally he noted something she had written that amused him, at one point writing in his diary

'My sister Mary says that women of the past generation have faces now out of fashion. Face expressions have their fashions, like clothes.'[4]

There is mention of her sharing a boating trip to Lulworth in 1868[5], while through their correspondence they shared an interest in art and literature, but otherwise their lives seldom crossed other than for gatherings back at the family home, occasions that would become even more important after Emma appeared upon the scene.

After two years at Denchworth, Mary was appointed to the North Hampshire village of North Waltham which she found to be in a chaotic state. After a disastrous inspection the inspector noted that *'The Present mistress has improved the order and discipline in the School, and I hope the state of the children's attainments will be more satisfactory after she has had time for her exertions to tell upon them.'* The Rector gave her no opportunity to do so, however, and reported on 17 January, 1867 that *'Miss Hardy having failed to satisfy the managers and having entirely lost the affection of the scholars through excess of severity, it was thought expedient that her connexion with the school should cease at the end of the year.'*[6]

It was a galling and humiliating experience for Mary, although Thomas felt being so self-effacing and unassertive that she could, or would, not try to defend her position did not help her. Instead, she was relieved to be back teaching in Dorset by the following year, first in a temporary position for six months at Minterne Magna followed by seven years at the National School at Piddlehinton, nearer to the family home. In 1875 she made her final move, to become headmistress of Bell Street Girls' School in Dorchester where she stayed until retiring in 1897, along with her sister Kate who had joined the school as a junior teacher, both ostensibly to be closer to their ailing mother.

Thomas's relationship with Mary inevitably changed after his marriage. She wrote to Emma and they saw each other at Bockhampton, but seldom socially. Despite her successful career, he felt sorry for her, *'having been doomed to school teaching and organ-playing in this or that village church, during all her active years.'*[7] In his article on her sister Kate, Winslow noted:

'Tom was especially close to Mary, only a year younger than he. In temperament, she was like him – quiet, rather shy, sensitive – and her special talent was painting, as surviving portraits of the family reveal. She was musical as well, and a church organist for a time. Tom's deep affection for Mary is shown in a number of his poems, yet Mary is the most difficult one for us to see and to know: we see her through others' eyes, especially those of Tom and Kate. Mary seems to be only one of the family who could be called lovable.'[8]

What form that deep affection for Mary took is difficult to ascertain with so little evidence to go on. We are led to the conclusion that while Thomas appeared to outwardly love his sister, he did so at a distance. He never appeared to compliment her on her ability as a portrait painter – an area where he could have projected Mary into a little of his limelight – or on her teaching career. Instead, he seemed content enough that her life as a spinster, and as a headmistress, was all she could or should aspire to. He had enough to deal with and she was her own person, even if too much so. Emotional attachment seemed reduced to words rather than time spent and from the 1880s onwards, there are few hints of a closeness that their proximity of birth would suggest.

In many ways, the relationship between Thomas and Mary reflected all his relationships: better on paper, better in the ideal than the reality, in the imagination than in the flesh. He was usually too distracted and gave her little thought or consideration as she made her own way through life, clearly proud of her older brother's achievements, but distanced from them. Tomalin wrote of their relationship that while outwardly devoted to Mary,

'his devotion to her had always been in the style of accepting her love rather than demonstrating his. He had made very little effort to involve her in his life even before the fall-out with Emma and there was a wistfulness in her awareness that he had moved into another world while she had remained in the old one.'[9]

Thomas wrote that even in retirement she lived like a hermit, still under the sway of her mother who she and Kate nursed for the next few years until she died in 1904.[10] Mary was in her early sixties now and her life of service, to her family and teaching had only a little over a decade to run, too late to escape the life she been afforded.

Could Thomas have done anything more for her? He described her as a *'hermit'*, unwilling to travel, uncomfortable away from the family hearth, and that was likely to be the case although he seemed to make little effort to test it. Later, he bought a house for Kate and Mary to share very close to where they taught in Dorchester on the increase in income he enjoyed following *Tess* and buoyed by changes to copyright law in the United States. Otherwise, he seemed to keep Mary at a distance, although this may have been due to her own reticence. His success as a writer potentially opened up a new world that she could have enjoyed, but the evidence is she was not invited to do so.

On the tenth anniversary of Mary's death, in 1925, Thomas wrote in his diary:

'She came into the world . . . and went out . . . and the world is just the same . . . not a ripple on the surface left.'[11]

Yet this sombre postscript on a life half-lived ignored a tumultuous event that happened in 1896, significant for its effects on Mary's health (she retired from her teaching post soon after), but also for its residual effect on her relationship with her brother. The provocation was a letter from Emma accusing Mary of having been a divisive presence in Emma and Thomas's marriage from the very outset. The language Emma uses is extraordinarily vitriolic and while Thomas managed to walk a tightrope thereafter, he must have rued this final breakdown in relations between Emma and the family at Higher Bockhampton.

'Miss Hardy' Emma wrote, *'I dare you or any one to spread evil reports of me – such as that I have been unkind to your brother* ... arguing, to the contrary,*' he has been outrageously unkind to me – which is entirely your fault'*. The letter went on to accuse Mary of drawing Thomas onto her side against Emma, by pandering to his weaknesses and foibles, concluding stridently with the accusatory sentence:

'You are a witch-like creature and quite equal to any amount of evil wishing and speaking – I can imagine you and your mother and sister on your native heath raising a storm on a Walpurgis night.'[12]

Thomas's response was to spend more time with Emma to placate her, but otherwise to ignore the incident. In *The Life* he noted of Mary that she *'never defended herself; and that not from timidity, but indifference to opinion'*[13] but the damage was done and the links between Max Gate and Higher Bockhampton, always tenuous, were finally severed for the remainder of Emma's lifetime.

How the incident impacted on Thomas and Mary is hard to ascertain. It is probable that everyone was so set in their ways that its effect, with all the protagonists now in their sixties, was less than could have been expected. Relations between the two households had been strained for some time and while Thomas must have regretted his wife's outburst, he would likely have sensed some justification for it. Yet Mary's 'crime' would have been no more than wishing to take the side of her brother against his carping wife who seemed not to appreciate her famous brother – a stance that her mother would have encouraged and approved of.

Mary and Katie continued to live their own life, often at odds with that of Thomas. They kept in touch with the Sparks family, especially their cousin Nathan, who disliked Thomas and the superior airs of the 'new' Hardy family. Like Thomas, they must have felt that they were walking a tightrope at times, keeping the balance between their extended family and their famous brother, knowing they were little more than by-standers on his life's trajectory.

Thomas continued to compartmentalise his life, as he always had when caught in the crossfire of strong women. After Emma's death in 1912, all their lives changed significantly. Thomas was consumed with guilt that manifested itself as grief for Emma at the same time that he was redefining his relationship with Florence. Moreover, he was trying to appease the overtures of the Gifford family and particularly Emma's niece, Lillian. It was at this point that the three siblings decided to move from Higher Bockhampton into the house 'Talbothays,' which Henry had built on one of his father's plots of land soon after the old man had died in 1892. For Mary the stay there was a brief one as she died three years later, the first of the siblings to die and the youngest at seventy-four years.

Later poems give us some indication of a certain fondness that Thomas felt towards his sister, albeit in his grieving, which was, after all, where he loved best. His memory of her 'young brown hand' half-way up a tree they had climbed in their childhood, is the most striking image of his elegy, 'Logs on the Hearth – A Memory of a Sister'. More typically, his response to her passing was doleful as expressed in another poem 'In The Garden'. Neither poem, however, gave more than a nostalgic nod at their shared childhood or regret of a life having ended with Mary being almost incidental to the setting and situation. One poem that did offer a memory of childhood was 'Molly Gone' written soon after her death, but only assumed to be about her. In it, there are verses on the *'singing'*, *'planting'* and *'jauntings'* of *'Molly and me'* and while it is explicitly a poem about time past (*'no more summer for Molly and me'*), it gives a glimpse into a happier world of childhood. Even the one poem in which Mary is mentioned by name gives little away. 'Conjecture', published in the 1917 collection, *Moments of Vision* sees Thomas group Mary with Emma and Florence, pondering what his life would have been without them (and like Mary, the life he conjectured could be like that of a hermit) before undoing the whole effect by speculating *'if not them, then perhaps others'* who could have filled his life. Such use of the imagination was hardly flattering to any of the three women, but then Hardy was not thinking of them when he wrote the words, but of himself.[14] Nevertheless, Mary's presence, alongside Emma and Florence does emphasise just how close she was to Thomas in interests as well as years. In his prose, we have fewer clues although it is very likely that he used Mary as the model for Faith, in *The Hand of Ethelberta,* who was a rather insipid character and again, hardly flattering.[15] It has also been suggested elsewhere that she may, at least in part, have been the model used for both Cytherea in *Desperate Remedies* and Elizabeth-Jane in *The Mayor of Casterbridge*.[16]

In many ways, Mary's life was in thrall to that of her mother's wishes. Jemima's influence on each of her children was such that three of her children ended living their lives, as she would have wished, looking after each other. They shared the home at Talbothays, albeit briefly in Mary's instance before she died in 1915, and there was no indication of any serious attempt by any of the three siblings to marry. The one sibling who broke ranks was Thomas and the unhappiness that caused within the family, and particularly with Jemima, was perhaps warning enough to the rest of them.

Thomas had left the family home when Kate was born in 1856 (albeit that he was to return to live at home for a period) and was a successful writer before she had reached adulthood. And yet despite the age gap, Kate was to become an important figure in the family's narrative, outliving all her siblings and immediate family, as well as Thomas's second wife, Florence, and not dying until 1940. While being of a different character and disposition to her older sister, Kate's life followed a similar path to Mary's. She was always the more sociable character and despite her seniority Mary appeared happy to defer to her in family matters. She ran Talbothays, nursed Mary through her final illness and did the same for her brother Henry, several years later. Kate was, by all accounts, popular and jovial and, in the view of one observer of the family, Donald Winslow, the *'most attractive and appealing member of the entire family.'*[17]

Kate's relationship with her older brother, however, was inevitably quite different to that of Mary. By the time Kate was sixteen years old, Thomas had published two novels and was fast acquiring a reputation as a promising young writer. This undoubtedly affected her opinion of her famous sibling as well as distancing him from her. Nor was Thomas averse to using information and insights he had gleaned from his own family; it would be interesting to know how they viewed the publication of *Under the Greenwood Tree* in the summer of 1872.

After school, Kate was destined to follow her elder sister and even spent some time living with Mary at Denchworth when she was only six years old. Back at Bockhampton, she attended a school in Dorchester by the age of ten and in 1871 was attending Dorchester Ladies' School for extra French lessons while helping her sister when time allowed. By 1874, at the age of eighteen years she was working as a pupil teacher at Piddlehinton Mixed National School before following her sister to the Salisbury Teacher Training College in the Close of Salisbury Cathedral, being awarded her teacher's certificate at the end of 1878. Her first teaching post was in the Dorset village of Sandford Orcas, a few miles from Sherborne, where she taught for a number of years before moving back to Dorchester in 1882. She joined the staff at Bell Street School, where Mary was headmistress, as the junior class teacher, and where she remained for the rest of her teaching career. She and Mary shared a house near the school that Thomas had bought for them. After they retired, they rented out the property and lived back in the family home at Bockhampton until Emma died, when they sold the house and joined their brother, Henry, at Talbothays. Kate had less appetite for continuing teaching and although she proved to be a competent teacher after an uncertain start, she decided to retire at the same time that Mary stepped down as headmistress although she was many years younger. Her desire to live a more leisurely life, and the opportunity to pursue her first interest, music, however, was not to be, with much of her time taken up caring for her ailing siblings.

Like Mary, Kate suffered from the fall-out with Emma that affected the whole family and which was exacerbated when they moved back to the family home after living together in Dorchester for many years, particularly while Jemima was alive to stoke the fires. After 1912, relations eased, especially after Thomas's second marriage although he was never particularly hospitable to any of his siblings. Nor do we see much evidence of a close bond between Thomas and Kate, despite the fact that they seemed to get on perfectly cordially, a situation no doubt aided by Kate's relationship with Florence, which was amiable enough. After she had thrown in her lot with Henry and Mary, Kate spent much of her time first nursing Mary, until she died in 1915 and then Henry, who died in the same year as Thomas. She continued to live at Talbothays until her own death in 1940, having reached the age of eighty-four and comfortably outliving all the family. She was comparatively wealthy and after Thomas's death donated a new organ to the church at Stinsford. She later bought Max Gate, which she gave to the National Trust. She enjoyed travelling, touring extensively around the north of England in 1934 and made friends easily. Her chauffeur on her motor trips, Harold Voss recalled *'She was a jovial soul and very fond of a joke'* before stating that *'Kate was my favourite of the Hardy family. I was very fond of her; she was a topping person.'*[18]

'Topping person' she may have been, but despite her efforts she was never particularly close to Thomas. It is likely from what we know that she would have liked a closer relationship with her older brother. After the fall-out with Emma in 1896, along with Mary, she felt unable to visit Max Gate until after Emma died. So for sixteen years, the onus was on Thomas to visit them after they had returned to the family home, which he did regularly while Jemima was still alive, no doubt enduring some sharp words from Emma for doing so. More upsetting, however, was the suggestion that while Kate harboured the desire to be closer to her famous brother, he was less inclined to see her in the same way. A diary entry on 10 February 1916 noted that she had gone to Max Gate to see Thomas and Florence, but 'he did not care about seeing me.'[19] Kate may have been unduly sensitive although two years later, she noted that when she was bringing flowers to the graves at Stinsford, Thomas and Kate Cockerell were looking around the outside of the building but *'either did not, or would not, recognise me.'*[20]

We should not be surprised by Thomas's behaviour. While family was important, he was always particular about keeping the various parts of his life separate, London from Emma, the family from Emma, Emma from his friends. That his sisters hardly feature in his *Life* or in his public life is hardly surprising either. Early on, there was a nod in their direction in *A Pair of Blue Eyes* when Hardy named the two little girls, Kate and Mary, but they were soon returned to anonymity. Given the dramatic changes that took place in Thomas's life it was, perhaps, inevitable that he would leave much of his old life in his wake, including his family. Undoubtedly, his loyalty to his sisters, apparent in the financial support he gave them, remained an essential part of his life, but not something that he could, or would even wish to, invest time in.

After Thomas's death, Kate provided the only link to his life at Higher Bockhampton. Undoubtedly she knew more about Thomas than she cared to tell or place on record.

For this reason, it is fitting that the last word should go to Kate who had seen the metamorphosis of her older brother over the previous half century from fledgling author to national celebrity. Following the opening of Hardy's reconstructed study at Dorchester museum in 1939 and having listened to a number of complimentary eulogies to Thomas, Kate reputedly smiled to herself before exclaiming *'if only they knew.'*[21] It seemed that Hardy had got away with it after all, (whatever 'it' was) and Kate was left as the last of those who had known his 'secrets' before taking them to the grave when she died the following year.

Chapter 3

Emma Hardy

'Mr Hardy had more than twenty years of insults, and apparently enjoyed them very much'[1]

'And there is always this extraordinary idealization of Mrs Hardy – whom he now says, and I think believes, was the sweetest, most gifted, most beautiful woman who ever existed.'[2]

Poor Emma. Even before she was married, Thomas was flirting with his illustrator and disparaging the institution of marriage in his writing. With three novels already behind him, a fourth, *Far from the Madding Crowd*, which contained Bathsheba's pessimistic observation that 'all romances end at marriage', and written during their courtship, was to be published soon after their own marriage. It was not an auspicious beginning.

While the novel ended happily enough for Bathsheba, after she had been suitably humbled, the book is littered with such observations about love and marriage. Emma must have wondered as she read it in its final form, how much of what Thomas had written pertained to them, newly married, or whether, in time, they would be any different from Bathsheba's parents, playing a mock game of continuous courtship to keep their marriage alive.

And it was not only through his writing that Thomas was vacillating, but also in his own nimble affections. In the months leading up to their nuptials, Hardy was showing a tendresse towards Helen Paterson, a young artist who had been commissioned to illustrate *Far from the Madding Crowd*. While the infatuation was brief and one-sided, forty years later in the aftermath of Emma's death (but before his marriage to Florence), Hardy recalled her in a poem entitled 'The Opportunity' dedicated specifically to her memory, which concluded:

Had we mused a little space
At that critical date in the Maytime,
One life had been ours, one place,
Perhaps, till our long cold claytime.

Apart from the slight to both Emma (and Florence who should have been in the forefront of his mind at this time) and setting aside the fact that Miss Paterson in no way encouraged his overtures (indeed, she was soon to marry the writer, William Allingham), it is a disturbing insight into the way that Thomas would commandeer the image or memory of someone he had met and drag it, invariably without their knowledge, into the heart of his poetry.[3]

Emma Lavinia Gifford was born in Plymouth on 24 November, 1840, the daughter of Emma and John Attersoll Gifford, a local solicitor who retired early to live off his wife's private income. She had enjoyed a comfortable upbringing with all the pursuits and privileges of middle-class life, including music lessons and French tuition which she would remind Thomas of throughout their lives to illustrate the social gulf between them. When she was twenty, her family's circumstances suddenly worsened and they moved to Bodmin from where Emma and her sister Helen sought work as governesses. Helen was the more successful, eventually meeting and marrying the Reverend Caddell Holder and moving to St Juliot near Boscastle in Cornwall. Before long, Emma joined her to assist with running the household and to help with parish activities although her passions were not so much the Church, but riding and playing the harmonium.

Thomas and Emma first met at the vicarage of St Juliot in March 1870 when he arrived on architectural business to look at the church, which was understood to be in need of restoration. He was greeted by Emma at the door and over the next few days made her better acquaintance. She was into her thirtieth year when Thomas rescued her from her life of isolation and servitude, which was as he saw it. Emma, however, saw it differently. For from the very start she believed – and made Thomas conscious of the fact – that her upbringing and her education were superior to his and whatever he might achieve in life, nothing would change that. And that it was she, who understood such things, who would support and encourage him to become a writer.

Over the next four years they were to meet sporadically with often-substantial gaps between meetings. For Thomas, in his imagination, Emma was a free spirit, riding across the hills on her beloved mare, Fanny, with her long brown habit flowing behind her. She was an unattached (and therefore to be yearned after), young woman who piqued his interest. It was to be this headstrong, carefree woman that he fell in love with. Once married, however, their relationship soon changed, first into companionship, then a fluctuating friendship, and eventually estrangement until the glorious resurrection of the young Emma after her death. Despite the relatively few weeks in total that they spent in each other's company over the next four years, their memory and the abiding impressions that the time left upon them were to provide the subject matter to which he returned time and again after Emma's death. Meanwhile in those first four years, they kept their romance alive through letter writing.

Several years after Thomas's death, Florence wrote to Howard Bliss about the letters Thomas had written to Emma:

'It was she who burned the letters and she told me he much regretted that at that time and since. She asked him for her letters to him which he had carefully preserved and she burned those too. He told me he thought the letters quite as good as the Browning letters and they might have been published.'[4]

It had all started off so well. In her 'Recollections', written in 1911, not long before her death, Emma recalled her early years and their first meeting with tenderness and affection – and this at the same time that she was writing her bitter denunciations of Thomas in the secret diary entitled somewhat damningly 'What I Think of My Husband'. Her words were warm and effusive and many of her paragraphs of their days spent together, the landscape, what she was wearing and the romance of her riding across the fields while he walked alongside, were tender and evocative. It is little wonder Thomas was overcome with grief and confusion when he discovered both books sitting alongside each other after her death.

Of the first moment of their meeting, she wrote: *'I was immediately arrested by his familiar appearance, as if I had seen him in a dream – his slightly different accent, his soft voice . . .. So I met my husband. I thought him much older than he was. He had a beard, and a rather shabby greatcoat, and had quite a business appearance.'*[5]

Their early days together seemed in retrospect a time that was almost mystical, suffused with a heightened sense of the romantic.

Even her words were warm and nostalgic: *'Scarcely any author and his wife could have had a much more romantic meeting'* before going on to describe the setting and her place in it with a sense of abandonment *'scampering up and down the hills on my beloved mare alone, wanting no protection, the rain going down my back often, and my hair floating on the wind.'*[6]

Of the period that followed, we know surprisingly little other than of his infrequent visits, a meeting in Bath, and her estrangement from St Juliot. They enjoyed a regular correspondence, which had it survived, would have given us an insight into the relationship. From the outset, and despite Emma's later recollections, their interest in each other seemed more companionable than amatory:

'We grew much interested in each other. I found him a perfectly new subject of study and delight and he found a "mine" in me he said.'[7]

He visited again in the summer, finding his young lady in brown of the previous winter having *'metamorphosed into a young lady in summer blue, which suited her fair complexion much better'* and that *'the visit was a most happy one.'*[8]

Whether it was Emma driving the relationship forward, we cannot be sure. Millgate mentions an episode recounted to Florence in which Emma's sister opened letters sent by Hardy to another woman while he was staying at St Juliot which suggest that her sister, at least, was keen for Emma to take this opportunity.[9] From the outset, Emma never saw herself as the lesser person in the relationship and felt that it was she that was making the sacrifice to help this fledgling writer. Even from their first meeting, Emma's relationship with Thomas was practical as well as romantic. It was she that encouraged him to give up his work as an architect's assistant and commit to his writing and she also, who helped him with his manuscripts, either as a copyist (in Thomas's memory) or as a significant contributor to his work (in hers). To Emma at least, theirs was an equal partnership in all senses.

Whether Emma and Thomas understood each other or the commitment that marriage involved was questionable. Over four years, they had seen relatively little of each other and, while Emma commented, *'The rarity of the visits made them highly delightful to both'* it was not necessarily the best preparation for married life.[10]

Thomas, by this stage, was busy writing his fourth novel to be published in book form in November 1874, just two months after his marriage to Emma. Submitted and published in instalments in *Cornhill Magazine* between late 1872 and mid 1874, the novel provides several controversial comments on love and romance which give us some insight into what Hardy at least conjectured about the institution of marriage although Emma, no doubt, was reassured by the book's happy conclusion.

Their marriage in March, 1874 receives a mere four lines in *The Life*, between a paragraph about sending off the manuscript of *Far from the Madding Crowd* and another, telling of its publication. The starkness of the statement, says much for Florence's editorial hand in *The Early Life* and her unwillingness to write expansively or generously about her predecessor:

'The next month Thomas Hardy and Miss Emma Lavinia Gifford were married at St Peter's Elgin Avenue, Paddington, by her uncle Dr E Hamilton Gifford, Canon of Worcester, and afterwards Archdeacon of London'.[11]

Whether his mother's exhortations against marriage were in Thomas's mind as he took his vows, we do not know although it is likely he would have attributed his standing there at the altar as down to the inevitability of where the romance had taken him and his inability to put a halt to proceedings rather than to any contravention of her wishes. Soon after meeting Emma, he had written in *Under the Greenwood Tree*,

'If we be doomed to marry, we marry; if we be doomed to remain single we do.' (Ch. 6) It was a very pessimistic view of marriage and one he returns to again and again in his writing, of the process by which a relationship moves inexorably towards matrimony. Time and again, Hardy writes on the impermanence of love and of marriage happening as the result of circumstance or expectation, not for love in any enduring shape or form. The whole process, instead, is random, as he attempted to explain in the same novel:

'When you've made up your mind to marry, take the first respectable body that comes to hand – she's as good as any other; they be all alike in groundwork: 'tis only in the flourishes there's a difference.' (Ch. 8)

On their honeymoon in Paris, Emma provided an insight into her own character through her diaries, and the contradiction between her shyness, her naivety and her own more privileged background. She noted that people seemed to stare at her in a way that made her ask herself, *'Am I a strange-looking person – or merely picturesque in this hat – women sometimes laugh a short laugh as they pass. Men stare – some stand – some look back or turn, look over their shoulders – look curiously, inquisitively'* before adding *'tenderly without my being mistaken'* while commenting also on the smallness and ugliness of some of the old women and working class people they saw.[12] Yet for all that, they enjoyed their time together although one suspects she would gladly have eschewed the visit to the morgue and having to view three cadavers, a morbid Victorian curiosity of the time that Thomas was keen to indulge in.

Settling back into London, Emma was confronted with a life she was not used to, of running a home for her husband and instead of being a companion in his writing and an equal, of being made to feel increasingly irrelevant. The first indication we get that things are not well in Hardy's writing is through his poetry. How sad for Emma that his first literary reference to her since their wedding was not a celebration of their communion, but a rather despondent poem called 'We Sat at the Window' which referred to their stop in a wet and grey Bournemouth on St Swithun's Day in 1875 and included the lines *'We were irked by the scene, by our own selves; yes'* (which only slightly improved on the original manuscript which read *'each other'* instead of *'own selves.'*)

The inspiration and energy that Emma provided as a fresh young woman full of gaiety had started to fade as she was transported further from her natural habitat in Cornwall. The countryside around Boscastle had been part of the allure to Hardy who placed considerable importance on his characters belonging to their surroundings. Before long, her interest in writing and literature, initially a point of commonality, became an irritation; her Anglican faith, her class-consciousness, her plainness, all became more pronounced as time passed, stripping the marriage of much of its essence. It seems even within the year of her marriage, her biographers are starting to tire of her – Tomalin alludes to Emma's *'inconsequentiality and chatter'* that could be wearisome becoming apparent as early as the first few months of marriage.[13] But the unravelling of their precipitous decision to marry was to take the rest of their lives, and beyond.

After a trip to the continent, one of three taken during the first ten years of their marriage, Emma and Thomas settled briefly in Surbiton. This was the beginning of eleven itinerant years, moving successively to Newton Road, Yeovil, Sturminster, Bayswater, Wareham, Yeovil again and back to Dorchester before finally moving into Max Gate in 1885, which was to remain their home for the rest of their lives. During those eleven years, we know comparatively little about the ups and downs of their relationship apart from what we can glean from *The Life*. They were most settled during the almost two years that they spent at Riverside Villa in Sturminister Newton overlooking the River Stour and about which we are told *'It was their first house and, though small, probably that in which they spent their happiest days.'*[14] This may have been true, simply because they were living in one place for a time, but the cracks in their relationship were already discernible. It is at this point that their hopes of having a family started to recede. In June 1877, Hardy noted that their servant girl was to have a baby before adding *'Yet never a sign of one is there for us.'*[15] Florence had no doubt it was Emma who was unable to conceive when she raised the issue of having a child with Thomas many years later, although there is no evidence to support her view.

A book published in 2017 may provide support for Florence's contention. It makes the extraordinary claim that in 1877, there was an illegitimate child, Augusta Humber, born to a maid who had worked for the Hardy's at Sturminster Newton, by the name of Elizabeth Humber and that Thomas Hardy was the father. While highly contentious and on the evidence, very unlikely (although the author of the book felt strongly enough to suggest a DNA test to resolve the matter), it would certainly cast new light on Thomas and the rumours of his philandering, real and imagined.[16]

The time between July 1876 and March 1878 that the Hardys lived in Sturminster Newton was the first time they had been properly settled for any length of time. If Thomas had any inclination to settle down, it was not to last. In the poem 'A Two-Years' Idyll' Hardy reflected on their time in the country town and asked *'What seems it now? / Lost: such beginning was all; / Nothing came after: romance straight forsook / Quickly somehow / Life when we sped from our nook ...'* Despite its outward meaning, it is possible that there was a souring of their relationship in the latter months that persuaded Hardy that they should return to London.

We know so little of their domestic life at the time. The earliest description we have of them as a couple is provided by Richard Bowker who visited them at their Upper Tooting address in 1880 for his American publishers. He met both Thomas and Emma, describing Emma as *'an agreeable, youngish English lady …'* before tellingly adding *' … immensely interested in her husband's work'*[17]

Later that year, Thomas was bedridden for several months with a serious illness which Emma nursed him through while providing practical assistance by writing out the drafts of *A Laodicean* for *Harper's Magazine*. It was a stressful time for them both and Emma balanced her role of caring for Thomas with her practical support to help meet the book's deadlines. Inevitably it seems, that once again she received little gratitude from her husband and it is no surprise that Hardy was so little enamoured of the novel. Before they were married Emma had taken considerable pleasure in assisting him with his writing and continued to do so up until his final novels. But on this occasion, with Thomas's illness, the door was properly ajar and, once again, Emma found she had a significant role to play, not only in caring for her husband, but in ensuring he could meet his publisher's deadlines. It was where Emma felt she belonged. Even before they were married, Emma had questioned Thomas about his inability to include her more in his life, noting in one letter *'your novel seems sometimes like a child all your own and none of me.'*[18] Now she was able to be properly involved despite the fact that in the meantime Hardy had become less inclined to share his ideas or his draft manuscripts. That short time over the Christmas of 1880, when she was able to play a significant role in assisting Thomas with his work allowed her to feel that one novel, at least, owed something to her help and ministrations.

It says much about Thomas that despite Emma continuing to support him with his writing, she never received any credit for doing so – never an acknowledgement, a mention or dedication, not even in the revised editions. He was intensely possessive of his work, later refuting any suggestion that Emma may have ever made a significant contribution as she had claimed, and dismissing *A Laodicean* as one of the novels that pleased him least. It seemed that Emma's frustrations at being kept at an arm's length, especially in the absence of a family of her own grew stronger in the years after they left Sturminster Newton and headed back to London where Thomas was beginning to establish his own social foothold without her.

Meanwhile, Thomas's mind and roving eye, always partial to female beauty, were starting to stir, as we can read in his jottings.

His observations in his letters and in *The Life* were more often than not about other women. Observing the Coronation Day on the town green in Sturminster Newton, it was the young women who captured his attention, noting in his diary, *'The pretty girls, just before a dance, stand in inviting positions on the grass. As the couples in each figure pass near where their immediate friends loiter, each girl-partner gives a laughing glance at such friends, and whirls on.'*[19] It was the carefree and flirtatious nature of the scene that appealed to Hardy and was to feed his imagination for fictional passages such as the opening scenes of *Tess*.

On their return to London, Hardy found himself in demand and soon succumbed to the invitations that came his way. His first surviving letters to Emma, from this time are full of references to women (women, in fact, their dress, their habits, their peculiarities dominate many of his letters) and are testimony to his abiding fascination, something that Emma must have found galling when it became more publicly known.

In March 1885, while visiting Lord and Lady Portsmouth, he wrote to Emma to tell her *'the young ladies are very attentive, and interested in what I tell them. Lady Portsmouth charges them to take care of me.'*[20] Two months later he wrote a further letter to Emma, and again it was his observations of the women who were there that caught his attention: *'Nearly all the ladies were wearing the same dresses as before. Lady Winifred's divine blue looking decidedly crumpled about the neck – the stuck up ruff I mean – not so well as when we saw it in all its new glory. Lady Margaret was in black lace, with gloves between salmon and buff, and a dull red fan – and necklace of brilliants and black ornaments between – dress low.'*[21]

In 1886, he met Lady Jeune, one of the leading London hostesses who took Hardy under her wing and introduced him into a new world of the literary and the well-connected including members of the aristocracy which meant that he was now meeting more and more women who, importantly, wanted to meet him!

In 1889, the relationship of Thomas and Emma took a more serious turn when Thomas received a book of poetry sent by the woman poet, Rosamund Tomson. He met Rosamund soon after in London and was clearly infatuated by her. It was, as Tomalin noted, *'. . . the first time in the fifteen years of their marriage that he had plainly shown he was attracted to another woman.'*[22] Florence dated the change in the marriage as 1891 when things started to go seriously wrong and even though he had renounced his feelings for Rosamund by 1892, there was no going back. It was around this time that Emma began her vituperative journal and that Thomas began taking himself off to London more and more often and became infatuated successively, with Florence Henniker, having met her in Dublin in 1893, and Agnes Grove. If this wasn't enough to undermine their marriage then Emma's full fury was most certainly provoked with the publication of *Jude the Obscure* for its irreligious and obscene content.

Up until 1895, Thomas's letters to Emma were warm and affectionate, his salutations usually 'My Dearest Em' or 'My Dear Em', and usually signed off, 'Yours (or Ever) affectionately, Tom' or just 'T'. By June 1903, the greetings had cooled in their ardour from 'My Dear Em, to 'Dear Em' and from 'ever affectionately' to 'yours' – and there they were to remain. From 29 November 1903, just before the appearance of Florence Dugdale into his life there begins a gap of forty-two months before the next extant letter appears in 1908.[23] By now, Emma knew about Florence and could sense the growing coolness of Thomas towards her. From this point on until the end of her life, Emma was only ever addressed as 'Dear E'. Nor does Thomas ever sign off 'Yours Affectionately,' hereafter only ever using one or both initials.[24]

It would be misleading to think that Thomas and Emma did not achieve some equanimity in their married life. They journeyed together often, especially in the south of England and managed to travel as far north as Scotland on one occasion. There is nothing to say that they did not enjoy each other's company although Emma's lameness meant she could not always walk as far as he and they often divided their time accordingly. They travelled abroad to Normandy, Holland, to the Rhineland and to Paris. In 1887, they visited Italy where they explored the great art galleries of

Florence and Venice. They both rode their bicycles around the lanes of Dorset and shared similar views on suffrage, on vivisection, on the Boer war and a host of other subjects. They both read and enjoyed keeping up with literature and while Thomas was engaged in his writing, Emma painted watercolours to a very respectable standard. Yet despite all they had in common, there were also subjects over which they disagreed, sometimes vehemently so, such as matters of faith and the subject matter of Hardy's later novels. Also, as the century moved into its last decade, Emma was becoming ever more aware of her husband's restlessness, his transitory nature and his penchant for young and attractive women.

Yet even apart from Thomas's flirtations, usually with young and attractive writers, Emma was beginning to feel sidelined. He gave her little encouragement to write while he was championing others. Nor was he taking her into his confidence about his own writing anymore. Despite the fact that, in the wake of *Tess's* success, he provided for her, improved the house according to her wishes, accommodated members of her family and supported her causes and interests, this did not compensate the yawning gap Emma felt from her husband's disaffection.

Since their marriage, Emma had grown more matronly, her limp more pronounced, and her hair parted down the middle rendered her face plain and shapeless.

In the early 1890s, an American writer, Gertrude Atherton described her as *'an excessively plain, dowdy, high-stomached woman with her hair drawn back in a tight little knot and a severe cast of countenance.'*[25]

Fanny Stevenson, the wife of Robert Louis Stevenson was particularly damning of Emma after meeting the Hardys at Max Gate in 1885, famously noting in a letter to a friend *'Did I tell you that we saw Hardy the novelist at Dorchester? A pale, gentle, frightened little man, that one felt an instinctive tenderness for, with a wife – ugly is no word for it . . .!'*[26]

Other observers were more generous. An old London friend who met her around this time described her as a *'nice, loveable inconsequential little lady of whom one grew very fond'* while Israel Zangwill, the British writer, Zionist and feminist who met the Hardy's in 1893 and whose movement she supported described her as *'Pleasant, pretty and un peu invalide.'*[27]

Perhaps the most telling description was that published in 1895 in the American magazine, *Ladies Home Journal*, that read, *'in appearance Mrs Hardy is striking: her hair is dark and slightly tinged with grey; her eyes are also dark. She is dignified and very graceful, and looks as though she might be the wife of some ecclesiastical dignitary'.*[28] It is by far the most flattering description we have of Emma. What makes it rather sad and pathetic is that it was Emma herself who wrote it.

Throughout the decade before her death, despite short periods of appeasement, the relationship between Thomas and Emma continued to be strained and their daily lives largely spent separately. The diatribe Emma had written in 1896 to Mary Hardy and the intensity of her attack on both sisters, as well as Jemima, closed the door between her and Thomas's family forever after. In 1899, her bitterness about marriage and her lot in life was given full rein when Elspeth Grahame asked her for some advice on married life:

'I can scarcely think that love proper, and enduring, is in the nature of men' . . . she began before alluding to what had happened to her own marriage by adding *' . . . at fifty, a man's feelings too often take a new course altogether'*[29]

By 1900 she has widened her target to include, first, male authors, writing to Louise MacCarthy, *'I fear I am prejudiced against authors – living ones! – they too often wear out other's lives with their dyspeptic moanings if unsuccessful – and if they become eminent they throw their aider over their parapets to enemies below & revenge themselves for any objections to this treatment by stabbings with their pen.'*[30]

During this period she had become more active in the suffrage movement, marching in London in 1907 and by the following year had all men firmly in her sights, when she wrote to her friend Lady Hoare,

'I have my private opinion of men in general & of him in particular – grand brains – much "power" – but too often, lacking in judgment of ordinary matters – opposed to unselfishness as regards themselves ! – utterly useless & dangerous as magistrates! & such offices – and to be put up with until a new order of the universe arrives, (IT WILL).'[31]

While Emma's marriage with Thomas was far from satisfactory for either party and for long periods of time, especially in its latter stages, almost non-existent, it is difficult to make judgements about how it affected Thomas's wider attitude to women and marriage. Even reading Hardy's early novels, there is a good deal of cynicism expressed about love and marriage when Hardy was at an age when such a pessimistic view seemed to properly belong to someone much older or at least damaged by life's travails. Capable of being charming, and being charmed, Thomas never allowed his marital state to blind him to the attraction of other women.

There are few letters extant from Thomas to Emma and, most disappointingly, none from the time of their courtship. The next letters we have – four in total – date from 1890 and are brief and informative, but give no real insight into their relationship. In January 1891, however, he is back at the Savile Club in Picadilly and writes most solicitously, perhaps compensating for feelings of guilt resulting from his on-going infatuation with Rosamund Tomson.[32] Only three more letters survive from that year, all sent in April from either the Savile Club or the Athenaeum Club in Pall Mall, each mainly concerned with correspondence, the garden, domestic matters and their respective health.[33] Similarly, in 1892, the two extant letters are brief and concerned with the funerals of James Osgood and Lord Tennyson. Although affectionate enough in their address, there is little insight into their feelings for each other.

While the correspondence is matter of fact, his novels are more helpful. Even while they were courting, Thomas was writing about love and marriage in a way that provides an insight into the way his mind was working. The heroine in his first novel, *Desperate Remedies*, Cytherea Graye is conventional enough, although by the time we get to Fancy Day in his next novel, *Under the Greenwood Tree* we are faced with a heroine vacillating between love and a comfortable, secure life, becoming engaged to one suitor while already betrothed to another. By his next novel, *A Pair of Blue Eyes* written and published during the time of their courtship (and not surprisingly, Emma's favourite) there are a number of precipitous quotes about love. It is the most autobiographical of Hardy's novels – something Florence argued against in *The Life*, although not convincingly so – and makes several observations on the course that love takes:

'Love frequently dies of time alone – much more frequently of displacement' (Ch. 27)

and adding another, by way of warning, *'Men may love strongest for a while, but women love longest.'* (Ch. 38)

However, more explicit were the observations from *Far from the Madding Crowd*, published in the same year as their wedding including his damning verdict on marriage (see Chapter 9 on Bathsheba). This is the first intimation of Hardy's long-standing opposition to the institution of marriage not properly outed in his fiction until the person of Sue Bridehead in *Jude the Obscure*. Even before committing to his own marriage, Hardy had stopped attending Church, the result of reading J S Mill and Comte and, more significantly, the French philosopher, Charles Fourier, whose strong anti-marriage views had a significant influence on him. It is no surprise, therefore, that marriage, including his own, was something he would rail against at various times in his life and literature while using his philosophical position as justification for his own actions and inclinations.

Apart from her husband's views on the sanctity of marriage, something that was further provoked by the publication of *Jude the Obscure*, the pleasure Thomas took in other women's company had become increasingly public and for Emma, ever more humiliating. The series of liaisons and infatuations that Hardy entered upon in middle age, beginning with Rosamund Tomson and continuing through both marriages, ended only when he was well into his eighties with his infatuation with Gertrude Bugler (and even then, he was busy trawling through his memory for other 'lost-loves' to write about). The relationships were usually conducted more in Hardy's imagination than in the flesh, though whether this was because the opportunity for a closer relationship did not present itself (and he certainly tried hard, especially with Florence Henniker), we can only speculate. He enjoyed dancing and being in close proximity with women and engaging in intimate conversation. Certainly, when it came to those women whose company he sought, there is little evidence of his reputed aversion of being touched – in fact, quite the opposite (Florence had written of Thomas in *The Life* that he *' . . . disliked even the most friendly hand being laid on his arm or his shoulder').*[34]

By 1900, relations between Thomas and Emma were at a low ebb and they were living largely separate lives. Thomas felt that the sympathies of their friends were in his court. Mrs Sheridan noted that Emma led Thomas *'a hell of a life'* and thought her *'half-tracked.'* Another acquaintance, Mr Moule opined *'Poor woman, she is phenomenally plain!'* and described her as *'a devil.'* Clearly Thomas thought likewise and saw no reason to hide his feelings; indeed, he fuelled much of the talk, for as Rebekah Owen concluded, *'his general outbursts against her general unbearableness amuse us all.'*[35] With the weight of opinion behind him, Thomas felt even less reason not to pursue his friendships with other women by openly flirting with them, disregarding any further embarrassment he might cause Emma who was still bitter about the views he had espoused on love and relationships in *Jude the Obscure*. And so, he was happy to dance the evening away with Agnes Grove at Larmer Gardens (again, managing to overcome his alleged sensitivity to touch); likewise, he was confident enough to exploit his reservations about the institution of marriage by separating his feelings, in life as in literature, from his relationship with his wife and other women he met. He appeared to accept the view of love as a temporary visitation as explained in *The Return of the Native*, where he wrote, *'Nothing can ensure the continuance of love. It will evaporate like a spirit'* (Bk. 3, Ch. 4). He even managed to provide a justification for his own inconstancy towards Emma and, later, Florence, by suggesting, *'The love of an inconstant man is ten times more ardent than that of a faithful man.' Desperate Remedies*, (Pt. 6, Ch. 1) as if such vacillations were part and parcel of 'love' as well as an excuse for his own aberrations.

Emma, meanwhile, continued to be marginalized although never muzzled. She kept herself busy with various public causes including joining a suffrage march in London in 1907. In a letter to the Editor of *The Nation*, on 6 May, 1908, she wrote *'Women have been sacrificed for ages to men . . . . Man's pride and woman's forced subjection and crushed condition have hitherto prevented acceptance of the necessity of this completed nature in a world of two sexes but the same humanity.'*[36]

It could have been the starting point for many of Hardy's novels, drawing attention to the plight and powerlessness of woman; instead, we can surmise, it is more likely an honest appraisal by Emma based on her own subjugation to Thomas.

Later in life, Emma polarised the opinions of many of those she met. Jacques Blanche writing in 1906 noted the physical and personality changes in her, writing poignantly that, *'Nothing remained to her of the full-blooded, rosy, jovial freshness attested by those who had seen her while still young. Instead, shrunken as if age had made her smaller, she adopted a defensive shield, retaining in stereotyped form the smile of former days as if fixed for all time by a photographer.'*[37]

The best known of her many detractors, the critic AC Benson was altogether less sympathetic and understanding of her situation. His description, even for an avowed woman hater, was unforgivably cruel:

In his view, Emma Hardy was *' . . . a small, pretty, rather mincing elderly lady with hair curiously puffed and padded and rather fantastically dressed. It was hard to talk to Mrs Hardy who rambled along in a very inconsequential way, with a bird-like sort of wit, looking sideways and treating my remarks as amiable interruptions... It gave me a sense of something intolerable the thought of his having to live day and night with the absurd, inconsequent, huffy, rambling old lady. They don't get on together at all. The marriage was thought a misalliance for her, when he was poor and undistinguished, and she continues to resent it... He (Hardy) is not agreeable to her either, but his patience must be incredibly tried. She is so queer, and yet has to be treated as rational, while she is full, I imagine, of suspicions and jealousies and affronts which must be half insane.'*[38]

Others thought more kindly of her and wrote sympathetically. Llewelyn Powys who met Emma in her latter years wrote that *'Mrs Hardy was a kindly woman whose forehead was adorned by two curls which appeared to my irreverent little boy's fancy like the feathers in the end of a drake's tail.'*[39] One could arraign a list of character witnesses on either side of the marital divide, but there is little doubt that before 1900, their marriage had broken down in all but name.

If Emma had been a more subservient, more obsequious wife, would she and Thomas have enjoyed a happier marriage? Perhaps. But perhaps also, it was their tempestuous relationship that gave fuel to Hardy's writing. Was it ever in Hardy's nature, after all, to remain monogamous in thought and print? It is hard, however, to underestimate her influence on Hardy's writing career. Even as late as the 1880s she was giving practical help to Thomas, yet still without ever receiving any acknowledgement for doing so. In the first novel completed at Max Gate *The Return of the Native* now held by the Dorset County Museum, one hundred and six pages of the manuscript are in Emma's hand. She was his companion and confidante even after their romantic feelings towards each other had faded. More significant, in the view of one of Hardy's biographers, Seymour-Smith, *'The Emma who tormented him from time to time was his true muse and therefore to an extent his own wilful creation'*[40] Whether that be so, it was clear that Hardy had relied on her a great deal from the early years of their relationship and even after it ran into trouble in the last decade of the nineteenth century.

Apportioning blame in the breakdown of a marriage is not always easy or obvious, especially for a successor to attempt, but there is little doubt that Hardy felt that, when in his literary persona, he should be exempt from charges of infidelity or disloyalty. When he remarked in his diary that *'The morality of actresses, dancers etc cannot be judged by the same standard as that of people who lead slower lives.'*[41], the clear inference is that he is asking for the same latitude be given to himself. It is doubtful Emma ever agreed with him. His attitude towards Emma and their relationship was full of contradictions: he depended on her to run Max Gate while he was being dined and feted in London; he stood by her when she launched her stinging attack on his sisters and mother; they discussed and shared common ground on the Boer War, on vivisection, on cycling and even latterly, on women's suffrage. But he neglected her, humiliated her, increasingly kept her at a distance, thereby contributing to the impasse that was to mark their last decade together. Her responses were often tactless and hostile so that by the time of her death, they were still living separate lives, she in her study, he in his. It is easy to blame Thomas for the breakdown by his unreasonable behaviour and intolerance of her many foibles, but undoubtedly Emma's agitation and increasingly bizarre behaviour and dress added to this alienation. Whether this was a response to, or cause of, Thomas's off-hand attitude is hard to ascertain.

Of Emma's mental state there has been considerable speculation. Dr Tony Fincham who wrote his doctorate on the medical aspects of Hardy's life and works conducted a careful medical assessment of Emma and concluded

'After a careful assessment of all the available evidence, concerning Emma's mental health, I consider she was psychiatrically unwell in the later years of her life. On the issue of hereditary mental illness in the Gifford family, my review of the family history implies a tendency to Schizophrenia. My Opinion: it is likely that Emma suffered from a schizoid personality disorder, the effects of which were compounded in her last years by a probable early vascular dementia and the overuse of a medication containing alcohol and opium.'[42]

Whatever her illness (and other writers have made rather more of the links and the propensity for mental illness in the Gifford family), there is little doubt that living with Thomas was unlikely to help.

By now Emma had become used to Hardy's modus operandi. He had moved from his

Wessex heartland to take his place amongst the literati in London society. Despite his humble upbringing, he was confident moving in exalted circles, critical of some, (particularly a number of the young ladies who frequented such parties) and admiring of others, although one suspects that his outward confidence hid an insecurity that became obvious when he wrote on matters of class in *Jude the Obscure*. There was a good deal of swagger in his letters from 1890 onwards and his social commentary on those he met at the many soirées and dinners he attended, people Emma would describe as his 'betters', could be scathing.

His nature, likewise, was hard to read. After his wandering eye became more and more apparent, and his propensity for falling into intense periods of infatuations more regular, so Emma was distancing herself from Hardy, decrying his fallen nature and flawed character, and revolted by his atheism and the obscenities of *Jude the Obscure*. Near the very end of her diaries, in a sentence written only six weeks before her death, Emma had noted that her father was right in her estimation of Thomas's character as being *'utterly worthless'*. [43]

For the last few years of their marriage, Emma was also ostensibly sharing her husband with Florence, something of which she no doubt was aware. At times he treated her very badly indeed. In 1912, he was presented with a Gold Medal from the Royal Society of Literature at Max Gate by W B Yeats and Henry Newbolt. Having enjoyed lunch together, Thomas asked Emma to leave, which she eventually did, carrying her cats with her, despite the pleading of his two guests for her to be allowed to stay. And yet it is difficult to see the provocation that Emma provided for him to act so, although we can infer that she had become exceedingly critical and tiresome. Florence Dugdale, although hardly a dispassionate commentator wrote of Emma in the hiatus between Emma's death and her own marriage to Thomas, that

' . . . nothing could be more lonely than the life he used to lead – long evenings spent alone in his study, insult and abuse his only enlivenment. It sounds cruel to write like that and in atrocious taste, but truth is truth, after all.' [44]

All this time, Emma was writing, assisted by Florence, and in April 1912, the last of Emma's published writings, *Spaces* appeared. One of her last poems, 'Time' gives us these prescient lines, written the year before her death.

'Of Time advancing
How' eer entrancing
No mind can know
What tides will flow,
Or winds will blow;
What airy chance
Or circumstance
Some day may show.'

While Emma's writing may lack guile and even be regarded as juvenile, one writer suggested that perhaps they were *' . . . a sort of puzzle left by Emma for a husband she seems to have believed unable or unwilling to hear her,'* hinting at what might become evident with the passing of time.[45]

Emma's relationship with Thomas had gone through five distinct phases. The first, from 1870 – 1874 was one of romantic attachment, occasionally bordering on fantasy; the second, a period of gradual acceptance, growing tolerance and an accommodation, each of the other as they learnt to live with each other's foibles; the third phrase starting around 1890 was one of hostility and bitterness, fuelled by the whiff of betrayal followed by a period of estrangement that lasted until her death in 1912; and finally, her resurrection in verse.

It was the first romantic overtures and memories that lasted. In the early days of their courtship during which the number of days and weeks they actually spent together were comparatively few, Thomas was writing *A Pair of Blue Eyes* which included the prescient lines:

'Every woman who makes a permanent impression on a man is usually recalled to his mind's eye as she appeared in one particular scene, which seems ordained to be her special form of manifestation throughout the pages of his memory.' (Ch. 3) And so it was with Thomas as shown by his elegies written upon her death in 1912, set in the memory of their early meetings in Cornwall.

Emma's final illness was quite sudden. In July 1912, according to the account in *The Later Life* she was at a garden party she was hosting in customary good health and vigour. By October she was complaining of occasional heart discomfort and the suggestion was that she knew something was seriously wrong when she presaged her impending death by announcing, after playing the piano in the sitting room, that she had played it for the last time. In late November she took ill and on the 26 November, the doctor was called who mistakenly felt she was not seriously ill, but undernourished through indigestion. The next day she was dead. [46]

And then came the funeral, the finding of the diaries and the outpouring of grief and remorse as Hardy professed to love Emma – the Emma of his imagining – as he best knew – under the cover of his verse, written at a distance in time and place.

Chapter 4

Florence Hardy

'Time will not help me for I know my own nature, and I shall miss him more and more. The thought of years that may have to be lived through without him fills me with terror. There was really nothing in my life except T.H. nor will there ever be.'[1]

Florence must have suspected what lay ahead of her when she married Thomas at St Andrew's church in Enfield on 10 February 1914. What she might not have anticipated, however, was that Thomas, seventy-four years at the time of their marriage, would live another fourteen years and that by the time he died, she would be old beyond her years, wracked by illness and the responsibility of caring for her often demanding husband. And that, despite the gap of nearly forty years that lay between them, she had less than a decade left before she, too, joined Thomas in the overcrowded family plot at Stinsford churchyard.

Florence Dugdale was born and brought up in Enfield along with her four sisters where she attended the National Infants School in Enfield before moving onto St Andrew's Girls School. Later she trained as a teacher at St Andrew's where her father was headmaster. She found teaching difficult and, not being of robust health, was keen to find a means to make her livelihood from writing. Early on, she met a young journalist, Alfred Hyatt who became the one friend who she later wrote *'was more to me than anyone else in the world'* and whom she lamented on his death in 1911 with the plaintive lines *'I think I lost, then, the only person who ever loved me – for I am unlovable.'*[2]

She had married Thomas as a comparatively young women and was soon weighed down by her position as the 'second wife', the early years of their marriage overshadowed by the Great War and the all-pervading presence of Emma that Thomas perpetuated through his *Poems of 1912-1913*. Although Florence had known Thomas for almost ten years and Emma as well for over half that time, she was still a shadowy figure outside of Hardy's immediate circle. Having stayed at Max Gate for extended periods of time, she had befriended Emma for whatever reason, helped her with her writing and become a companion of sorts. She had also had time to see for herself just how entrenched was the estrangement between husband and wife, and no doubt had to listen to Thomas speak ill of his wife when they had time alone. The shock of Hardy's turnabout following Emma's death and the sudden outpouring of grief and remorse, therefore, would have come as a considerable shock and something she would have struggled to comprehend, even before her marriage. Writing to a friend and confidante of both her and Thomas some three months after Emma's funeral, her anger at Hardy's response to Emma's death was palpable:

'I must say that the good lady's virtues are beginning to weigh heavily upon my shoulders. I had three pages of them this morning. Chief among the virtues now seems to rank her strict evangelical views – her religious tendencies, her humanitarianism (to cats I suppose he means). Thomas says "it was, of course, sheer hallucination in her, poor thing, and not wilfulness." I feel as if I can hardly keep back my real opinion much longer.'[3]

Worse was to follow with the publication of his moving elegies to Emma's memory. Whereas it was Thomas's novels, especially *Jude the Obscure* that had finally severed the semblance of a relationship between Emma and Thomas, with Florence it was his outpouring of poetry extolling the virtues and enshrining the memory of the woman from whom he had been effectively estranged for many years before her death that marred the beginning of their married life.

To understand the background of Florence's appearance in Hardy's life, it is noteworthy that she was the fourth in a succession of women writers whom Thomas courted in some form or another over the sixteen previous years. The first was the twice-married Rosamund Tomson who sent a copy of her poetry to Thomas in the summer of 1889 leading to a flirtatious relationship that continued for three years. When Hardy decided that she was using him for her own purposes, he moved on to a fresh relationship with another published writer, Florence Henniker, again, alas, married although that didn't dampen Hardy's ardour. Not surprisingly, his overtures were unsuccessful in enticing her from the security of her own marriage although it is possible that he would have been willing to disturb the sanctity of his own. When that relationship passed from the romantic to the cordial, Thomas soon found another fledgling writer, in Agnes Grove who he befriended before that attraction too wore off under the watchful eye of her husband, although he continued to offer her support in getting her work published. And finally, in 1905, Florence Dugdale appeared, another aspirant woman writer, another admirer, who came to pay her dues to the sixty-five-year-old Hardy at Max Gate.

Florence may not have been physically strong, but she was both serious and determined. In *The Second Mrs Hardy*, the authors noted that *'As a young woman, Florence had a fragile beauty which continued to haunt Thomas Hardy for years'*; more important for Thomas, however, she was single and vulnerable and this time he resolved to keep her closer to him, at least until the opportunity presented itself to advance their relationship – possibly even one day to marry should there be a reason to do so.[4]

Although Florence was an admirer of Thomas Hardy's, the most popular version, possibly apocryphal, of their first meeting was that she first wrote to, and then visited Hardy at Max Gate sometime during 1905. She did so at the bidding of her close friend, the journalist Alfred Hyatt to try and persuade Hardy to allow the young man to publish an anthology of Thomas Hardy's writing – on which brief she was ultimately successful when a selection from his novels and poems was published by Alfred the following year. From there the relationship grew. Several meetings were arranged surreptitiously over the next two years, usually in London, ostensibly for Florence to help Hardy with his research for *The Dynasts*. In 1909, their relationship was such that she accompanied him to his friend, Edward Clodd's house in Aldeburgh where she spent the weekend in Thomas's company, an entertainment that was repeated several times over the next three years. In addition to the intermittent work Thomas provided for her, Florence also travelled to Dublin on several occasions to take up employment as a companion, to Lady Stoker, wife of the eminent surgeon Sir Thornley Stoker, with whom she also developed a close and abiding friendship. She returned to Enfield less and less often, foregoing her close friendship with Alfred Hyatt, who was now suffering with tuberculosis, although it is likely that Florence had little idea how serious his condition had become. Undoubtedly, the loss of both Sir Thornley and Alfred in the year before Emma's death were grievous blows to her, especially considering the delicate situation she found herself in with Thomas at this time. How both deaths impacted on Florence, and affected her subsequent decision-making is hard to ascertain, but it is reasonable to suspect that she felt under considerable pressure for a variety of reasons when Emma died.

For the few years from Thomas's and Florence's first meeting until the years immediately prior to her death, Emma was probably unaware of the relationship and certainly of its intimate nature. Eventually, however, Thomas felt confident enough to introduce her to Emma and Max Gate and by the last two years of Emma's life, Florence had become a familiar visitor to the house and had even inveigled her way into Emma's affections. Emma was grateful to the young helpmate and saw her as a companion and one, moreover, prepared to show an interest in her writing. Whatever Florence's initial disquiet and her own feelings for Thomas, she was not altogether acting disingenuously when she wrote to Emma early in the summer of 1910, *'I cannot find words to thank you sufficiently for all your goodness to me. Believe me I am most truly grateful and if at anytime there is anything you wish me to do for you it will be a great joy.'* [5] She wrote again in September, promising *'as soon as I get home I am going to start typing "The Maid on the Shore" and will just stick to it until it is done'* before concluding by writing *'I fancy though your great triumph will be with "The Inspirer"'*.[6]

At the same time, Florence was enjoying a clandestine relationship with Thomas including their weekends at Aldeburgh. This double life no doubt weighed heavily upon her and despite managing the disparate parts of the marriage on one level, she still found herself drawn into what she ironically described as part of the Max Gate ménage à trois. In a letter to Edward Clodd in November 1910 she wrote:

'The Max Gate ménage always does wear an aspect of comedy to me. Mrs Hardy is good to me, beyond words, and instead of cooling towards me she grows more and more affectionate. I am intensely sorry for her, indeed sorry for both.'[7]

What gives a much better insight into Florence's place in the household, indeed, into the intimacy of their relationship in the years 1910–1912 can be found in her correspondence with Edward Clodd. In the same letter in which she spoke of the ménage à trois, she confided in Edward how she had been distraught at hearing of the death of Lady Stoker in Dublin, having looked after the old woman at the family home in Dublin. On imparting the news to Thomas, however, she wrote, she received scant sympathy from Thomas who was himself in mourning for one of their cats, Kitsey, and who merely commented to Florence *'was there ever so sad a life as mine.'*[8] Florence was incensed when sometime in the following week she went into Thomas's study and found him working on what she described as a *'pathetic little poem describing the melancholy burial of the white cat. I looked over his shoulder and read this line 'That little white cat was his only friend.'* [9]

Her reaction is interesting for a secretary / helpmate, reputedly of timid disposition: *'That was too much even for my sweet temper and I ramped around the study exclaiming: "This is hideous ingratitude." But the culprit seemed highly delighted with himself and said smilingly that he was not exactly writing about himself, but about some imaginary man in a similar situation.'* [10]

Apart from the ingenuous explanation that Thomas no doubt used in similar situations with other women, the sense of familiarity that she enjoyed with Thomas while living under the same roof as Emma casts a new light on their relationship. Even when Florence showed her duplicitous nature in writing to Emma two months later about the death of another cat, hoping she had recovered from the shock and suggesting *'you should write one of your delightful poems to his memory'* she was in no mood to forgive Thomas. [11] In December, 1911 she noted that the poem about 'Poor Kitsey!' was coming out in the next *English Review* although *' . . . in deference to my feelings he has altered it a little. Nonetheless, he has retained the line: "that little cat was his only friend." I tell him that it is monstrous ingratitude on his part.'* [12]

How close they were at this point is a matter of conjecture although it is interesting to note that less than four months after Emma's death, she made the comment in a letter to Edward Clodd in reference to Emma Hardy's grave at Stinsford,
'There he will lie, when the time comes, and a corner, I am told, will be reserved for me.' [13]

On the more personal question of the nature of their relationship prior to marriage, Thomas and Florence were careful in covering their tracks. Thomas made great play of the friendship between Florence and Emma, evident in the support that Florence gave Emma with her writing, encouraging her, typing her manuscripts and helping to get them published. At the same time, however, Florence was sharing her concern about Thomas having to live with Emma's insults and abuse with a no doubt curious Edward. It is quite possible that she felt truly sorry for Emma before her death. What happened after 1912, however, fuelled by Thomas's monstrous and hypocritical reaction to Emma's death propelled her dislike of Emma into a visceral hatred that clouded the early years of their marriage and was never properly vanquished.

What most biographers struggle with, however, is in defining the nature of the love and affection that Thomas and Florence felt for each other. To many observers, Florence was portrayed as the dewy-eyed sycophant, a quiet, retiring admirer, and a literary groupie, happy to do Thomas's bidding, content to wallow in the shadow of greatness. She had no vocation, having given up teaching, no independent means, no ambitions of her own other than a misplaced one, to write, and was happy to dedicate her life to the world-famous author whose company she first sought as an admirer and, perhaps, as someone who could help her friend in his career. Later, she saw her own life's purpose through his; to look after the old man, to help protect his literary legacy and to be seen vicariously, as someone without whom he would not cope, let alone be able to write. In return, Florence appealed to Thomas as someone who would care for him and allow him to get on with his writing, a helpmate dedicated to himself and his work, who would also be a companion to him and not compete with, or embarrass him, as Emma had.

Both views are far from the mark. Florence was no shrinking violet. She was quiet, insecure, a worrier, neurotic, seemingly without humour, a view at odds with the dry wit that she often showed in her letters. By 1912, thanks to a bequest from Sir Thornley Stoker, she was financially independent although this resulted in her husband behaving parsimoniously towards her on occasions. And she had loved and been loved, before and after meeting Thomas, by Alfred and possibly Sir Thornley, even if she deemed herself 'unlovable'. Meeting her soon after the War, Llewelyn Powys described her as *'a dark, nervous woman of an awkward carriage, but one who possessed an odd distinction of her own'*. His abiding impression however was her *'hopeless attitude of life-avowal'* remembering the meeting: *'As I stood by her side in that room emptied of its company I received a draught of Bronte-like melancholy the strength of which I have never forgotten.'*[14]

Like Emma before her, Florence looked to Thomas to help her own writing career and like Emma, was disappointed. Eventually she did manage to get a commission from the Oxford University Press and published two children's books: *The Book of Baby Beasts* in 1911 and *The Book of Baby Birds* in 1912, but her ambition to write was never encouraged by Thomas. Yet as a wife and companion, she gave her husband the care and companionship he craved and supported him in his writing and correspondence.

In a recently discovered letter to a former pupil. Harold Barlow, Florence wrote

'Perhaps you have read, if you have the English papers, that I am now the proud and very happy wife of the greatest living English writer – Thomas Hardy. Although he is much older than myself it is a genuine love match – on my part, at least, for I suppose I ought not to speak for him.'

Andrew Norman in his book, *Behind the Mask* went so far as to suggest that *'Florence Hardy was, in many ways, the complete antithesis of Emma, and in consequence, the changes which she brought about to Hardy's life were truly remarkable... Florence did all in her power to make Hardy's life bearable.'*[15]

Despite being cognizant of the fact that he needed someone to look after him, Thomas seemed unable to appreciate how to treat his new wife. He saw Florence as a tender companion, someone who would look after him, but did not see it implicit upon him to give much in return. We know of his meanness when Florence was ill when he expected her to pay for her treatment. We also learn from the parlour maid, Ellen Titterington that they occupied separate bedrooms with a common dressing room between although this was by no means an unusual situation, especially given the age difference. We should not, however, assume they did not have a physical relationship. According to Hermann Lea, Florence had clearly considered the idea of having a child before she was married although she was concerned whether it would safe to do so because of his age and certainly it seemed that Hardy might still have been hopeful of having a child with Florence. There are few other clues apart from an extraordinary letter to Dr Marie Stopes in late 1923 which indicated Florence had not altogether dismissed the idea, writing, *'I find on talking to him that the idea of my having a child at his age fills him with terror'* and that Thomas had said that *'he would have welcomed a child when we married first ten years ago, but now it would kill him with anxiety to have to father one.'*[16]

The early years of marriage were difficult for Florence. She noted in a letter to Sydney Cockerell that the day Emma died was the day that she turned from *'youth into dreary middle age'*.[17] Overwhelmed by the train of events, including her own recent losses of Alfred and Sir Thornley, she could not have foreseen the consequences of Emma's sudden passing. Before that happened, it is possible that Thomas was hoping (with her compliance) that she would provide the same role of companion for Emma as she had for Lady Thornley, while being there for him as his secretary and confidante or even possibly, as his mistress. Emma's unexpected death may have been propitious for Hardy as his home circumstances had became increasingly intolerable, but for Florence, emotionally fragile and with the other possible stays of her life removed, it was the worst of times. Before she knew it, she found herself locked into a battle for Thomas and for Max Gate with Emma's manipulative niece, Lillian, (who before the end of the decade was diagnosed as insane). Not wanting to give up Max Gate, without a career of her own and adrift from her own family, notwithstanding her own strong feelings for Thomas, marriage probably seemed for Florence, indeed for them both, as the best option.

The early weeks after Emma's death were difficult for them both. Having read Emma's diaries and especially that entitled 'What I think of my Husband', Thomas was consumed with guilt. In March 1913, he headed off to Cornwall where he had first met Emma (*'his late espoused saint'* as Florence called her) for the sake of the girl he married and who had died 'more than twenty years ago' although his family doubted if such a girl had ever existed. Florence, meanwhile, was left at Max Gate, noting in a letter that she kept *'a loaded revolver'* under her pillow for protection, while cursing the diabolical diaries and the effect they had had upon Thomas.[18] He was little improved on his return and although he assured her that he had laid Emma's ghost to rest, Florence was dubious that it was so and became increasingly agitated and upset by Thomas's mental state. At one point he had suggested to her that she should always wear half mourning in future as *'a mark of devotion to (Emma's) memory'* a remark that led Florence to write *'Sometimes I wonder if there is not something in the air of Max Gate that makes us all a little crazy.'*[19]

While the trip to Cornwall passed without incident, Florence was locked in a struggle with Emma's niece, Lillian who was intent on keeping her aunt's memory alive. Thomas was averse to taking sides and tolerated Lillian's interference although Florence noted, when she was not there, there was a remarkable change in his spirits. Eventually Florence delivered an ultimatum to Thomas that either the niece left or she would, which had the desired effect of Lillian leaving Max Gate for good in late 1913.

The departure of Lillian was also the removal of the last impediment to their marriage which duly took place on the 10 February, 1914, a mere fourteen and a half months after Emma's death. It was attended only by the officiating vicar, Florence's father and her youngest sister and Henry, Thomas's brother and was kept secret from family and friends prior to the event. In a response to a letter from Sydney and Kate Cockerell, Florence confirmed the rumour of their marriage to writing that *'I did indeed marry him that I might have the right to express my devotion – and to endeavour to add to his comfort and happiness.'* Tellingly, she went on: *'Had I not married him I realized that I should not be able to remain at Max Gate and I dreaded that, when the time came when he most needed my care, I should not be able to be with him.'*[20]

The first weeks and months of their marriage may have given Florence some hope that she had superseded Emma in Thomas's affections. In March she wrote to Lady Hoare, *'I think he really needs affection and tenderness more than anyone I know – for life has dealt him so cruel blows. I remember, some years ago, he said to me pathetically, "I do not ask for much – I only want a little affection."'*[21]

She was soon to be disappointed. In September 1914, *Satires of Circumstance* was published with its elegies to Emma that threw her back into a slough of despondency and made her question Thomas's love for her and even her own worthiness. Not long after its publication she wrote to Lady Hoare
'The Book pains me horribly and yet I read it with a terrible fascination. It seems to me that I am an utter failure if my husband can publish such a sad, sad book,' before asking herself *'If I had been a different sort of woman, and better suited to be his wife, – would he, I wonder, have published that volume?'*[22]

Desperately unhappy and alone, not sure who to turn to or confide in, Florence became increasingly indiscreet. As it transpires, most of what we know of Florence, from her feelings about Thomas to her despair about Emma's constant presence in their lives came from her own pen and often to her detriment.

A letter to Lady Hoare written in 1914 beginning with the personal admission *'But I must confess to you – and I would confess this to no one else . . ..'* was only one of several that contained a plea for confidence.[23] There were many similar requests. Soon after Emma's death she had concluded a letter to Edward Clodd by writing *'I ought not to write all this I know but it is a most tremendous relief to do so, and to know you won't ever breathe a word to anyone.'*[24] Later, she wrote in the same vein to Rebekah Owen, *'I wouldn't write as I do to any woman in the world but you, for you have always seemed to me the truest and most high-minded woman I ever known'*[25]; before realising, at last, that few of those who received her letters had any intention of destroying them or even of not betraying their confidence by speaking about them. By 1917, Florence wrote again to Rebekah Owen noting that *'I have come to the conclusion that many people . . . try to inveigle me into a correspondence so they can boast of being in constant touch with Max Gate and my husband'* before urging *'if anything should happen to me I entreat you to burn every scrap of my writing. I do write so carelessly and injudiciously that I fear there are letters of mine preserved that I should hate to have seen.'*[26] Yet in 1918 she is still at it, concluding a letter to Sydney Cockerell with a caution on talking about the proposed biography, writing *'Perhaps I have said too much about it all already – but I would not breathe a word about it to anyone except yourself.'*[27] Sadly, as is evident from these surviving sentences, fuelled by her own injudicious nature and lack of judgement, it was those closest to her that let her down.

The first few years of married life were difficult for Florence. Thomas kept lamenting his late wife, which hurt her deeply: *'And there is always this extraordinary idealization of Mrs Hardy,'* she wrote to Edward Clodd, *'whom he now says, and I think believes, was the sweetest, most gifted, most beautiful woman who ever existed.'*[28] It was to take some time for their marriage to gain any equanimity or common ground; ironically, it was the shared pessimism and grief resulting from the war years that eventually helped assuage the despair she felt.

By 1916, Florence was aware of Thomas ageing and noted that he never wanted to go anywhere or even see anyone again. Both she and Thomas had grown close to a cousin of Thomas's, Frank George, before he was killed in the Dardanelles casting them into further gloom. He had met Gertrude Bugler for the first time in 1916, an event which would lead to a later crisis in their marriage, but by 1917, Florence was able to tell Sydney Cockerell that Thomas was keeping well, and that he could *'cycle five or six miles with ease if he takes his time.'*[29]

By the last years of the War, the idea of a biography was also starting to take shape. Thomas had written notes of his early years, which Florence had read although she was nervous of his habit of burning anything he did not want known. She wrote to Sydney of the need to keep the existence of the manuscripts secret and that *'. . . on no account must we mention the word "autobiography" or call them autobiographical'* for she felt if they were regarded thus Thomas would promptly destroy them as *'he would never write an autobiography and that the mere idea – or suggestion – annoys him.'*[30]

She was very aware of Thomas's penchant for covering his tracks for any prying biographers, present and future, who might follow. Early in January 1919, she noted that he was *' . . .busy with his letter sorting, having reached 1893. Quite four-fifths or more have to be destroyed – some I rather regret, but when he wants to burn, he will burn and not all the King's horses nor all the King's men could prevent him'* before concluding *'And I expect he is right.'*[31]

Meanwhile, while their own relationship was taking on a more business-like footing, with Florence taking on more of the role of custodian of his works, as well as wife and carer, she was to receive another reminder of her husband's inconstancy with his imaginary dalliance with Gertrude Bugler to whom Florence noted, he lost his heart entirely. But apart from that rather awkward and embarrassing episode, their life had settled into a pattern with Thomas revelling in his role as the grand old man of English Literature, receiving visits from the Prince of Wales and enjoying the friendship of younger literary men, particularly T E Lawrence and Siegfried Sassoon. Since the end of the War he had grown more dependent on her and did not like being left alone, which had the effect of drawing them closer so that in 1921 she could write to Sydney that *'We are a cheerful pair – TH and I'.*[32]

Such cheerfulness, however, was only ever fleeting. In November 1922, she confided in Sydney that *'He said that he never felt so despondent in his life. And he told me that if anything happened to me and he would go out and drown himself, which, considered rightly is a compliment, isn't it?'*[33]

The palliative cure she offered was rather refreshing: *'It is wonderful how quickly he got over it, and I think that was the result of taking two bottles of champagne – not all at one go, but two glasses twice a day. That seems always to do him more good than anything.'*[34]

Whether it lasted long enough to see him through the anniversary of Emma's birthday towards the end of the month was doubtful for the anniversary was inevitably a sombre time at Max Gate. Florence recalled that Emma had once told her that she was the only living person who remembered her birthday, but now Thomas made sure that neither of them was able to forget it, along with other significant dates that related to Emma (most notably that of their first meeting on 7 March, 1870 that was frozen in time on his desk calendar).

As the decade progressed, Hardy continued to be feted for his literary achievements although Florence noted the disappointment he felt in 1926 when the Nobel Prize for Literature was awarded to George Bernard Shaw instead of himself. His fame was such that they were accustomed to visitors at Max Gate. Always, she was protective of her husband's health and suspicious of those who she felt were prying or likely to write anything critical about him. She was already starting to look at the prospect of life after Thomas and could feel the cold winds of pending widowhood. Her ambivalence towards Max Gate and their possessions, especially anything that might betray them, led her into moments of introspection, once leading her to confide in a letter to Marie Stopes, *'I think I am really a disciple of Mahatma Gandhi. I want to get rid of worrying possessions.'*[35] Thomas, also, was unable to let himself enjoy the fruits of his literary life, telling Florence not long before his death that, had he his time over again, he would *'. . .prefer to be a small architect in a little country town . . . He would have been a much happier man.'*[36]

Florence had suffered from various illnesses throughout her life and there was no doubt that the marriage exacted a toll upon her health. Hardy's death and the debacle that followed upset her considerably. Immediately following Thomas's death there was a proposal, led by James Barrie and Sydney Cockerell, for his funeral to be at Westminster Abbey and for his ashes to be laid in Poets' Corner. Cajoled and bullied to act contrary to her wishes, Florence reluctantly agreed to the exhortation that her husband belonged to the nation. Meanwhile, Hardy's heart was extracted and buried in a ceremony that was held at the simultaneous ceremony at Stinsford churchyard near his birthplace.

After the funeral was over, Florence made it her business to destroy every trace of Emma's life at Max Gate. With the help of the gardener she achieved this *'by carrying out the entire contents to the garden, and setting light to it in bonfire pyres. Everything, including even Emma's old corsets, is remembered going up in flames.'*[37]

The year after Thomas's death she visited Cornwall, like a penitent setting out to exorcise her own ghosts of Emma. The circumstances of the burial at Westminster Abbey continued to haunt her. She felt the solitude deeply and in August 1929 wrote to John Cowper Powys that she hardly knew *'what to do with the remnant of my life that is left'* (she was still only forty-nine years old!)[38] Max Gate was both a home and a prison and she recognised her ambivalence in continuing to live there, telling Powys *'sometimes I feel nothing would induce me to leave Max Gate and at other times I feel it will be death to remain here.'*[39]

Florence was now a rich woman and able to fulfil her wish of having a flat of her own in London. She was also able to help her family and for a time, also enjoyed the attentions of James Barrie, who was solicitous in her widowhood, offering his flat in London before she got her own and writing her what she took to be flirtatious notes. Barrie was complicated, however, and Florence emotionally vulnerable. She mistook his words of sympathy and read too much into his letters (including one written while Thomas was still alive that asked *'I forget if I ever told you how much I like you, No, too shy, but I do like you very much'*[40] and eventually, to the disappointment of Florence (but not of those, like Lawrence, who knew Barrie rather better), she resigned herself to a single life.

The publication of Somerset Maugham's *Cakes and Ale*, widely seen as a parody of Hardy caused her a good deal of unhappiness as did the editing of the material and subsequent writing of the second volume of the biography which was eventually sent for publication in late 1929. Emma continued to haunt her and in 1934 she wrote *'today is the 22nd anniversary of the death of Emma and she has been in my mind all day – and I have been up in the sad little attic where she died – still full of her presence.'*[41]

In the meantime, she had fallen out with Cockerell, Thomas Hardy's other literary executor. Ill health continued to dog her and at Christmas, 1936 she wrote to Frederick Adams, *'I am spending Christmas here alone and quietly, and will try to begin sorting papers and burning some.*[42] Presciently, she added, *'I often think it is time for me to begin my packing.'*[43]

As her health deteriorated, more and more papers, letters and diaries of Thomas as well as her own, were consumed by yet more bonfires in the gardens of Max Gate, taking their secrets into the skies over Dorchester. Within a year she was dead.

In looking at her life in relation to Thomas, we are left with many unanswered questions. What was the nature of their love? How did Florence fit in with Thomas's view of women? How did he treat her? Was their relationship one built on companionship or a deep abiding affection?

Of their intimate lives, we have so little evidence to go on. Thomas and Florence were both obsessed with privacy and the protection of Thomas's legacy so that we can only presume that the bonfires consumed whatever secrets they must have had especially in the years leading up to Emma's death. But we know enough to suspect their subterfuge from when Thomas first asked Florence to help with some research he was conducting for *The Dynasts*. Apart from the weekend away at Edward Clodd's house at Aldeburgh, without Emma's knowledge, she went touring with Thomas and his brother, Henry, and even later, with her own father, who was impressed to be included in the author's company (and undoubtedly Thomas helped to raise Florence's status in the eyes of her own family). As his helpmate and secretary, Florence had become part of the household at Max Gate for weeks at a time and ingratiated herself with Emma, helping with her writing and getting her poems published. And yet she was more than just a secretary, meek and obliging. She could stand up for herself and while she noted Emma's niece Lillian's own admission that the Gifford's all had tongues that could *'cut to the bone'*, she was also capable of being direct and forthright.[44]

The issue that caused her the greatest sadness was Thomas's devotion to the memory of Emma. Almost certainly, Emma had pricked a nerve by leaving her written accounts of their life together, both her bitterness towards his alleged betrayal of her in 'What I think of my Husband' and the nostalgic jottings of their early years together, as if she knew that Thomas was more susceptible to words on paper than words spoken, that they would etch themselves onto his conscience. Yet Florence could console herself in the knowledge that Thomas's elegies to Emma fitted a pattern that reoccurred throughout his life. There are relatively few poems to Florence or Emma written while they were married to him; indeed, the vast majority of his poems to women were written when they were either dead or removed from him or otherwise denied him: Emma, of course, after her death, Tryphena, Jemima, Agnes, Florence Henniker and many other lesser known women friends. As he wrote through the mouthpiece of Jocelyn Pierston in *The Well-Beloved*, he *' . . . loved the woman dead and inaccessible as he has never loved her in life.'* (Pt. 2, Ch.3) The most attractive, the most romantic, the most amorous and erotic gesture a woman could make for Thomas Hardy, it seems, was to die, if not for him, then as grist for his poetry. Like so many writers, he used grief as a salve, writing his best poems in the absence of the subject. While many of the poems he wrote about women he had known were elegiac, it was not only humans who were so treated.

In 1922, Florence wrote to Sydney Cockerell about a new collection of poems that Hardy was about to publish which she felt incomplete without a poem on 'Wessie': *'TH says he could write one if Wessex was dead – but why should the poor little animal have to die before a poem is written to him?'* Concluding with a little black humour of her own by writing *'Wessex flourishes although a poem awaits him if only he had the thoughtfulness to pop off.'*[45]

Even into his eighties, Hardy kept harvesting his memory for those early moments of infatuation, posing as either love or affection. And when he could not glean enough from the past, he could become infatuated with someone more than fifty years younger than himself, in the form of Gertrude, harmless in itself, but real enough for Florence to be sorely wounded by it. The pattern was there. The observer might say was that all Florence needed to do was either leave him or predecease him and, had he still the wit to write, she would have received her poetic due – a not unlikely supposition.

And so what of their love? What of Thomas's attitude to Florence as distinct from womankind in general? Or those other women that had piqued his interest? Did Florence become the second Mrs Hardy only because of the circumstances in which both she and Thomas found themselves, both mourning for lost lives? Tomalin felt that Florence was grateful to Thomas for all he did for her, but while she was fond of him, she *'was never in love with him'*[46] Likewise, Seymour-Smith felt Thomas *'never loved her as he had loved Emma, but he was deeply attracted to her gentleness, her modest love of literature and her air of quiet hopelessness.'*[47] She had become a good companion and confidante for Thomas, looking after him and protecting his literary reputation and in light of this role, she was overwrought by his death and the aftermath. Her tragedy was she never replaced Emma in Thomas's affections nor ever felt completely at home at Max Gate. She confided to Siegfried Sassoon that she even disliked being called Mrs Hardy for the name *'always seems to belong to someone else whom I knew for several years and I am oppressed by the thought that I am busy in her house, using her things and, worst of all, having even stolen her name."*[48]

Time has not been kind to Florence, invariably focusing on her possessiveness, her secrecy, her betrayals, the disloyalty she displayed in her letters and her jealousy of Gertrude Bugler. She has been depicted as devious and deceitful carrying on an affair with Thomas Hardy even when living at Max Gate. Seymour-Smith is particularly scathing, labelling her duplicitous and treacherous, questioning her word on the date Emma had started her 'diabolical' diary, accusing her of starting the rumours of

Emma's mental health while suggesting the strong likelihood of her conducting a sexual relationship with both Sir Thornley Stoker and Thomas Hardy.[49]

Yet such judgements are unduly harsh. After a few difficult years, Florence and Thomas settled down to life at Max Gate after the War. Always haunted by the presence of Emma, constantly challenged by Hardy's own views and demands, she did what she could as his companion and confidante to make his life as comfortable as possible and to protect him.

After his death, she struggled to find happiness. In his letter of condolence to Florence in 1928, George Bernard Shaw wrote:

'You must feel lost for a moment with nobody to take care of; but you know, there are lots of things for you to arrange; and before you arrange them, just go to bed and stay there until all your arrears of sleep are made up and you feel the return of spring making you jolly and selfish and lazy. That may not seem possible yet; but it is inconceivable that Thomas Hardy's widow should be unhappy or unblest.

Only, don't marry another genius; they are not all sound at the core; and anyhow he would be an anti-climax. Marry somebody who has nothing else to do than to take care of you.

Meanwhile, what an . . . adventure it was, wasn't it?'[50]

It was an adventure, but not one that brought much happiness to Florence, either then or in the future. Despite moments of equanimity and joy, no doubt, hers was not a happy life. Yet we owe her a debt despite the bonfires and censorship, the excising, and the editing. Her despair at his death may not have been that she had lost her great love, but that she could no longer add to his comfort and happiness, for she was always best in her role as a helpmate to genius.

Chapter 5

Tryphena Sparks: 'Dear Phena'

Amongst the number of young women romantically linked with Thomas Hardy during the 1860s, the name of Tryphena Sparks is the most often mentioned – and the most enigmatic. Yet even before her, there were a number of real and imaginary friendships and amours that Hardy referenced and returned to throughout his life.

In his poem 'A Middle Gate in February' written in 1889, Hardy fondly recalled the time as a youth with the bevy of young women in their *'curtained bonnets and light array'* who, sadly, were *'now underground.'*[1]

Prior to that he had recalled four local beauties and identified them by their distinguishing features including Lizbie Browne with her bay-red hair (Hardy described her in the poem 'To Lizbie Browne'), while of another, Rachel Hurst, Hardy made reference to her artificial dimple-making, making use of the detail in describing the person of Arabella in *Jude the Obscure*.[2]

One who made a more significant impact upon Hardy was Louisa Harding. In her person and memory we see some of the contradictions about Hardy and women, the preservation of images and the durability of memory. A friend of the family recollected *'Hardy's youthful speechless admiration for Louisa Harding'* and that *'even in old age, she said, he blushed and became boyishly enthusiastic whenever her name was mentioned'*.[3]

According to Florence in *The Life*, Hardy became infatuated with the attractive farmer's daughter on sight alone and having once managed to say 'good evening' in passing her in the lanes, subsequently tried to find other ways to meet her. When she left for school in Weymouth, he followed her in order to gaze at her over the church stalls, only ever eliciting a shy smile. Seymour-Smith asserts that Tom was in love with her, but that her parents had forbidden her to have contact with him on the grounds of his 'social inferiority'.[4] Yet despite the lack of contact and the paucity of information, we have one observation, expunged from the final draft of *The Life*, that Hardy had written of her grave that *' . . . a nameless green mound in the corner of Mellstock Churchyard was visited more than once by one to whom a boyish dream had never lost its radiance.'*[5] When Louisa died in 1913, a year after Emma, Hardy wrote the poems 'Transformations' and 'Human Shows' where Hardy talks of Louisa and Emma sharing the same churchyard, *'Long two strangers they and far apart; such neighbours now!'* Louisa was an abiding memory and just a few months before his death he was again recalling her with his poem 'To Louisa in the Lane' bemoaning that he had to wait *'till with flung-off flesh I follow you'* into the graveyard at Stinsford where she would share Thomas in due course with Emma and later Florence. Even in death, it appears Thomas was not beyond concocting a little dalliance.

Other girls he had brief flirtations with included the sisters Eliza and Jane Nicholls. It was probable that Thomas was unofficially engaged to Eliza and wrote several poems to her (including 'She to Him' and 'Neutral Tones'). In 1866, the relationship soured as Thomas became infatuated with Eliza's younger sister, Jane, who was possibly the subject of Thomas's poem, 'The Wind's Prophecy' although it is unlikely that she ever took her mischievous flirtation with Thomas very seriously. Eliza, who never married, re-appeared at Max Gate in 1913 much to Thomas's and, no doubt, Florence's chagrin, armed with the ring and portrait of Thomas, both of which he had once given her and offering herself up as the second Mrs Hardy.[6] Millgate, in particular of all Hardy's major biographers felt she was a significant presence in his writing and the original of the heroine of 'Desperate Remedies' (Cytherea), remarking in an article co-written with Stephen Mottram that, *'Of Eliza's importance to Hardy there can be little doubt – so many aspects of his early life and early writings seeming to fall into place around her – but the details of the time, place, character and intensity of their shared moments and the contents of their exchanged letters are likely to remain for ever unknown. As Hardy would surely have wished, Eliza perhaps not.'*[7] What we do know is that Hardy visited Eliza in Findon on a number of other occasions during the mid-1860s and that the relationship between Hardy and Eliza, again according to Millgate *'seems at first to have developed slowly, in part, perhaps, because of the infrequency of their meetings and of Hardy's lingering feelings (such as they may have been) for Louisa Harding.'*[8]

So even before Hardy became enamoured with Tryphena, he had been busy exploring his fascination with women. As a young man, he was physically immature and his lateness of development in virility could explain much of his character and behaviours. His fascination with the fairer sex, however, both in the flesh and in his fantasies, continued throughout his life as the number of women who had poems written about them attests.

Tryphena, Thomas's cousin on his mother's side, was born in 1851, the youngest daughter of Jemima's oldest and closest sister, Maria. She was an attractive and clever girl and while much younger than Thomas, their paths often crossed, particularly in the period between 1865 and 1869. According to Gittings, the relationship reached a climax in the summer of 1869, or, if we are to accept Hillyard's exhaustive detective work, as early as the summer of 1865, although what form their relationship took has been open to speculation ever since. Biographers have worked hard to establish her place in Hardy's life, not altogether successfully, and there is still conjecture about just how important she was. Certainly, early indications were that she played hardly any role at all which should make us suspicious knowing what we know now. Tryphena is not mentioned at all in *The Life* and her place in the Hardy canon rests on the poem, 'Thoughts on Phena' published soon after her death in 1891, the only poem that was indisputably about her and their family connection.

Which may have been where Tryphena remained, on the periphery of Hardy's early life, a passing footnote in the biographies as one of the three Sparks sisters, a dear cousin, befriended by Thomas. Nor would it have been a surprise if she had been the subject of flirtations from her cousin eleven years her senior, nor that she had enjoyed a dalliance with him. In her biography *Thomas Hardy The Time-Worn Man*, Claire Tomalin noted, after all, that cousins fulfilled a social and a sexual role in Victorian England suggesting that:

'They were accessible, flirtable with, almost sisters, part of the family, and that it is likely that . . . Tom thoroughly enjoyed the company of all his girl cousins, flirted with them and made as much love to them as he could get away with when he had the chance.' [9]

Whether Thomas Hardy took things further as Tomalin suggests makes the possibility of an illegitimate child less unlikely than has been suggested, but we simply don't know and as Tomalin concluded,
'. . . there is no evidence she and Hardy met in London, and the friendship or flirtation between them cannot have lasted long.' [10]

Gittings, possibly naively, doubted whether any relationship had taken place for she would have known that any blemish on her moral character would undo her in her chosen career – not that that has often dissuaded would-be lovers. The question as to whether Thomas and Tryphena were in any sort of meaningful relationship, however, or whether she was a major influence on Hardy and his writing continues to intrigue and trying to find the answer has led to a good deal of speculation. Regardless, when Thomas was living in Weymouth in the summer of 1869, it is likely that he and Tryphena spent time together alone. It was clearly a significant time whether or not we believe the story, almost certainly true, of Thomas buying her a ring. It is almost certain, too, that the sadness he expresses in the poem 'At Waking' in which he bemoans the 'prize' he has lost (and here, fast forward to the lost prize in 'Thoughts of Phena') relates directly to her. If it was the start, or the dying fall, of their relationship remains a matter of conjecture, just as much in the view of many writers as to whether there was a relationship at all.

Looking at what is known of Thomas and Tryphena tells much about how we see Thomas and his relationships with women thereafter. A number of Hardy scholars and biographers believe that the events of the years 1865–1870 provide the key to Hardy's relationships and influenced both the way he conducted himself, and how he wrote about women, for the remainder of his life. If only to address their claims even if no other reasons exist, we need to take Tryphena's claim to Hardy's affections seriously.

So what do we know about Tryphena? That she was born in 1851, the youngest of six children. That her mother, Maria, Jemima's sister, was aged forty-six years at the time and the birth must have been as unwelcome as it was unexpected, considering the financial pressures the family laboured under. Tryphena was, by all accounts, a bright and clever girl as well as being both pretty and lively. She was twenty-two years younger than her oldest sibling, Rebecca who had been born in 1829; in fact, all of her other siblings were much older with the closest in age being Nathaniel born in 1843. The other three siblings, Emma, Martha and James had attended school in nearby Puddletown, only a short distance from Hardy's home in Higher Bockhampton so over the years the families saw a good deal of each other.

When Thomas was young, his mother would often take him to see her sister, Maria and his young cousins, before Tryphena was even born. As an adolescent, it was the attractive Martha who Thomas was drawn to although she was six years older than him. When he went away to London, Tryphena was still a young girl, but by the time he had returned she was sixteen years old and a student teacher at Puddletown School and an independent and spirited young woman.

Having worked as a pupil-teacher at Puddletown School in 1866 (where she was once reprimanded for a neglect of duty), Tryphena moved to a non-conformist school at Coryates in 1868.

In January 1870, Tryphena entered the Non-conformist Stockwell Teacher Training College in South London on a scholarship. So successful was she that at the end of her two years, she was appointed as Headmistress of Plymouth Day School, a large school for girls in Plymouth, Devon on a salary of close to £100 a year.

During her training in London between 1870 and 1872 when she moved to her headship in Plymouth, aged twenty-one, she and Hardy remained close. Gittings felt it highly probable that Thomas had visited her in Plymouth in 1872 on the way to meeting Emma's father, ostensibly to ask for Emma's hand in marriage.[11] It is a passage in Hardy's life we know very little about, apart from stories of the hostile reception Hardy received from Emma's father, John Gifford in Bodmin, but it may also have been Thomas and Tryphena's last meeting alone. We can only speculate whether it was at this point that they ended their relationship. Gittings suggests that the Christmas of 1872 may have been the last time Thomas saw Tryphena, and then only *'if indeed his own mother let him.'*[12]

Soon after she took up her post as Headmistress, her eldest sister Rebecca came to live with her as housekeeper and remained on, even after Tryphena's was married, before dying in 1885. Rebecca had only been married for three months to a saddler in Puddletown, Frederick Pain, when she absconded and the shock of this to her family and acquaintances helped fuel the unsubstantiated theory that Rebecca was actually Tryphena's mother rather than her sister.[13] Martha, meanwhile, with whom Thomas had flirted when he was an adolescent, despite their age difference, had moved to London and taken up a position as a lady's maid, become pregnant to the butler and married. Hardy retained an old affection for Martha and it is likely that her experiences as a servant were used by Hardy in *The Hand of Ethelberta*. Tomalin suggests that the novel was amongst other things, *'a farewell to Martha'* who emigrated to Australia with her family soon after. [14]

In 1873 or possibly early 1874, Tryphena met Charles Gale, the proprietor of a public house in Topsham, a village some 35 miles northeast of Plymouth and they were married on 15 December, 1877. Soon after, they began a family, having four children in all: Eleanor Tryphena (Nellie) in 1878, Charles in 1880, George in 1882, and Herbert in 1886. Following the birth of her last child Tryphena suffered a 'rupture' from which she died just three days before her thirty-ninth birthday.

That much we know. There is, however, much more, the story of another Tryphena based on a variety of sources, some more reliable than others, fuelled by hearsay, oral accounts, speculation, research and textual analysis.

The first salvo in the campaign to push Tryphena into the foreground of Thomas Hardy lore came with the publication of a book published in 1966 titled *Providence and Mr Hardy*, written by Lois Deacon and Terry Coleman, that made a number of speculative claims about Tryphena and Thomas, including, most contentiously, that she had borne him an illegitimate son. Other claims made included that Tryphena was, in fact, the daughter of her twenty-two-year-old sister (the same one Thomas was alleged to have flirted with briefly at a party while still a boy); that the two were engaged for a number of years and even the suggestion that Rebecca was in fact the daughter of Jemima.[15] Despite the strength of some of their arguments, based on family testimonies, their unsubstantiated and extravagant claim that:

'For sixty years he (Thomas) had lived in a multi-caverned hell, into which he had been plunged by a score of hideous ironies of circumstance. The complex tragedy of "concatenated affections" between himself, Tryphena Sparks, Horace Moule, Emma Lavinia Gifford and Charlie Gale had devastated the lives of three of them during the decade 1867–77 and had, perforce, to be hidden during the lifetime of Hardy's whole family'.[16]

– strikes the reader as melodramatic until we remember that Hardy was a purveyor of secrets and that this period of his life is one he made sure we knew almost nothing about. Kate's comment after the opening of Hardy's recreated study at the Dorchester Museum and its inference that people did not know all or much of the truth about her famous brother should have told us as much.

Not surprisingly, such claims and the publicity they generated, prompted a vigorous response from Hardy's biographers. Gittings, in his first volume of biography, *Young Thomas Hardy* summarised the claims made as monstrous and especially that Hardy

'. . . had a child by a very young girl, ostensibly his cousin, but really his niece. Apprised of this, he reproached himself (inaccurately) with the sin of incest. Guilt, atonement, and disillusion over this, it is said, lay at the bottom of his work, and of his whole attitude to life.'[17]

In his response, which consisted of a ten-page appendix to his biography of Hardy, Gittings began by recounting what was commonly known and substantiated by an earlier pamphlet by Lois Deacon, that Tryphena Sparks was in a relationship (understanding? Engagement?) with Hardy, that he gave her a ring that her future husband, Charles Gale, whom she met in 1873 persuaded her to give back (arguing that she and Thomas were cousins) and that after Tryphena's death, Thomas and his brother Henry, visited her grave in Topsham, Devon to place a wreath on her grave and that her widowed husband refused to see him, to all of which Gittings noted

'There seems little doubt that most of this story is true.'[18]

Thereafter, he goes on the attack, refuting Deacon's claims in detail, even challenging the claim that the summer of 1867 was particularly long and hot by citing the daily forecast from *The Times* for nearby Weymouth by the day. While there was a suggestion that he protested too much, probably in an attempt to redress the balance (an observation later made by Larkin), he dismantled the more extreme claims of Deacon and Coleman, particularly concerning the unsubstantiated account that Hardy had a son, ostensibly with his cousin who was more likely his niece.

Yet when we return to Gittings' text, it is clear from the number of references alone (42 compared with 6 in Millgate including his appendix devoted entirely to debunking the theses of *Providence and Mr Hardy*), that he sees a significant role for Tryphena.

To support this assertion, Gittings refers to the happiness of a summer the couple spent together in Weymouth in 1869, the emotional turmoil and unhappiness wrought in Hardy and the guilt he felt in sending out two Valentine cards in 1871, to Emma and Tryphena (an unsubstantiated claim made by Gittings). All of these issues were facing Hardy that he, apparently, spent considerable time wrestling with. Gittings scoured the poems and novels, seeing Tryphena as Fancy Day in *Far from the Madding Crowd* and being the subject of various poems, including 'At Waking', 'In the Vaulted Way' and others from the 'She to He' sequence. He refers to Tryphena as a 'former lover' in linking her with Elfride in *A Pair of Blue Eyes*[19], an association normally reserved for Emma. While rebutting the outlandish claims made by Deacon and Coleman, Gittings does ascribe an important place for Tryphena in Thomas's life, albeit much later than Hillyard who argues that Hardy came of age around 1865, when he first dallied with Tryphena, while Gittings placed the date nearer to 1870 when Hardy was already thirty.

Armed by Gittings' research, other biographers boldly followed, including Millgate, still regarded as Hardy's definitive biographer.

He acknowledged that Hardy was attracted to Tryphena, but in terms echoed by Tomalin that almost certainly there was

'no child, probably no formal engagement, and perhaps not even a dramatic parting, but simply a gradual erosion of intimacy, an eventual relapse into the friendly and cousinly terms of the past.'[20]

although, like Tomalin, he noted that

'The two were often alone together, and it would not be extraordinary if they made love.'[21]

In his biography, Millgate argues that it was Eliza Nicholls, not Tryphena, who was the most important figure in Hardy's early emotional life and diminished her further by listing various other belles, including Cassie Pole, Mary Waight, Louisa Harding as well as Martha and Rebecca Sparks, and Eliza's sister, Mary Jane.[22] Hence, Tryphena is relegated to the status of just one of his romantic attachments and not an important one at that. In contrast to Gittings, little is made of her significance, personal or literary, and as a result, the weight of scholarship turns against Tryphena and sees her recede from the front line. The biography of Hardy by Seymour-Smith supported the view of Millgate over Gittings

'that Tryphena's passage through Tom's life was fairly, if not absolutely, unimportant'[23] and completely dismissed the rumour of her having a baby son, called Randolph, in the summer of 1868 while demolishing much of the speculation and mystique that was commonly spoken about Tryphena.

In the most recent book on the subject, Nicholas Hillyard set out to look for evidence about Tryphena through Thomas Hardy's own work. At the outset, he argued that

'Deacon's recreation was enlivened by a few risky speculations which were seized upon by her critics and with their demolition, Tryphena was once again relegated to the status of footnote.'[24]

His attempts at rehabilitation, however, contain a substantial number of his own speculations, almost all interpretative, many fascinating in the links and assertions they make, but without being truly compelling.

As the smoke clears, we are none the wiser. Our intuition, cautious or otherwise might lead us to pronounce one way or another, but perhaps the last word should lie with Philip Larkin in a review of *Young Thomas Hardy* who wrote that the Deacon-Coleman solution

'may have been wildly and ludicrously wrong, but it felt true.'[25]

I trust his poet's instincts and his writer's understanding of Hardy. But if that sounds feeble compared to the cases put up by Deacon and Coleman or by Hillyard, there are the strands of evidence, however small and tenuous, that lead to the conclusion, that Tryphena played a much more important role in the life and writings of Thomas Hardy than her major biographers give her credit for. It is in the detail of the writing, (and we should give credit to the detective work of Nicholas Hillyard, even if we disagree with his deductions), the unusual behavior, the clues provided by Hardy himself, as in the last verse of 'On a Heath' (below) on which Hardy was quizzed in 1920 on the 'other life', only conceding that there was 'one':
(There was another looming / Whose life we did not see; / There was one stilly blooming / Full night to where walked we; / There was a shade entombing / All that was bright of me).

There was Hardy's own illustration of a dead body covered by a sheet accompanying his poem on Tryphena in the collection of poems, an image Tomalin calls 'distinctly weird' – or his self-professed prescience of her death.[26] There is the visit Thomas and Henry paid to Topsham after Tryphena's death to pay their respects where her widowed husband refused to receive them. If we look carefully, we can also find various textual clues – the publication of *The Well-Beloved* with its three generations mirroring the Sparks' sisters; or Hardy starting the novel soon after Tryphena's death with Pierston burning her writing and a lock of her hair in direct imitation of the opening lines of, 'Thoughts of Phena'. Most of the evidence is speculative when taken on its own, but collectively it forms a strangely compelling body of evidence of dates, places, events, many suggested by Hillyard, which seem to support Larkin's hunch, if not about Tryphena's parentage or a child, at least about Tryphena's influence on Thomas Hardy and his work.

In answering the questions about Hardy's attitude to women and their influence upon him, there is little that is explicit. Tryphena could be the key that unlocks everything. If we believe Hillyard, she is woven through many of the heroines of Hardy's novels and a good number of his poems. She undoubtedly influenced Thomas and that influence lingered although whether it only appealed to the romantic in Hardy, the writer or the 'other self', or Hardy himself, we just don't know. Although family, she also represented the new woman, full of ambition and capable of breaking away from the poverty of family and aspiration, as she showed in securing her first headship straight out of teaching college. On the other hand, she may belong where Tomalin and others have put her, at the periphery of Hardy's life and writing. Even the obvious links with Sue Bridehead in *Jude* (a cousin, trainee teacher) are countered by claims the character was based rather on Florence Henniker, quiet, intellectual and altogether less demonstrative rather than the more earthy Tryphena, although Hardy's own evidence in his preface to the novel, that

'some of the circumstances of the novel were suggested by the death of a woman in 1890' [27]

cannot be ignored. Hardy drew his characters from a variety of sources as well as his own imagination and each was a composite of the conscious and unconscious. We can only conclude that it is from not knowing that we continue to be teased, unsure that when Hardy wrote of becoming a 'young man in 1865' a phase he argued lasted until he was 'nearly fifty', the period from his alleged dalliance with Tryphena to her eventual death, he was relating his life directly to hers. That might be too much of a supposition to make, but the suggestion is still worthy of consideration rather than dismissing it altogether as others were inclined to do.

Recent writers on Hardy have also tended to dismiss any idea of Thomas and Tryphena being particularly close. It is unfortunate that the writings of Deacon and Coleman with their extravagant claims resulted in a backlash relegating Tryphena's place in Thomas's life as being no more significant than other local girls he had dallied with, including her own sisters. Deacon and Gittings, however, undoubtedly opened the way for a much closer examination of Tryphena's possible relationship with Thomas in the future. It is clear that while Jemima loved her sister, Maria and her nieces, it was quite a different matter to Thomas forming any romantic attachment with any of them. What's more, Thomas was very conscious of his mother's disapproval of the possibility of any such thing happening. He was also becoming aware of the gap between the local Dorset girls he had grown up amongst and the 'new 'women he had seen in London and who, like Emma, appeared much more sophisticated and alive. We can only speculate about whether in 1872 Thomas made a choice between continuing to pursue Typhena or to set his store on Emma, although knowing what we do of Tryphena it is altogether more likely that it was she who determined the course of their future relationship. Regardless, from 1872 Tryphena disappeared from Hardy's life and while she lived the remainder of her days in Plymouth, not so very far away from Dorset, they did not meet up again. But she was never out of Hardy's thoughts and after her death, he wrote the poem in her memory entitled 'Thoughts of Phena' in which he recalled their time together:

Not a line of her writing have I,
Not a thread of her hair,
No mark of her late time as dame in her dwelling, whereby
I may picture her there;
And in vain do I urge my unsight
To conceive my lost prize
At her close, whom I knew when her dreams were upbrimming with light
And with laughter her eyes.

What scenes spread around her last days,
Sad, shining, or dim?
Did her gifts and compassions enray and enarch her sweet ways
With an aureate nimb?
Or did life-light decline from her years,

And mischances control
Her full day-star; unease, or regret, or forebodings, or fears
Disennoble her soul?

Thus I do but the phantom retain
Of the maiden of yore
As my relic; yet haply the best of her – fined in my brain
It may be the more
That no line of her writing have I,
Nor a thread of her hair,
No mark of her late time as dame in her dwelling, whereby
I may picture her there.

It is hard to overestimate her importance to Hardy. Nicholas Hillyard suggests that *'Without Tryphena, it is just possible Hardy would have become the poet we recognise, but certainly not the novelist'.*[28]

The savage reaction by Hardy scholars and biographers to the Deacon-Coleman thesis succeeded in pushing Tryphena into the background, but in the clamour, possibly buried much else besides. Tryphena was a significant presence in his life, especially during the mystery years from 1865–1870 and her reputation is long overdue for a fresh appraisal.

As someone who took pleasure in collecting photographs of the women he met, the absence of any tangible reminder of Typhena must have upset Thomas. Yet she remained, in his words and affections, as well as in his verdant imagination, the 'lost prize' that had somehow eluded him.

Chapter 6

Florence Henniker 'Dear Fellow-Scribbler'

In 1889, the poet, Rosamund Tomson sent Hardy a book of her poetry *The Bird Bath* that had been published using her pseudonym, Graham R Tomson. She was reputed to be a striking beauty, a fact that her portraits bear out, already onto a second husband who she was also soon to abandon on the way to taking up with the novelist H B Marriott Watson who she stayed with until her early death.[1]

For the next three years, Hardy was in her thrall. He seemed to lose all sense of propriety, behaving flirtatiously when in her company and through their regular exchange of letters as he enjoyed '*. . . a far season of / Of love and unreason*' that '*turned his life upside down*'.[2] Hardy asked for her photograph very early on in their relationship, as was his wont, and it was this that became the keepsake he used when writing 'An Old Likeness', first published in 1922 in Hardy's collection entitled *Late Lyrics*. At the time, Rosamund was both pleased and flattered by the attention that she had managed to elicit from Hardy and paraded her association with him. Eventually, Hardy decided she was merely exhibiting him as 'an admirer' for her own purposes and broke off the friendship 'with considerable disgust' as he recounted to Florence Henniker, although possibly that was said for her benefit. [3] In 'An Old Likeness' written after her death in 1911, clearly all has been forgiven (or forgotten) as Hardy calls up the passion which had taken him 'by storm' twenty-two years previously and led him to pick up the painting he had been given and kiss it '*as if I had wist it / Herself of old.*'

What was significant about her sudden appearance in Hardy's life was that she enticed Thomas to shake the cage of his marriage and realise just how dissatisfied he had become with Emma. Such was Hardy's libido and imagination he needed little encouragement to respond to Rosamund's overtures. She was to become the first of a succession of four women writers who were attached to Thomas to a greater or lesser degree over the following twenty years, concluding eventually with Florence Dugdale.

Rosamund's relationship with Hardy, tenuous as it was, signalled a turning point in Hardy's personal life and that following the thwarted romance, Hardy began to look, in the words of Millgate, '*quite deliberately outside his marriage for emotional satisfaction, and potentially for sexual satisfaction.*' [4]

It was with this back-story in mind that Thomas met Florence Henniker in 1893.

Florence Henniker was to become Thomas's closest female friend for thirty years and a constant correspondent and confidante until her death in 1923. They met at a propitious time of his life, as his marriage to Emma was experiencing difficulties and after an initial period during which Thomas hoped for a romantic attachment, or at the very least an intimate relationship, conducted through letters interspersed with assignations, they were to settle into a long-term and close friendship that continued throughout her life. Clearly besotted from their first meeting, Thomas's feelings for her eventually mellowed after he found his deepest feelings were unrequited, and it was to Florence's credit that she gave Thomas pause enough to allow for a cordial and close friendship to grow out of her rebuttal of his early amorous and inappropriate advances. She was, after all, a happily married woman, albeit independent of thought and spirit, and was to remain so throughout her life.

Their long friendship and correspondence continued after the death of both her husband and Emma in 1912, with the tacit approval of Florence Dugdale, the second Mrs Hardy, who, unusually (for she was both possessive of Hardy and suspicious of women who tried to get too close to him), approved of Mrs Henniker. Soon after her marriage in 1914, the new Mrs Hardy wrote of Mrs Henniker in a letter to Lady Hoare,

'She has always been a sincere and affectionate friend to him, staunch and unfaltering' before adding *' . . . and I am glad to say, she is my friend too'* [5]

This was in contrast to Emma in the seventeen years until her death in 1912 who was frosty towards the younger woman (no doubt stirred by seeing the full flowering of her husband's infatuation) which may, in turn, account for why so few of Florence's letters to Thomas survive from that early period.

Florence was born in 1855, the daughter of the 1st Lord Houghton. She married a British army officer in 1882, (Major, later General) Arthur Henry Henniker-Major, but rather than settling into life as an army officer's wife, with all its duties and expectations, she was determined to write. Having been raised in a household filled with the intricacies and intrigue of British politics, Florence was a strong, independent woman, more handsome than classically beautiful and both intelligent and well informed while possessing all the social graces and charm of a society hostess. While early in her life she had a reputation for being both fast and clever, by the time she and Hardy met she was a mature, confident woman of thirty-eight years and a published writer, quite unlike anyone he had met before.[6] Nor was her family all it seemed: Despite their outward piety, her father, Lord Houghton, a conservative Member of Parliament, was also a literary man, a publisher and writer (he wrote a biography of Keats and possessed an unsurpassed collection of erotic literature, later bequeathed to the British Library). His liberal views, fuelled by his time at Cambridge where he was a member of the Apostles' Club, rubbed off on Florence although in her personal life she took a rather more traditional standpoint, especially when it came to fidelity and marriage.

Florence and Thomas first met at the Vice-Regal residence in May 1893 where Thomas and Emma had been invited for Whitsuntide. Thomas had known Florence's father, Lord Houghton as far back as 1880, and it was this connection that lay behind the invitation for Thomas and Emma to visit them in Dublin. Florence was there to act as hostess for her younger brother, Robert, the second Lord Houghton, now Lord Lieutenant of Ireland, who had been widowed six years previously when his wife died at the tragically young age of thirty leaving him with three young children. As well as her official duties, Florence was also keen to meet Thomas Hardy whose reputation had been considerably enhanced following the publication of *Tess of the D'Urbervilles* in book form the previous year.

Like both of Hardy's wives and several of his women friends, who saw in Thomas a possible supporter of their own writing careers, Florence was keen to pursue their mutual interest. Prior to meeting Thomas she had had two novels published: *Sir George* in 1891 and *Bid Me Good-bye* in 1892 with another published later in 1893. In that respect, at least, she differed from a number of his other admirers who saw Thomas as a possible help in getting them started on a writing career (including both his wives) although she was grateful for the help he seemed only too keen to offer. Florence was already recognized in literary circles, well connected and comfortable in society; indeed, arguably, she had significantly less need of Hardy than he did of her. Yet when they began to know each other, they found they had many mutual interests and views, even in such matters as vivisection, although some subjects, such as architecture and romance, were more probably in his mind than hers.

The impact of this Whitsun visit upon Thomas was immediate and dramatic as was the impression that Florence, a charming and well-bred woman, made on him. Her family connections, her interest in him and her admiration of his writing (an essential pre-requisite for any reciprocation), allied with her affectionate qualities, aristocratic upbringing and her broad literary and humanitarian interests drew him to her. In his diary, from his first introduction, he described Florence as a *'charming, intuitive woman'* [7] who displayed the qualities that allowed them to build a lasting friendship once Thomas had navigated the hormonal storm that seemed to precede any equanimity he might be able to achieve. At the time, he was busy writing *Jude the Obscure* which would do so much to destroy the last vestiges of trust and affection between Emma and himself, and it is not surprising that the person and views of Florence Henniker can be seen in both the novel (particularly in the embodiment of Sue Brideshead) and also, in a number of his later poems. Their time in Dublin, meanwhile (without her husband, but with Emma lurking about) was busy including a visit to the Guinness brewery with Mrs Henniker and several of the vice-regal guests, a trip to Killarney, as well as attending the races, and the Queen's birthday review which he described as *'a romantic scene, pathetically gay.'* [8]

For Thomas the physical attraction was immediate and he made every effort to capture her attention and show her how she could benefit from his person and reputation. He seemed to blunder into situations without any thought for the feelings of Emma (or the absent husband) with an emotional impulsivity as if believing such behaviour was acceptable. Impervious to how foolish and insulting he could seem, he was constantly trying to emphasise what he could offer Florence. As Dalziell noted,

'The intensity of his feelings . . . led him to adopt any stratagems—from architectural lessons to literary discussions—which might help to establish an intimate relationship.' [9]

The early letters give a good idea of the intensity of Hardy's pursuit and how quickly he had lost his head and heart. Within days of returning from Ireland on 29 May 1893, their letter writing was in full flow. On 3 June, he wrote *'My Dear Mrs Henniker' 'I much desire to go somewhere with you.'* And later in the same letter, he made a *'dreadful confession'* that he was going to a luncheon to meet another writer, adding *'she is very pretty, they say, but on my honour that had nothing to do with it – purely literary reasons only.'* [10]

By 7 June, they were exchanging books and Hardy was arranging tickets for the theatre and by 10th June felt encouraged to write (having known Florence for a matter of a few weeks), *'I sincerely hope to number you all my life among the most valued of my friends.'*[11]

By 20 June, he was installed in the Athenaeum Club, and working hard to impress Florence with his social connections, in this instance the indefatigable London hostess, Lady Jeune:

'Lady Jeune has a dinner on the 9th July – I wonder if you are to be there. I have accepted also an invitation to Lady Shrewsbury's dinner on the 29th (of June), but I can throw her over if necessary.' In the same letter he arranged to meet Florence early on the following Saturday morning, knowing she was to be at a ball the previous night and exhorting her: *'Don't fag your self out at that dancing. Promise you won't.'* Of Emma, during this time, or Arthur Henniker, there is never a mention.[12]

In a letter to Florence in June 1893, only a month after they met, Hardy provided an insight into his views of society women (possibly with half an eye towards impressing Florence). In a letter to Florence dated 29 June, he wrote a revealing description of the Academy crush he had just attended and where he met a 'great many vain people':

'One amusing thing occurred to me. A well known woman in society, who is one of those despicable creatures a flirt, said to me when I was talking to her: "Don't look at me so!" I said, "Why? – because you feel I can see too much of you?" (she was excessively décolletée). "Good heavens!" she said. "I am not coming to pieces, am I?" and clutching her bodice she was quite overcome. When I next met her she said bitterly: "You have spoilt my evening: and it was too cruel of you!" However, I don't think it was, for she deserved it.' [13]

What Florence made of Hardy's callous comments is not known, but she must have been surprised at Hardy's willingness to pass judgement on those who had welcomed him into London's inner sanctum and the apparent social confidence he exhibited in writing so freely about them.

Throughout the summer of 1893, the correspondence continued unabated so that by July, he was comfortable enough to write that *'You seem quite like an old friend to me'.* [14] However, it was evident that Thomas's passions had not waned; indeed, he seemed ever hopeful that something illicit or at least complicit would evolve from their close and intimate correspondence. He was soon to be let down for the last time although the revelation of his feelings (and the rejection) was not made explicit until the publication of *Wessex Poems* in 1898. Included amongst its number, was a poem, 'At an Inn' that described a meeting Thomas had engineered in August 1893 when, for some hours during which his, *'love lingered numb,'* his hopes were finally dashed. Thomas had learned that Florence was staying at the family's seaside house in Southsea and proposed that they meet in Winchester so that he could show her the Cathedral, to which she agreed. Even so, she must have had some reservations having received a letter from Thomas written on 3 August (since destroyed) only a few days before their meeting in which he had transgressed the propriety of their friendship. Thomas travelled alone from Dorchester by train and met Florence at Eastleigh station from where they caught a train to Winchester. It was on that journey, in the privacy of the train's compartment, that Hardy's fervent overtures were repulsed and, no doubt, the contents of his letter discussed as well. Clearly, Florence saw that visiting the Cathedral was a ruse to provide Thomas with the opportunity to get Florence on her own. Her rebuttal to his words (for it was always with his words that he wooed best) was to mark the end of Thomas's hopes and while they stayed that night at the George Hotel, the city's smartest hotel, he must have felt the ignominy of his situation, alone in his room, possibly drafting his poem.[15] He noted as much in his letter to Florence of 17 August when he wrote:

'You allude to the letter of Aug(ust) 3rd. If I sh(oul)d never write to you again as in that letter you must remember that it was written before you expressed your views – "morbid" indeed! Petty rather – in the railway carriage when we met at Eastleigh' before concluding, perhaps in hope, *'But I am always your friend'* [16], no doubt bruised and unsettled by the failure of his suit.

It is to the credit of Florence that she was able to rise above this potentially excruciating lapse and build such an enduring friendship both with Thomas and, in time, his new wife. It could be, of course, that she had briefly harboured some affection for Thomas also, by entering into a correspondence that was both personal and intimate. Her devotion to her husband and her Christian faith was never likely to allow her to entertain any impropriety, however, and the time quickly passed when she may have felt tempted by Hardy's overtures. We may be uncertain of her feelings or intentions in entertaining an intimate friendship with Thomas, but of his desires and hopes for her, we can have little doubt.

Three weeks were to elapse before his next letter, the longest gap so far in their correspondence. By the autumn, however, Thomas and Florence had decided to collaborate on a short story *The Spectre of the Real,* which was eventually published in 1894. The initiative came about, one suspects, as a pretext to spend time together. From what we know, both through their correspondence and based on its stylistic features, Thomas produced the draft to which Florence made a number of contributions, by providing some of the descriptive passages and other suggestions regarding the storyline although the plot bore all the hallmarks of Hardy's short stories.

On 28 October, Thomas wrote to Florence, in part to thank her for another photograph she had sent him:

'I must let you know that the story is finished' adding later in the paragraph, *'If anything in it is what you don't like please tell me quite freely – and it shall be modified. As I said last time, all the wickedness (if it has any) will be laid on my unfortunate head, while all the tender and proper parts will be attributed to you.'*[17]

The story received few plaudits. Regardless of who wrote what (and they agreed to keep their 'parts' secret), it is certain that it was Thomas who had first proposed the collaboration for his own non-literary reasons and that the process of writing with Florence was, certainly for him, more important that the story's publication and reception.

Throughout the first few months after they had met, we can follow Thomas and Florence's burgeoning relationship by their surviving exchange of letters (although,

sadly, almost all of Florence's letters to Thomas were destroyed, whether by Hardy himself or by Florence Hardy in one of their innumerable bonfires). Nevertheless, there are enough left for us to see the intimacy of their relationship and how quickly it developed. In the first few months it was undoubtedly Thomas making the running as he acknowledged in a letter of 10 September, 1893:
'You may be thankful to hear that the one-sidedness I reminded you of is disappearing from the situation. But you will always be among the most valued of my friends as I hope always to remain one at least of the rank and file of yours.' [18]

In early letters, Florence was usually addressed as *'My dear Mrs Henniker'* or *'My dear friend'*, only on one occasion slipping into the more colloquial *'My dear little friend'* once before reverting immediately to 'my dear friend', which is where it stayed. In signing off, Thomas was more consistent in style although he used a variety of forms (*'yours ever' 'ever yours', 'your affectionate friend' 'always your friend', 'ever affectionately yours'*).

What was not so conventional was some of the intimacy of their exchanges and the personal details they shared. Thomas often included flirtatious, even inappropriate, comments in his letters, while Florence, more cautious in what she wrote, regularly sent Thomas photographs of herself and a number of significant gifts (an inkstand was one that Thomas most treasured). Clearly, at times, the closeness of the relationship unnerved Florence and made her doubt the appropriateness of the friendship, and her own behaviour. One letter from Thomas (sent to *'my dear little friend'*) highlighted various concerns that Florence has raised about herself and prompted Hardy to write: *'Of course, I shall never dislike you . . . I won't have you say there that there is little good in you'* touching on the *'ethereal, intangible'* features of her character before concluding *'If you only have one good quality, a good heart, you are good enough for me. Believe me, my dear friend'* and signing off *'always yours Tom H.'* [19]

Thereafter, the letters dry up, partly after the uproar that followed the publication of *Jude the Obscure,* partly through illness, and partly through other demands on the time and attention of each from other parties. Initially, there was little sign of any diminution of affection, especially on the part of Hardy; in time, however, a subtle change took place in their relationship. By the time Thomas wrote in August 1895, *'I am overwhelmed with requests from editors for short stories. Why didn't you go on being my pupil so that I c(oul)d have recommended you as a substitute'*, he had resigned himself to a platonic, rather than a romantic friendship, albeit one that would more likely endure. [20]

While the initial amour, such as it was, had faded by 1896 (by which time Hardy had met the subject of his next infatuation), Florence and Thomas settled into a regular and still often deeply personal correspondence, maintained even when Thomas and Emma were touring the continent on their bicycles. Occasionally there are little snippets that give us an insight into their on-going relationship and the intimacy of their conversation. Sadly, we only have Hardy's response in a letter of 1 June 1896 to a previous conversation and can only wonder what had provoked Florence's comment: *'By the way, I have been offended with you for some time, though I have forgotten to say so, for what you said – that I was an advocate for "free love".'* [21]

But on the whole the letters focused on literary matters although there was always a desire, usually unsuccessful, for Thomas to engineer meetings with Florence. He was often asking where she was and occasionally called on her at her home. He was often encouraging her down to the West Country and reacting rather petulantly on being told she was too busy to see him.[22] He had taken the liberty to befriend her husband, Arthur Henniker, whose name came up more in their correspondence (as did Emma's). By the turn of the century, his letters were full of pessimism, full of details on such mundane subjects as a visit to the dentist or health matters (he concludes one in January, 1899 with the sentence *'But my pleasures are all past, I fear!'* [23] His own hypochondria often featured. In a letter to Florence on 23 August, 1899, in response to one of her own describing a pain in her eye, he spent some time, by way of consolation, in telling her, *'To my disappointment, also, the weakness in my own comes back at intervals of a few days – a rheum – left by the influenza I had in London'* [24]. Over the years, health matters, including references to rheumatism, toothache, headache, neuralgia, violent colds, depression, influenza, putrid throat and sciatica, featured prominently as the subject of their correspondence regressed from the personal into the mundanity of everyday life.

Apart from literary subjects and vivisection, The Boer War, in which Florence's husband (now) Major Arthur Henniker served, (and which led Thomas to write to Florence to ask for a photograph of her husband to be framed with the 'other celebrities') now dominated their correspondence. Arthur Henniker was to serve in South Africa for three years, not returning until late 1902, and yet, rather than to present itself as an opportunity for Thomas to see more of Florence, a combination of illness and reserve on both sides, saw them spending even less time together. Moreover, Thomas's agnosticism clashed with Florence's faith and he could not avoid being provocative: *'We (the civilised world) have given Christianity a fair trial for nearly 2000 years, and it has not yet taught countries the rudimentary virtue of keeping peace: so why not throw it over, and try, say, Buddhism.'* [25]
Through it all Florence kept her equanimity; she had learned how to cope with Thomas and was not going to let his occasional silliness get in the way of their friendship.

It is the appearance of Florence Dugdale that marked the final phase of their relationship. The two women became friends soon after Florence Dugdale came onto the scene (indeed, there is a view – unfounded – that Florence Henniker had first introduced Florence Dugdale to Thomas as early as 1904) and even though any romantic interest had long passed, her approval meant a great deal to Thomas. In 1910 Thomas wrote to Florence of his new friend: *'I am so glad you like her: she quite likes you – indeed you have no idea what a charm you have for her.'*[26] When Thomas and Florence Henniker lost their respective spouses within several months of each other, there was no suggestion of trying to recapture the intimacy of their early years. When, in early 1914, Thomas and Florence Dugdale married, the other Florence only found out through reading the newspaper.

If it is in the early correspondence with Florence Henniker that we get an insight into Thomas Hardy's hopes and desires and his thoughts on women and society, it is in his writing, notably in *Jude the Obscure* and through a number of his poems written in the last years of the nineteenth century that Hardy acknowledges his feelings for Florence and the debt he owed her.

There is no doubt that Florence made an immediate impact on Hardy's writing. Busy with *Jude the Obscure* one of his characters, the intelligent Sue Bridehead, who displayed traits of Emma and Tryphena was at least in part modelled on Florence. This was most obvious in the inclusion of her own name in the name of the character (Susanna Mary Florence Bridehead), as well as in her essential character trait of seeming emancipated, but ultimately deceiving on that point by being quite conventional as well as ethereal (a word Hardy uses to describe both Sue and Florence). If we are not convinced by the descriptions, we can turn to the testimony of Hardy's second wife, Florence Dugdale, who confirmed that Sue Bridehead was, indeed, based, at least in part, on the person of Florence Henniker. [27]

It was in Hardy's poetry that we find other references to Florence. In 'A Broken Appointment' Hardy writes of the grief he felt when Florence failed to appear at an arranged meeting, bemoaning her lack of courtesy, and her lack of feeling and compassion, concluding:

'Once you, a woman, came
To soothe a time-torn man; even though it be
You love not me?'[28]

Thomas wrote a number of poems about unrequited love, either directly or obliquely to Florence, including 'A Thunderstorm and 'In Tenebris' [29], but by 1896, he had come to terms with their relationship as best expressed in 'Wessex Heights':

'As for one rare, fair woman, I am now but a thought of hers
I enter her mind and another thought succeeds me that she prefers;
Yet my love for her in its fullness she herself even did not know;
Well, time cures hearts of tenderness, and now I can let her go'.

At the outset of their relationship, according to Seymour-Smith, Florence was to *'excite his love, his lust, his love and finally, if only temporarily, a fierce involuntary resentment'* [30] It was his frustration that having found a new, enlightened woman, one of spirit and independence that he would discover she was bound to convention by her faith and family.

In time Florence was superseded in his affections by Agnes Grove, temporarily, and then by Florence Dugdale yet she was to remain his longest surviving friend. In his diary, reproduced in *The Later Years*, Thomas made the following entry:

April 5. In today's Times*: "Henniker – on the 4th April, 1923, of heart failure, the Honourable Mrs Arthur Henniker. R.I.P." After a long friendship of thirty years!'*[31]

Her death was a sad loss to both Thomas and Florence. On the day of the funeral, Florence wrote to a friend: *'We feel very sad today as our dearest friend – Mrs Arthur Henniker – has been laid in her grave this afternoon.'*[32] Florence had grown inordinately fond of her namesake who was, she felt, their 'dearest friend.' Soon after the funeral, she paid tribute to her friendship in a letter to Sydney Cockerell, stating: *'She was beautiful and gifted and the kindest woman that one could conceive'* adding *'I miss her so much'* [33]

Thomas and Florence had met at a difficult time in his life, but after an initial period of embarrassment in which Hardy had to make the difficult adjustment from ardent suitor to companion, Florence became a valued confidante and the closest and most loyal of all the female friends in his life.

Chapter 7

Agnes Grove: The Dear Little Pupil

By 1895, Thomas's social life was settling into a pattern that had repeated itself several times over since he had first been introduced to London society by Mary Jeune (later Lady St Helier) a decade earlier – first with Rosamund, then with Florence Henniker and now, with another writer, Agnes Grove, who was to become his 'dear little pupil'.

Thomas and Emma had first met Mary Jeune in 1886 at one of the growing number of soirées and social occasions to which members of London society were inviting him. Mrs Jeune had remarried three years after being widowed by the death of her first husband, Colonel John Stanley in 1878, to Francis Jeune, a judge and conservative MP, later to become Lord St Helier. The couple had a young son, Francis, born in 1883 only three years before the couple first met the Hardys, as well as Mary's two daughters, Madeleine and Dorothy, from her earlier marriage. While not herself a writer, she was a patron to many authors and poets, notably Edith Wharton, and as the hostess who was primarily responsible for introducing Hardy to London society, she was an important person in his 'coming out' and the development of his more cosmopolitan outlook.

Mrs Jeune's significance to Hardy was three-fold: first, she provided an entry into London social life. As one of London's best known hostesses, full of joie de vivre – 'irrepressible' as Hardy called her – residing first in Wimpole Street and later in Harley Street, she was famed for her lunches, crushes and soirées and providing Hardy with an entrée to London society; second, she was rich, attractive and interested in literature and was keen to spend time with Hardy, talking literary matters as well as introducing him to her own circle; thirdly, Mrs Jeune provided the company of a young family in particular through her two daughters, who adopted him as family and called him 'Uncle Tom' throughout their lives, some compensation one could imagine, for the family he had never had with Emma. Interestingly, Emma's uncle, Dr Edwin Gifford, who had married Thomas and Emma while a canon at Worcester Cathedral and later became Archdeacon of London, had married Francis Jeune's sister, Margaret in 1873, linking the two families some thirteen years earlier, although it was Thomas, not Emma, that the family took to their bosom, and Thomas who spent most of the time in their company.

Thomas was increasingly finding himself drawn to attractive women, preferably society ladies who either wrote themselves (as did Rosamund Tomson, Florence Henniker and Agnes Grove – and indeed his two wives) or who were interested in literature. With each of his various liaisons, real or imagined, Thomas's response followed a similar pattern, first of infatuation, often embarrassingly demonstrative in its manifestation, an often intimate (and usually one-sided) correspondence before a gradual cooling of affection. Inevitably, after the first flush, head replaced heart, whether it was real emotion that Hardy had felt or some romantic notion of love that he conjured up, but it was a pattern that characterised his whole life, of perpetual adolescent feelings and responses. Hence, when he realised Rosamund was using his literary reputation to try and enhance her own, he lost interest in her; similarly, when Florence, modern woman though he judged her to be, would not countenance a relationship and brushed aside his advances, but offered him another, by way of close friendship, he responded in a way that was protective of self as well as of her. He had adapted remarkably well to the opportunities afforded by the London social scene with an enthusiasm that ran contrary to his earlier views on the aristocracy, often displaying an outward confidence that bordered on swagger. And now, through meeting Agnes Grove in 1895, he was also to discover another truth about just how interwoven were the upper echelons of society in which he chanced to mingle, by blood as well as by association. For not only was Agnes Grove Lady Jeune's niece by marriage, but she had also met Florence Henniker's brother, Lord Houghton at a party hosted by Lady Jeune. Indeed, sometime later, at his residence in Dublin where Agnes and her husband had been invited to stay, Lord Houghton had been described as being *'unduly attentive'* towards her.[1]

Thomas Hardy's first dalliance with Agnes was on the 4 September 1895 when he and Emma were staying at Rushmore in Dorset as the guests of the archaeologist, General Pitt-Rivers, Agnes' father. Hardy had met Pitt-Rivers at the Athenaeum club where he was a fellow member and had previously been a guest at their London residence. The occasion of the visit coincided, probably intentionally, with the annual fête that took place in the Larmer Tree Gardens, which had been created by the General.

On this particular night, as the evening drew in, hundreds of Vauxhall lamps were lit to allow for the evening festivities, the band struck up, and dancing commenced. Before long, Hardy had invited Agnes, the youngest and most beautiful of the General's daughters, to dance.

And so, as it was described by a local reporter, amid a scene of *'extraordinary picturesqueness and poetry'*, in the heightened atmosphere of music and dancing, under *'thousands of vauxhall lamps'* and *'the mellow radiance of the full moon,'*[2] Hardy was entranced, dancing the evening away, seemingly without a thought for Emma or Walter Grove, her husband. It was a night that stuck in the memory, the last time he trod on the greensward and it would sustain him for many years. Even on the occasion of her death, in 1926, Thomas could recall the night very clearly indeed, some thirty-one years later (although he did get the month wrong; perhaps an example of poetic licence to help the verse scan:

'Yes, I am stopped from hoping what I have hoped before – Yes, many a time! –
To dance with that fair woman yet once more
As in the prime Of August, when the wide-faced moon looked through
The boughs at the faery lamps of the Larmer Avenue.'

More telling even was the second verse which took the evening out of the realms in Thomas's memory of dancing to something, potentially more, at least in his imagination:

'I could not, though I should wish, have over again
That old romance,

And sit apart in the shade as we sat then
After the dance
The while I held her hand . . . '

From Agnes, we have very little recollection of the evening apart from a diary entry that *'she met and talked to Thomas Hardy, found him interesting.'* [3] Six months previously, she had tragically lost a new baby boy, two days after he was born, and she was still coming to terms with her loss. The next morning, Thomas would have felt his own disproportionate sense of loss in finding that she had left for London and that the connection made whilst dancing would have to be sustained through Hardy's determination to inveigle himself into her world by the only way he knew how: through evoking their common love of literature and writing.

Later the same month, Thomas wrote to Florence to tell her in his tactless way *'It was a pleasant visit, . . . the most romantic time I have had since I visited you at Dublin.'* [4] But his feelings for Agnes Grove were never of the same intensity as those he felt for Florence and nor was there ever the promise of more, but that did not stop Thomas encouraging Agnes into an intimate correspondence by championing her literary ambitions, much to the annoyance of Emma.

Agnes was to be very much in his thoughts over the coming months as he tried to find a way to make himself indispensable to her. While the relationship would be of a different nature than that with Florence Henniker, it nevertheless followed the same course that was true of all Hardy's relationships with his favoured women. A more significant problem for Thomas was the reaction he received from Emma who was irritated and embarrassed by his public infatuation and immediately proposed they went away on holiday together. Likewise, when Hardy's second wife, Florence Dugdale, who later became a good friend of Florence Henniker, edited *The Life of Thomas Hardy*, Agnes received short shrift. Indeed, there was one other reference to Agnes in the *Life of Thomas Hardy* and that was some ten months later at the Imperial Institute in London where he and Emma would listen to the famous bands of Europe. On that occasion, it was noted, in July 1896, they met

'with other of their friends, the beautiful Mrs – afterwards Lady – Grove; and the "Blue Danube" Waltz being started, Hardy and the latter lady danced two or three turns to it among the promenaders, who eyed them with a mild surmise as to whether they had been drinking or not.' [5]
Hardy was in thrall, later in life recalling her beauty and especially her violet eyes.

Agnes was the fifth of eight children born to Augustus Lane Fox, and his wife The Honourable Alice Stanley, between 1855 and 1866. Along with her siblings, Agnes had taken the surname of their father, being baptised either as Fox or Lane-Fox. While her father was not initially a popular choice of suitor for Baron Stanley, due to his modest prospects, his fortunes changed dramatically in 1880 when he inherited the vast estates of his cousin Horace Pitt-Rivers and, as part of the bequest, was required to adopt the surname 'Pitt-Rivers'. Agnes was a spirited girl partly fuelled by the fact that she was unusual in having received a good academic education while boarding at Oxford High School and also from the example of her mother's family, particularly her grandmother Baroness Stanley, who was a noted women's education campaigner.

After their father's elevation and their move to Rushmore, the family soon became acquainted with the Grove family at nearby Ferne House.

Walter Grove was one of the six children of Sir Thomas Grove. An Old Etonian who would have been satisfied living the life of a country squire, he was an unlikely partner for the headstrong and privately educated Agnes. Nevertheless, though eleven years older than Agnes, he had set his sights on his pretty new neighbour and by the end of 1881, when she was still only eighteen, they had started to plan the prospect of a life together.

There were, however, the interests of the families to negotiate, and these were not to prove easy. General Pitt-Rivers wanted some surety for Walter's prospects including an allowance from his future son-in-law's father and an acknowledgement that Ferne House would in time, pass on to Walter.

Sir Thomas was less forthcoming, knowing his own precarious financial position. He had been widowed three years previously and had already set about wooing an heiress to help secure his family's fortunes and had expected his son to do likewise.

In the deliberations between the two fathers, Walter decided to keep his own counsel. Agnes, however, was of an altogether different timbre. She was a true heir of her mother's reforming family and was to be deeply interested in the social and political issues of the day, notably the suffrage movement and was not afraid to stand up to her father in matters of the heart.

By late 1881, the growing relationship between Agnes and Walter was causing deep divisions between Agnes and her parents. In her diary, she had started to call her father 'the man' and her mother 'The minor one.'

In 1882, while staying at their London residence in 4 Grosvenor Gardens, matters came to a head. Agnes recorded in her diary on 27 February, *'Late for breakfast, considerable disturbance. I got very angry. Really angry. With the man too.'*[6] It was not only her own predicament that concerned her but that of her sister Alice also, for as she concluded *'I have a faint chance of escape from this tyranny and misery but she seems to have none . . . . '*[7] The domestic battles continued with little respite. In March, Agnes noted *'Grand row. The man swore etc. I had dinner up in my sitting room.'*[8]

But behind the scenes there were signs of movement between the two families and eventually a financial deal was brokered including a guarantee from the General that Agnes would receive an allowance of £300 p.a. With the impasse broken, the wedding between the nineteen-year-old Agnes and her thirty-year-old husband duly took place on 20 July and after honeymooning in New York they returned to find Sir Thomas had remarried in their absence.

Over the next few years, Agnes settled into her married life and despite a growing family, continued to develop her range of interests. She was a devotee to the Liberal cause, keen on debate and social issues, as she was on the society pages. Her life consisted of moving between the Dorset countryside and London, watching the growth of the Larmer Gardens that her father had established in 1880 for public enlightenment and entertainment and seeing her own three children grow up – a period of relative happiness that was brought abruptly to a halt with the death of their baby boy in March, 1895.

Agnes, like Rosamund and Florence, was a writer and Thomas soon established that the way to develop their friendship, and to create a dependence upon him as her confidante, was to inveigle his way into her affection by acting as both mentor and tutor. According to her biographer [9] Thomas was probably responsible for persuading Agnes to begin writing an article which he then offered to critique, while at the same time sending her a copy of the recently published *Jude* which included the note that he knew Agnes to be *'sufficiently broad of view to estimate without bias a tragedy of very unconventional lives'*.[10]

By admitting Agnes as his new muse, Thomas was acknowledging that his relationship with Florence Henniker was unlikely to progress any further. He had realised that Florence was never the potential mistress he had once hoped she might become and was both more righteous and principled than he had once thought – nay hoped – of her. Fearful of her reaction to the publication of *Jude the Obscure*, he had not yet sent her a copy of the book, an omission she took exception to accusing him of thinking her 'narrow', which may well have been the case (and she would have been annoyed to know that he had sent Agnes one in her place).

Thomas refuted the charge by suggesting that as Florence had lived through the writing of the book, he had presumed it would hold less interest for her, but it was clear that he had lost confidence in being able to count on her unconditional support and approval.[11] A month before, in a letter to her, he had accepted the impasse they had reached, commenting rhetorically on another suggestion of spending time with her, by writing, with faded hope, nay resignation, *'But that's all over, I suppose'*.[12]

Before the Larmer Garden party, Thomas didn't know much about Agnes, her character and her relationship with her husband and her family – especially those with her father and father-in-law, strong characters both. She had been a headstrong girl and the tumultuous on-going relationship with her father leading up to her wedding, only softened in the two years before his death.[13] As a young bride she had travelled to New York, started to learn the banjo and shown a penchant for shopping and partying. [14] After the death of the Sir Thomas in 1897, Walter assumed the baronetcy and at that point Agnes become Lady Grove. Walter was a fairly genial, yet hapless, man and his struggle to maintain the two great houses of Rushmore and Ferne was to consume him and Agnes for much of their lives. Ferne's future was soon determined and the property was first let, and eventually sold and in 1899 Walter and Agnes moved to Sedgehill, a smaller property owned by the Grove family. Later, as she became more aware of the deficiencies in her husband's character, she realised that he was unable to provide for her emotionally or financially. With her family's flagging fortunes, she sought to find a source of livelihood until ill health forced her into retreating from public life. Thereafter, for most of her latter years, money and debt dominated her life and by the end Hardy was just another intermittent correspondent, an old friend and admirer who had been lost to her.

The first flush of enthusiasm generated by her newfound relationship with Thomas provided an important impetus to Agnes's writing career.

Having worked on one article without success, she decided to write another on a subject dear to her heart entitled 'What Children Should be Told' which was published in July 1896. It was, by all accounts a forthright and challenging piece that was published in the *New Review* and established Agnes for a career in journalism. Hardy's contribution to her writing was likely to have been significant, both his advice and help with editing while his personal encouragement would have meant a great deal to her. As typical with Thomas, there was a seductive edge to his letters to Agnes, full of persuasion and flattery, making sure that she knew his abiding interest in her. It was present in his phrases, in words, in intimations, in making his subject feel that what she felt and thought mattered: *'I have often thought of the pleasant conversation we had at the Larmer, & shall hope to renew it some day'* he wrote to her in November 1895.[15] Four days later he was writing again, returning an article he had edited for her and saying about the novel he has just sent her, *'Don't let it depress you . . . or I shall not forgive myself for having written it'.*[16] He continued to correspond regularly through the early months of 1896 still taking his editing role very seriously and was so pleased by her improvement that in April, he concluded a letter with the well-known epithet, *'You are such a good little pupil'.*[17] They remained close throughout the summer of 1896 and in August he wrote to her again in response to an invitation to a play in which she was performing, *'I would have given anything to have seen you, as you know very well, even in a character not your own'.*[18] Three months later he was still attempting his unsubtle overtures, informing her *'I was in London last week. I wish you had been!'*[19]

In 1899, he wrote to her that he was going to be at the Woodbury Hill fair and that he would *'treat her to all the penny shows if you come!'*[20] Early 1900 he was still pursuing her, even making the promise *'I am intending to bicycle to you next summer.'*[21] Likewise, we sense the changing landscape by his forms of address, ranging from 'Dear Mrs Grove', 'Dear Lady Grove', 'My 'Dear Lady Grove' to 'My Dear Friend.'

At the same time, he continued to write flirtatiously to other women, including Florence Henniker and even to Mary Jeune, writing to her in 1897,

'My dear friend, I am intending to arrive at your door about 5 Wednesday. Could any other woman in London have attracted me thither this weather I wonder! Remember I come to see you rather than for the dinner. . . . . Your affectionate friend, TH.'[22]

Neither Agnes (nor any of them) was ever on their own in Hardy's mind. For each woman he befriended, sought after, there are so many solicitudes, meaning little on their own, but collectively illustrating his unflagging enthusiasm for the pursuit. There is no doubt his help was invaluable to Agnes, even as she allowed his flirtatious comments to wash over her.

By 1900, Agnes had become an accomplished writer, concentrating on topical, even controversial, issues, and developing a style of journalism that Hardy felt was her forte. She had ingratiated herself with both Thomas and eventually with Emma through their shared views on women's suffrage, even staying overnight at Max Gate in 1900. And yet, despite her appreciation for the unstinting support he gave her to help extend her writing career, her affection for Thomas was no more than that and it was rather to a younger coterie of men, capable men, admirers loyal to her, and of her class and background that she turned to for support and friendship.

During the next two years, the Groves spent time in Tangier. From their experiences of their first sojourn, Agnes published *Seventy One Days Camping in Morocco* although 'camping' may be putting too fine a point on it, full as it was of polo matches, hunts and social occasions reminiscent of their tea parties in England. Most of 1901 was spent in Morocco while back home, their family's financial struggles continued. Ferne had been sold, temporarily assisting the family's flagging fortunes, but their long-term prospects were not looking positive. They were back in Morocco in 1902 where their time was tragically cut short when their youngest son, eight-year-old Terence, fell into a pool and drowned.

After a period of grieving, and with Hardy's encouragement, Agnes returned to her writing. In 1903, she was offered a salary to become a regular contributor to the *New Magazine* and soon immersed herself in the London literary scene, albeit with the interruption in 1904 of the birth of another son, named Walter after his father.

During the Edwardian years, Agnes was busy writing, contributing to local and national publications and publishing three further books. Having lost contact while she had been abroad, Thomas was quick to take up his previous role and include Agnes in his social circle in London where she took on a role as hostess, often alongside Emma, and became a *'regular and intimate member of Hardy's circle of friends at the time'*.[23] In 1907, it was to Hardy that Agnes dedicated her most substantial book of essays to date, *The Social Fetich* based around the theme of social solecisms and various associated writings on such diverse subjects as tipping and social and class customs. By now her writing had matured and her tongue in cheek comments and gentle irony, even her disassembling of the aristocracy of which she lay at the heart, with her advice that it was open to anyone *'to learn the fetichistic pass words and practices of contemporary society'.* [24] It was this clever writing that provoked admiration, even from such a polished commentator as Hilaire Belloc. [25] Such was her burgeoning reputation that she took to light-hearted intellectual jousting with George Bernard Shaw in the letter column of *The Academy*, while her relative Sir Bertrand Russell added his judgement on both of them for good measure, which no doubt amused her.[26]

In 1908, Agnes published her most substantial book, *The Human Woman*. Thomas had not seen it in its entirety before publication – indeed, because the Hardys had eschewed London the previous season, they had seen less of Agnes, but on reading it, he described it as *'a series of brilliant and able essays which all who favour woman suffrage should be grateful for.'*

Hardy then added, not altogether sincerely, *'I, of course, who have long held that in justice women should have the votes, whatever may be said of the policy of granting them to the sex (from a man's point of view), need not convincing, though some of your ingenuous arguments had not occurred to me.'*[27]

By her mid-forties, Agnes had matured as a writer and carved her own niche, but before long the winds would change once more. In 1910, she published what was to be her last book, *On Fads* which was very well reviewed before her life turned inwards yet again, consumed by financial and health worries. Her links with the Hardys, after Emma's death, loosened further and while she wrote occasionally, sending congratulations on his marriage to Florence in 1914, and always corresponding at his birthday, the intimacy of their friendship, such as it was, faded, so that her death in 1926 brought him up with a start, casting his mind back to their evening together at the Larmer Gardens.

Agnes had had a troubled life after her formative years and the circumstances of her early marriage squeezed the joy out of her. It was propitious that she met Thomas in 1895, and that he had been able to give her the encouragement she needed. Always inclined to write, it was Hardy that encouraged her to put to pen to paper and with his support, her writing attained a quality that won the admiration of her patron [28]. After the tragedy of losing their son, Agnes had become more involved in public affairs, campaigning against vivisection and vaccination (she was later taken to court and fined in 1905 for failing to have her son vaccinated without registering a conscientious objection). Since the 1890s, she had become involved in the suffrage movement, but the latter part of her life and her burgeoning career as a journalist and essayist, sadly, lasted for only the first decade of the twentieth century. She had contracted tuberculosis in 1906 and did not enjoy good health for the remainder of her life. Worse, the last sixteen years of her life were blighted by financial uncertainties that had clouded her courtship and marriage and the warnings she had been given that presaged what lay ahead, were slowly realised. When she died in 1926 of tuberculosis, six years before Walter, she was unrecognizable from the feisty writer and agitator of twenty years before. Her letters were increasingly despondent noting that she saw few people and that her life was *'save and scrape the whole time.'* [29]

What do we learn about Hardy from Agnes? That whatever he hoped for, there was no romance, no intimate relationship, and that what evolved was no more than a mutual fondness. Thomas's penchant for being foolhardy over new female acquaintances to whom he took a shine, was evident in his relationship with Agnes, from his first infatuation, to the realisation that what he could offer the attractive young women whose company he sought was just intellectual stimulation, a meeting of minds and not the physical companionship or contact he had once hoped for. He was learning to deal with less.

Throughout the first few years, Hardy's engaging and intimate letters to Agnes were bookended with similar letters to Florence, equally flirtatious. Inevitably, Hardy sat on the edge of propriety, as was his wont, until the signals were clear that he was overstepping the mark. Once Florence had made her position clear, he turned to Agnes who took his kindness and support to heart and responded as she could. She was always grateful to him. In turn, Agnes helped him through the aftermath of *Jude the Obscure*, and the disappointment of Florence Henniker's rebuttal. Moreover, she succeeded in overcoming Emma's initial hostility by showing she was not a threat to the Hardys' marriage and by joining with Emma in embracing the cause of women's suffrage she found herself included in Hardy's literary circle in London for the halcyon years of the early twentieth century. After that, she largely disappeared from view, diminished by worry and ill health only to be resurrected in the elegy 'Dear Agnes' that Thomas penned in her memory soon after her death in 1926.

Chapter 8

Gertrude Bugler

To include Gertrude Bugler in a book of Hardy's women is to give credence to the idea that Thomas Hardy, aged eighty-three years, was capable of making his wife, Florence, aged forty-six years, so jealous by his infatuation with a married woman twenty years even younger than herself that she felt in danger of losing her husband's loyalty and affection. Florence's response to what she perceived as the threat of Gertrude to the sanctity and reputation of their marriage exposed her own poor judgement and actions to public ridicule, and significantly shaped her public reputation, then and now. By giving the friendship undue significance when it was, in the eyes of friends and contemporaries, nothing more than the emotional and nostalgic meanderings of an old man is to accept that Florence, once the usurper, felt herself to be in real danger of being similarly displaced in Hardy's affections. Yet to see Gertrude and her relationship with Hardy in such a prism is to underestimate old emotions that it stirred up in both Thomas and Florence. Unlike Pierston in *The Well-Beloved*, it tells us that emotionally, Hardy never did properly grow up and accept his fallibility while the paucity of emotion and care that he showed to his wife throughout their married life is laid bare. Gertrude's presence here, therefore, is important in understanding Hardy's relationship with Florence and his attitude towards women and the separation of his roles as spouse and writer.

Gertrude Bugler was born in Dorchester in 1897, the daughter of Augusta and Arthur Bugler, who at the time was a confectioner in the town. In her youth, Gertrude's mother, Augusta Way and her sisters had been milkmaids in the Stinsford meadows and at the Kingston Maurward estate working for their father, Thomas Way, who was identified by Millgate as a model for Dairyman Crick in *Tess of the D'Ubervilles*. It was in the late 1880s that she first unknowingly attracted the attention of the then young Thomas Hardy. In unpublished material in the possession of Richard Little Purdy, Millgate refers to an interview with Harold Child in which he claimed that Hardy had confessed that the striking resemblance of Gertrude to Tess was *'made more poignant by the fact that it was Augusta Bugler . . . who first suggested the figure of Tess to his imagination'* It is very likely that having used Gertrude's mother as the model for the heroine, he found the past revisiting him in the person of her daughter.[1]

From her youth, Gertrude was touted as a rare beauty in the local district and a keen amateur actress. She first came to prominence in 1913 when she had been chosen to take the part of Marty South in *The Woodlanders* at the annual Hardy play at the Dorchester Corn exchange, a tradition that had started in 1908. Gertrude's appearance even caught the attention of the *Mail*, which included a photograph of her in their London edition, such was her beauty.[2] Gittings described her as *'a natural actress, slender, with expressive and very dark eyes'* and undoubtedly capable of catching Hardy's ever-roving eye.[3]

In 1920, the annual Hardy play, a tradition instituted some years earlier, was *The Return of the Native* in which Gertrude, now aged twenty-three years, was cast to play the part of Eustacia Vye. Such was the play's success that the players were invited to Max Gate to recreate the mumming scenes where, again according to Gittings, Gertrude charmed both Thomas and Florence, with Florence writing to her friend, Louisa Yearsley, soon after that *'she is a beautiful creature, only twenty-four, and nice and refined.'*[4]

A truer indication of what lay ahead, however, was reflected in a letter to their old friend, Stanley Cockerell, to whom Florence had written,

'TH has lost his heart to (Miss Bugler) entirely, but as she is soon getting married, I don't let it get me down too much.'[5]

There was no play in 1921, the year in which Gertrude married her cousin, Ernest Bugler at Stinsford (conveniently requiring no change of name), an event that should have calmed Florence's anxieties. Gertrude's new husband had bought a few acres to set himself up as a farmer near Beaminster and was a war hero, having been awarded the Military Cross for his exploits on the North West frontier of Afghanistan during World War One.

In 1922, having been set to take the leading role in the production of *Desperate Remedies*, Gertrude found herself to be pregnant and reluctantly withdrew from the cast. It was at this juncture that Gertrude's relationship with Florence, previously perfectly amicable, outwardly at least, turned sour.

According to the sources available (mainly the self-incriminating letters of Florence and, writing in her own defence, the much later published recollections of Gertrude), Hardy had written to Gertrude to express his personal sadness that she would not be able to take her part in the production, *Desperate Remedies* and inviting her to call on them at Max Gate, as he had an inscribed copy of a book for her. When she did so, early in June, 1922, she was met by a hostile Florence who not only sent her away with a rebuke, but followed the visit up with a letter a few days later in which she criticised Gertrude, stating *'It is simply "not done" in our station of life for any lady to call on a gentleman'.*[6]

Gertrude responded, judiciously and sensitively, but although matters went quiet for the next eighteen months, Florence's disquiet was merely simmering beneath the surface. Both Wilkins and Nicholson, in their respective novels, make great play of the relationship between the two women, seeing Gertrude as almost entirely blameless, as she undoubtedly was, while portraying Florence at best as temporarily demented and at worst, evil. Certainly, they had licence to do so based on Florence's own actions and her embarrassing letters and from the various biographers that have painted Florence in a very poor light since. Even the death of Gertrude's first-born did not blunt her pen, writing to Cockerell about the agonies that Gertrude would have experienced at being *'cut out by a rival leading lady'* (a disassembling of the truth) and the fact that *'the tragic climax is that she had a still-born son on the day of the performance'* before concluding with the ironic confession, *'What a gossip I am.'*[7] Even this personal tragedy did not appear to soften Florence's pen; rather, it seemed that the suggestion gave her some grim and morbid satisfaction.

Much of the material that damns Florence as being paranoid about Gertrude comes from her own letters collected and published by Michael Millgate in 1996 and quoted extensively by all subsequent biographers, notably Pite, Gittings and Tomalin. Having already shown her true feelings about Gertrude, Florence was about to descend further into the well of jealousy.

In 1924, Hardy's own production of *Tess* was performed in Dorchester to general acclaim, with considerable praise lavished on Gertrude's acting from Cockerell himself and even Florence's friend and confidante, J M Barrie. As she saw her husband's growing infatuation with his new star who he identified more and more as the personification of 'Tess', so her jealousy grew until in January 1925, it boiled over. The provocation was the suggestion that had been made that Gertrude would headline the London production and that she would do so with Thomas's personal endorsement.

The first intimation Gertrude had that she was being considered for the role was when she received a letter from Frederick Harrison from the Haymarket Theatre who wrote, *'I believe Mr Hardy has told you how much I would like you to play "Tess" in a series of matinees which I am arranging to do here, probably in April or May.'*[8]

Not long after, Gertrude was invited to Max Gate for luncheon with Frederick Harrison and Professor Sydney Cockerell, Hardy's literary executor, under the pretext of seeing a new fore-scene to the play and some new lines that Thomas had written. [9] The discussions were amiable, and contracts signed, although Gertrude remembered Thomas pushing her on whether she could bear leaving her new baby. When she came to leave, Thomas insisted on walking her to the car, saying to her when they were alone *'If anyone asks you if you knew Thomas Hardy, say yes, he was my friend.'*[10]

Sadly, this was to be the last time the two of them met.

Excited by the prospect of performing on the stage in London, Gertrude set about learning her new lines. Soon after, however, she was to receive a telegram from Florence informing her that she would be calling on her at her home in Beaminister.

Our initial record of the meeting is from Gertrude herself and is notable more for what she didn't record. According to Gertrude, Florence merely noted:

'Among other things she said, Mr Hardy was very excited about the play going to London, he was in a nervous state. She feared he would want to go up to town to see it and, at his age, it would not be good for him, nor for his name. She asked me not to go to London, saying I was still young and might have other chances later on. So, in the end, I wrote to Frederick Harrison saying I had decided not to play Tess after all.' [11]

Other accounts fill in the gaps and turn the meeting from a strongly worded request to something akin to blackmail. Principal amongst these was a letter from Gertrude to William Blunt, written in 1964, some two years after the publication of her own recollections. Blunt was publishing a biography of Sir Sydney Cockerell, and included part of the letter which expanded on the meeting between Gertrude and Florence. In it, she wrote, *'Oh what a cloud there must have been at Max Gate! And I knew nothing then of this "infatuation for the local Tess". As I read those words a line from* Tess of the D'Urbervilles *came into my head: "It is in your own mind what you are angry at, Angel, it is not in me." It was only in the mind of F E H. Yes, I am happy and proud of the perfectly innocent pleasure that T H found in my company, and proud of his friendship.'*[12]

Tomalin described Florence's reaction to Gertrude Bugler as *'the biggest drama of her marriage'* and fills some four pages with its machinations, centred on her letter to Gertrude in 1922 (later returned to Florence after Hardy's death and, presumably, destroyed) and various missives with Cockerell as well as Gertrude's responses.[13] Central to her account was the suggestion that her husband *'had been writing poems to her in which he spoke of running away with her – poems Florence had destroyed.'*[14] Whether true or not (and Tomalin hoped not for she felt destroying the poems would have been the greater sin), it is clear that she was so persuasive that Gertrude wrote her letter of resignation immediately after the visit.

There was an attempt at a reconciliation between Gertrude and Florence after Hardy had died. In the summer of 1929, Florence, perhaps affected by guilt, invited Gertrude to call at Max Gate where as the recently widowed wife of Thomas Hardy, she invited Gertrude to play Tess in a new production at the Prince of Wales theatre in London. After due and careful consideration, Gertrude accepted and the short season, her only one spent in London, was a moderate success. She remained wary of Florence, however, and later recalled one incident that showed she was right to be so. Florence had warned her of the way that London critics might treat an amateur actress, naming two in particular, one *'a horrid man and would probably be merciless'* and the other, *'a friend'* who she thought *'would do what he could to help.'* In the event, as Gertrude noted in her *Personal Recollections, 'The Horrid man said the nicest things about my acting – the other, certainly did not!'*[15]

There is a common refrain in all the biographies and recollections that Florence behaved ridiculously, that it was absurd that she could imagine that there might be a romantic attachment between her husband and Gertrude. The fact that it did generate the jealousy it did was seen as a reflection on both the character and the mental state of Florence. The very thought that, even in his eighties, Thomas's penchant for pretty ladies and his propensity to become besotted with some young, married woman who never showed the slightest personal interest in him, was able to hurt Florence deeply implies that she was both unsure of her husband's affections and fearful of the public humiliation that might result, but it was also an insight into the off-hand and dismissive way that Hardy would often treat her.

To understand Florence's initial response to the presence of Gertrude, we need to go back to the early years of her relationship with Thomas, the covert years when Emma was still alive and the awkwardness of being befriended by Emma while spending time alone, at Max Gate, but also discreetly elsewhere in Hardy's company and most notably at Aldeburgh. Florence was wracked with self-doubt at the time, as she had been in the aftermath of Emma's death and the ensuing battle with Lillian, Emma's niece, for the control of Max Gate. Her confidence was no doubt further eroded by the discovery of the diaries soon after Emma's death and that likely exposed the couple to the uncomfortable truth by what Emma had written about them both. Even the security of marriage, which Hardy was determined to keep as quiet as possible, was undermined by the publication of the *Poems of 1912-1913*. Little wonder, then, that Florence was not confident about what place she held in Hardy's affections.

What is more, there was little thereafter to give Florence any sense of self-worth or even economic security. When she needed medical attention during the war years, Hardy expected her to use her own savings for the purpose. He continued writing, meanwhile, often poems about women he had known in his younger days. The death of Florence Henniker in 1923 and the return of Hardy's letters to her (inadvertently opened by Florence when they were delivered to Max Gate), were a stark reminder of other women with whom he had communicated, often intimately, over the years. Moreover, they reminded her how easily Hardy was able to slip from the commitment, as well as the intentions and obligations, of matrimony.

It is hardly surprising that Florence found it hard to humour her ageing husband, to see him as the harmless old rogue that others saw, for reasons that were tied in with Thomas's duplicitous nature. Undoubtedly, it was the intensity of feeling and interest that Hardy exhibited towards Gertrude and the fact that he appeared oblivious to the feelings of those closest to him that irritated her most. What seems to us ludicrous now, is that a wife, herself more than thirty years younger than her husband, displayed jealousy of a perceived rival in such an overt and public way. It demonstrates as no other relationship ever did, the transience of his affections and his apparent disloyalty, albeit rooted in a growing disinterest, towards both his wives. Yet the fact that his infatuation for the young actress was in his own head, while not a mitigating factor, does serve to emphasise yet again, how Hardy separated parts of his life at his own convenience and his lack of empathy with those closest to him. He saw no contradiction in what he wrote or said and would have meant Florence no harm; but by acting as he did, Florence felt he was saying to her that she was not sufficient to nurture his soul and imagination or feed his libido; for that he needed a Gertrude.

There was, therefore, some understandable justification for Florence to feel irked by Hardy's obsession, reaching its peak by mid-1922, and then spilling over in public two years later. We read, from one of the cast, of a silver vase of carnations delivered covertly to Gertrude following her miscarriage and of gossip that gathered strength in late 1924 of a growing intimacy between them.[16] Gertrude and Thomas regularly shared tea between the matinee and evening performances and were often seen to be indulging in what Florence interpreted as 'intimate whispering'.[17] At the production in Weymouth production on 11 December, Hardy was again in the wings, pointing out that Gertrude had her wedding ring on which he removed before slipping it back on her finger at the appropriate point in the play 'as in the wedding ceremony.' [18] Each single action or observation was innocent enough, but collectively and when fuelled by the lavish praise being showered upon Gertrude at home and in the press, was enough to upset Florence into making an intemperate response. It is well to remember that at this stage, Florence was still recovering from an operation to remove what was seen as a potentially cancerous tumour, only returning from London, where the operation was carried out, in mid-October 1924. It is likely that she was also clinically depressed. Despite her husband's well-meaning letters written when she was in London following her operation, as she lay there, she would have been very aware of her husband's emotional philandering in the past, which allied with feeling so insecure and neglected, led her to react as she did.

By early 1924, Florence was becoming more and more upset by Hardy's obsession with Gertrude. Cockerell, who was staying with them at Max Gate, begged her to see the humour in the situation, noting Hardy's considerable age (he was eighty-four) at the time. In response, Florence said she had tried to do so, but apart from the embarrassment she was enduring, she confided in Cockerell that Thomas *'spoke roughly to her and showed her she was in the way.'*[19] The following day, the two of them spoke again, and Florence drew attention to the fact that while it was her birthday, Thomas had made no mention of it.[20] Considering that Thomas was almost obsessive about birthdays and anniversaries, especially those of his close family while keeping his desk calendar fixed on the date when he first met Emma, Florence understandably felt slighted and unappreciated. The poignant note Hardy made in his diary on 23 December 1925, recognising the tenth anniversary of the death of his sister, Mary, gave the unappreciated Florence a good idea of what she was up against.[21]

Before we look to see what others made of the spat between Florence and Gertrude, it is useful to turn to *The Life of Thomas Hardy*, ghost-written by Hardy, but edited and published by Florence, to get Florence's view several years on. Understandably, there is not a mention of Gertrude although there are several references to the Hardy Players, for whom Gertrude was a lead actress in many of their productions and the star of the Dorchester production of *Tess*.

There are, however, a number of references to the various Wessex Scenes produced over several years by the Hardy Players based in Dorchester, including those from *The Dynasts*, *The Mellstock Quire* in the castle ruins in Sturminster Newton[22] and *The Famous Tragedy of the Queen of Cornwall* at the Corn Exchange at Dorchester 1923.[23]

Of *Tess* though we are told little only that the play was then performed by the Hardy Players in London in February, 1924, but without the anticipated success.[24]

The final mention of the company was likewise dismissed by Florence: *'the company, self-styled "The Hardy Players", produced* Tess *to such unexpected success at Dorchester and Weymouth that it was asked for in London and the following year produced there by professional actors for over a hundred nights, Miss Gwen Ffrangcon-Davies taking the part of "Tess".'*[25] What is not mentioned is that in the local production at Dorchester, Gertrude was the star and part of why the show had been invited to perform in London and that she was only replaced in the London production at Florence's instigation. In a letter to Sydney Cockerell in August 1925 Florence mentioned that a new London production was planned with Miss Gwen Ffrangcon-Davies playing Tess before commenting *'He may fall in love with Miss Ffrangcon-Davies as much as he likes and the more than the better.'*[26]

We don't know if Thomas ever recorded his admiration of Gertrude in the book's drafts, but if so, there was nothing surer than that any such felicitations would be struck out by Florence. While it might seem strange that Florence should be so jealous having herself behaved with such impropriety when Emma was alive, undoubtedly her knowledge of Hardy's inconstancy and duplicity in the past lay at the root of her jealousy. While Hardy displayed what Seymour described as *'strong emotion on the part of a romantic poet'* [27], and that this emotion was inclined to run away with him, it was never a threat; indeed, it can be argued that Hardy's infatuation with Gertrude was not with who she was, but with what she represented. In the light of her own experiences, it is not so surprising that Florence's obsession with Thomas, having given up her life for him, bordered on the paranoid, viewing any threat to her role as his protector or wife with a level of suspicion and fear.

Of the works of fiction about Hardy, two refer to the relationship between Thomas Hardy and Gertrude, to a greater or lesser extent. In his novel *Winter*, Christopher Nicholson managed a whole storyline based around 'Gertie' and her relationship with Thomas and its effect on the household at Max Gate. Nicholson makes play of the parallels drawn between Gertrude and Tess, a fascination that had its roots in Hardy's memory of her mother, Augusta, the behaviour of Thomas towards Florence and the physical and psychological state of Florence, with Gertrude the unwitting provocateur.[28]

Damien Wilkins in his novel *Max Gate* focused on the events of Hardy's final year and death, and also drew on the legend of Thomas and Gertrude, including a scene of contrition after Hardy's death when Florence breaks down in front of Nellie, the housemaid and narrator of the story, launching into an extraordinary and scarifying self-assessment of the damage she did to Gertrude, beginning with the description that *'I'm a wretched person'* and concluding after some four pages of self-purging and confession with *'I'm as good as a murderer.'*[29]

If nothing else, the unspoken relationship between Thomas and Gertrude has provided speculation and intrigue, if only for writers of fiction and not surprisingly, much has been made of it. The facts tell us otherwise, however. Gertrude's role was almost entirely passive, being a peripheral player in all that went on. After all, this was a battle that took place in Florence's mind, provoked and fuelled by Hardy's long-term treatment of her. We also learn something about Hardy and his own perpetual adolescent longings. The fact that he was over eighty when the crisis took place and that, unlike Jocelyn Pierston in *The Well-Beloved*, who escaped the anxiety of searching for an ideal of beauty (*'Thank heaven I am old at last. The curse is removed'*), Hardy never gave up his quest. (Pt. 3, Ch. 8) Yet, while age seemed not to affect his libido, Hardy's infatuation with Gertrude was to act as a final bookend to Hardy's imaginings as well as a sad reminder to Florence that because of his wandering eye, she had never been comfortable in thinking his affections were ever for her alone.

By the time life at Max Gate took on some normality once again, Florence was unwell. Used to the fickleness of her husband's affections, she was also physically weakened from her treatment and had become morbidly concerned about her own health. Gertrude, inadvertently, had provoked a crisis between husband and wife, serious enough to persuade Florence to stir herself so as to defend her husband's reputation and the sanctity of their marriage with disastrous results to her own reputation.

There is little question that Gertrude was an innocent and passive recipient of Hardy's attentions, and arguably that he saw her simply as the embodiment of Tess and as her mother's daughter. Her appearance, her attachment to the area (being born in Dorchester and married at Stinsford), the earlier evocation of Tess through her mother, Augusta, all lay behind Hardy's fixation with her. The whole sad episode, which was no more than an affair of the mind, however, laid bare the state of the marriage of Florence and Thomas and the characters of both: one, paranoid, obsessed with preserving her hard-won husband's reputation and not wanting to see it, or her role in his life, coloured by some dalliance; the other, living in his world in parallel to hers, and not seeing anything he did as a betrayal to either.

After playing Tess on the stage in London, Gertrude returned to their farm in Beaminster with her husband, Ernest and their daughter, Diana. When Ernest died in 1956 she was living in Dorchester where she was cared for by her daughter and becoming something of a local celebrity in her later years. After the death of her nemesis, Florence, in 1937, she was more confident about sharing her memories of the Hardys and in 1962, the Dorset Natural History and Archaeological Society published her *Personal Recollections of Thomas Hardy*. She died in Dorchester in 1992, at the age of ninety-five years.

To understand Hardy's response to Florence and Gertrude, it is useful to revisit Hardy's own peculiar views on the transitory nature of love. In 1926, there was an entry in Hardy's notebook that Tomalin picked up in her biography about how Marcel Proust had used a theory of Hardy's by which *'the lover creates an image of the beloved in his mind that may bear little resemblance to the real person'*.[30] It was a theory that we see reoccurring time and again in Hardy's fiction – and in his life. It is apparent that Gertrude in the guise of Tess was one such image and as such, not to be seen as a threat to Florence, but part of the writer's imaginative process that needed to be understood. Florence would not have been surprised at Proust's words, *'Desire arises, satisfies itself and disappears – that's all there is to it. So the young person you marry is not the person you fell in love with'* for she had seen this with Hardy in the past. [31]

What upset her, rather, was not the absence, or even the transference of desire, but the lack of attention Thomas paid her and the absence of any sympathy and kindness towards her, especially when she had been ill. This, in turn, fed her paranoia, making her susceptible to other doubts, which manifested itself in such embarrassing incidents as her cruel response to Gertrude's stillborn child that was picked up by Hardy biographers. Certainly, if we look more sympathetically at Florence's plight, we can start to understand why she saw Gertrude, or what Gertrude represented, as a threat to the stability of her relationship. Assailed by doubts of her own self worth, there was little that Hardy wrote about on the married state that could give her comfort.

Florence's reaction to Gertrude made her a subject of scorn and derision with a number in her immediate circle, alienating her from Cockerell who was later to describe her as *'. . . dull beyond description – an inferior woman with a suburban mind, but very ambitious to be well-off.'* [32]

Poor Florence. Thomas continued to rely on her in his day-to-day life and kept her at his beck and call, but she received little in return other than the reflected glory of being Thomas Hardy's wife. There is no doubt she looked after him despite the lack of affection shown her and before long he was back writing poems about Emma, ('If It's Ever Spring Again' 'West of Wessex Girl' to name but two), cycling about the countryside and entertaining visitors to Max Gate, and showing a new lease of life described by one biographer, rather generously, as *'entirely attributable to the presence of Florence'* [33]. If it was so (and she did greatly improve Hardy's comfort, especially in making Max Gate more liveable) Thomas was not the one to ever give her credit for doing so.

At the very end, it must have been distressing for poor Florence to be at Westminster Abbey, against her will, on the arm of Cockerell for the state funeral of her husband while Gertrude was at same time in the churchyard at Stinsford for the burial of Hardy's heart in the family grave – how fitting, how symbolic that they should have been cast in their respective places.

Chapter 9

Bathsheba Everdene and the Novels of 1871–1874

Desperate Remedies (1871), Under the Greenwood Tree (1872), A Pair of Blue Eyes (1873) and Far from the Madding Crowd (1874)

'All romances end at marriage'

(*Far from the Madding Crowd* Chapter 41)

Hardy's career as a novelist got off to an inauspicious start. His first manuscript *The Poor Man and the Lady* was read by his publisher William Tinsley, turned down and was later destroyed (although some of the material was saved and later re-worked). For his second offering, Hardy entered into negotiations with Tinsley for the publication of *Desperate Remedies*, his first published novel, and eventually agreed to an arrangement by which Hardy would contribute £75 towards the publication of the book, a very significant sum of money for the time.[1]

Hardy was by no means able to afford such an amount, having only £123 in total savings at the time and with his new romance just a matter of months old, it placed a considerable strain upon him. But in the end, encouraged by Emma, he agreed the terms and on 25 May 1871, the book was published.

The term 'vanity publishing' is seen by some as pejorative implying that an author's only reason for taking this route was that their manuscript was not good enough to attract a publisher. This was not always the case, however, then or now and Hardy was not alone in subsidising his own books along with a number of well-known writers who also self-published part or all of their work.[2] But while some authors could afford the outlay required, it undoubtedly placed a great strain on Hardy's resources even though he did eventually retrieve close to £60 from the book's sales.

Its follow-up, again published by Tinsley, and titled *Under the Greenwood Tree* for which Hardy sold the copyright for a paltry £30 (in retrospect one of the better bargains in publishing history), also failed to sell in sufficient numbers and was considered another commercial failure. [3] By this stage Hardy was despondent even though Emma was doing her best to encourage him. She was also offering him practical help, checking, critiquing and, most importantly, spending a very considerable amount of time in making a fair copy of the manuscript. It was not surprising, however, that when Hardy's third novel. *A Pair of Blue Eyes* also failed to achieve the sales required to satisfy the author or publisher, Tinsley, that they agreed that their partnership, such as it was, had run its course. In spite of interest from Macmillan, Thomas decided to take a different route for his fourth novel and in 1874 had his first major success with *Far from the Madding Crowd* initially published in instalments by *Cornhill Magazine* and later in a single edition by Harper.

Of the four early novels Hardy wrote in the years before his marriage, it is the heroines who catch our eye. From the outset we are introduced to women whose life and sexuality are far from straightforward and whose views and circumstances are presented in a way that were seen by some contemporary literary critics as shocking. One heroine after another is placed by Hardy in an uncertain, often hostile world where, by a combination of female guile and pragmatism, they strive to make the best of their situation. Almost invariably, however, they are squeezed by opposing forces, beaten down by life, punished by fate and marriage, or afflicted by both circumstance and the traits peculiar to their sex. No doubt, Hardy's own experiences of women, limited though they may have been, fed into his writing, and especially his early heroines. The women he depicted give us our first insight into how Hardy saw contemporary women and the issues that they faced. What he wrote both surprised and shocked his audience and critics, even in the early throes of his career.

The greater part of *Desperate Remedies* had been written prior to Thomas meeting Emma with the first draft of the novel being sent off to his publisher immediately before Hardy had travelled to St Juliot in May 1870. His life was already complicated as he struggled to juggle his architectural work with his writing. The previous year, he had returned from London and taken lodgings at Weymouth, although his personal life still centred around the family home in Higher Bockhampton. He enjoyed his new found independence, which included bathing off Pebble beach in the mornings and rowing in the bay in the evenings, away from his parents' watchful eyes. At the same time, it is likely he was spending a good deal of time with Tryphena and it is likely that her presence is reflected in the novel. Hardy was reading more contemporary literature around this time, including Wilkie Collins, whose influence is evident in *Desperate Remedies* as part of a popular genre of the time called the 'sensation novel,' designed to shock the readers – something Hardy certainly managed to do.

Desperate Remedies begins with a mysterious illegitimate birth and goes on to include references to blackmail, murder, bigamy, attempted rape and prostitution. Most surprising to the modern reader was the very explicit reference to lesbianism in the scene in which Miss Aldclyffe gets into bed with Cytherea and where there is reference to undressing and passionate kissing. Because lesbianism was not publicly acknowledged, nor ever a crime – the Act of Parliament in 1885 that made sex of two people of the same gender a crime only applied to men – the scene escaped both the heavy hand of the censor and the opprobrium that fell on other similar sexually charged scenes in Hardy's canon.

The heroine of *Desperate Remedies,* published anonymously in March 1871 was Cytherea Graye, a young woman who worked for the eccentric Miss Aldclyffe, who had been the beloved of Cytherea's own father until propriety forbade their marriage on the grounds that she had had an illegitimate son by another, wholly unsavoury man. The only other significant female characters in terms of the plot are the first and second Mrs Manson, the first murdered by Miss Adclyffe's illegitimate son, Aeneas Manston and the second, of similar appearance, who took her place at Aeneas's cajoling to deflect any suspicion of the murder.

Despite positive reviews in the *Athenaeum* and the *Morning Post*, the plot of the novel immediately raised the hackles of some of his critics, inviting a crushing review in the *Spectator* asking how Hardy could even think it possible that *'an unmarried lady owning an estate could have an illegitimate child.'* [4] While it was the issue of class that became the target, the social issues raised in the novel were more compelling. As well as the reference to lesbianism, other issues such as bigamy, murder, poverty, incest and loveless engagements all surfaced at some stage in the novel. It was this combination which led to a more personal attack later in the review on the author's anonymity: *'By all means let him bury the secret in the profoundest depths of his own heart, out of reach, if possible, of his own consciousness'* [5]

In the novel, Cytherea is in love with Edward Springrove, a young architect who is already engaged to another woman. Miss Adclyffe persuades Cytherea instead to marry her own illegitimate son, Aeneas which Cytherea agrees to before the son's crime of murdering his first wife is discovered. In the end, Aeneas commits suicide in prison and Edward, freed from his earlier engagement, marries Cytherea.

Through the person of Cytherea, Hardy proceeds to highlight a number of social and economic issues facing women of the day. In the development of her character, we are able to detect elements of Hardy's own views and opinions about women as well as seeing signs of the duality of his role as a writer and husband to be.

It is a book far removed from his West Country roots and from his later reputation as a writer on rural life. Written after his return from London and amidst the period of which we know comparatively little, we can only speculate whether aspects of Cytherea's personality or character are drawn from Tryphena (or from Louisa Harding or the Nicholls sisters); we can, however, assume from what we learn later on, that many of those he met and developed an emotional attachment to influenced his writing in some way.

If we trawl *Desperate Remedies* for clues to Hardy's own state of mind at the time, we can see evidence of many of the issues that he is wrestling with including the challenge of dividing his time between writing and architecture, and his shifting affection between Emma and Tryphena. When Cytherea turns to her brother, Owen, whose illness is a reason for her financial woes and suggests *'it is difficult to adjust our outer and inner life with perfect honesty to all!'* Hardy is most probably giving voice to his own private thoughts and the struggles in his own life. (Ch. 13, Pt. 4)

From the outset, Hardy's views on women and on women's issues sit at the fore of his writing, especially those on love and marriage. In *Desperate Remedies* there are several examples of Hardy's views (albeit through his role as narrator), on the subject of love. Early in the book we are presented with the idea of transient love, and especially his constant searching for lost love or the unattainable when he laments *'With all, the beautiful things of the earth become more dear as they elude pursuit; but as with some natures utter elusion is the one special event which will make a passing love permanent for ever.'* (Ch. 1, Pt. 2) It is not difficult to see Emma as a case in point and, in retrospect, she was never as desirable to Hardy as when she was roaming freely on her mare, Fanny, above Beeny Cliff, an unharnessed spirit. It also encapsulates Hardy's own life-long chase for the ideal woman that culminates in the fiction of *The Well-Beloved* with its rather creepy premise. Looking further afield, there are many examples, particularly in Hardy's poetry, of love that eludes him and therefore remains pure and unsullied, very often by the very fact that the love has become unattainable or is lost forever. With Hardy, distance in time and space served to grow the attachment and sense of longing even, as we find out in his novels and poems, over the passing of decades. Yet he may already have been thinking of opportunities lost, perhaps even of Tryphena, as he was writing.

Cytherea's life and the choices available to her are determined by circumstance, as in so many of Hardy's novels. She is not without fault and Hardy alludes to her impulsivity as being common to her gender, of acting first and thinking later.[6] In differentiating the gender from his own Hardy is inevitably guilty of engaging in a certain stereotyping (pride and vanity are two more traits he attributes to women) and while it raised the ire of feminists who felt he seldom gave his heroines much chance, Hardy was ahead of most writers of his age in drawing the readers' attention to the plight of women.

There is much that is admirable about Cytherea who sees her first responsibility as a moral one, that of helping support her sick brother. She is soon given another, that of managing her outpouring of love or as Hardy put it succinctly, cultivating the 'art of renunciation.'[7] Yet throughout the novel, Hardy continues to define women by character flaws or traits, at times using words that now seem clichéd and patronising while at other times, contrarily, full of empathy and insight. How much more important a love letter is for a woman than a man? he asks. How much more important are a woman's clothes which compared to a man are so much 'a part of her body'? At one point, Owen, Cytherea's brother reminded her *'You know as well as I do . . . that with women there's nothing between the two poles of emotion'* (Ch. 9, Pt. 3) thereby emphasising the impulsive above the rational as part of the makeup of women. Hardy, elsewhere, mentions the cleverness of women who delight in indulging in the women's pleasure of recreating defunct agonies and manipulating emotional situations. As characteristics, they are not out of place in Victorian literature although they read less well today, but it was not to take Hardy long to develop his women characters in more sophisticated and sympathetic ways and to empower them to challenge their circumstances.

Rosemarie Morgan in her book *Women and Sexuality in the Novels of Thomas Hardy* contends that Cytherea is a *'thoroughly orthodox creation. Part angel – self effacing, noble, sexless, self-abnegating – and part Gothic personification of sensibility under pressure.*[8] Without in any way contradicting that view, on another level, Cytherea is a new age woman, who exhibits sexual feelings and delights in physicality. Several critics and reviewers make much of the erotic in the novel and imply that it was only Hardy's clever use of allusion and metaphor that allowed the book to escape the censor. Probably the most memorable of such scenes is the alleged lesbian love scene between Cytherea and her namesake, Cytherea Adclyffe, a scene described by Morgan as one *'that many readers have been unwilling to accept for what is so obviously is'*.[9] Tomalin referred to the scene as being of social as much as sexual significance noting that while *'no modern reader can be unaware of the sexual element . . . the line between physically demonstrative displays of innocent affection and conscious eroticism was not easily drawn in the mid-nineteenth century.'*[10] The fact that she knows that Cytherea is the daughter of the man the older woman once loved gives a further uncomfortable twist to the passage although the vagueness and ambiguity allows the scene to escape censure. Early on, Hardy had learnt what was deemed acceptable although he was to continue to push the boundaries over the next twenty years.

Other scenes that could be used to evidence the idea of an erotic charge in the novel include the spontaneous kiss between Edward Springrove and Cytherea Graye on Budmouth Bay *'She breathed more quickly and warmly: he took her right hand in his own right... He put his left hand behind her neck till it came round upon her left cheek... Lightly pressing her, he brought her face and mouth towards his own... '* (Ch. 3, Pt. 2)

Of course, there is a temptation to read too much into the passage. Richard Sylvia insinuates further evidence of Cytherea's sexuality by describing the passage below as sexually charged with *'its phallic implications of the lifted finger and the self-induced pleasure'* although one might also note, with rather less imagination, that it is also the wedding ring finger to which she refers, giving the passage an altogether different meaning:

'The contemplation of her own left fourth finger by symbol-loving girlhood of this age is, it seems, very frequently, if not always, followed by a peculiar train of romantic ideas. Cytherea's thoughts, still playing about her future, became directed into this romantic groove. She leant back in her chair, and taking hold of the fourth finger, which had attracted her attention, she lifted it with the tips of the others, and looked at the smooth and tapering member for a long time. She whispered idly, "I wonder who and what he will be?"'[11]

The problem the reader faces is one of interpretation. Clearly different writers and scholars start with the same text and yet come to very different conclusions. Words can often be interpreted or can change in meaning over time according to social convention. We start with a heroine who is seen as honest and well-meaning yet find also a woman charged with sensuality and eroticism (the two, of course, are not incompatible). Hardy had to choose his words carefully, to express what he wanted his characters to say, but also to walk the tightrope of what was acceptable to the sensitivities and sensibilities of Victorian readership. It was an auspicious start for Hardy's catalogue of heroines and one that prepared the ground for those that followed. Adding to the presentiment of what lay ahead for Hardy's heroines, but applicable, one senses, to women in general, is this passage that appears late in the novel:

'Of all the disingenuous and cruel satires that from the beginning till now have been stuck like knives into womankind, surely there is not one so lacerating to them, and to us who love them, as the trite old fact, that the most wretched of men can, in the twinkling of an eye, find a wife ready to be more wretched still for the sake of his company.' (Ch. 16, Pt. 4) From the very outset, Hardy's views on the lot of women and on marriage it seems were profoundly pessimistic and as we look ahead, we can see this 'satire' acted out in the desperate remedies taken by others of Hardy's women, in the disparate relationships of Grace and Fitzpiers, Tess and Alec, Bathsheba and Troy.[12]

By the time Hardy came to publish his next novel, he had known Emma for over a year and his life had taken on a different aspect. The savaging he had received for *Desperate Remedies*, especially from the *Spectator* took its toll on him and in late 1871,

Jemima Hardy aged sixty

Jemima Hardy in her eighties in a Bath chair

Emma – young

Older Emma

Kate Hardy

Mary Hardy

Florence – young

Thomas Hardy fully bearded in his mid thirties

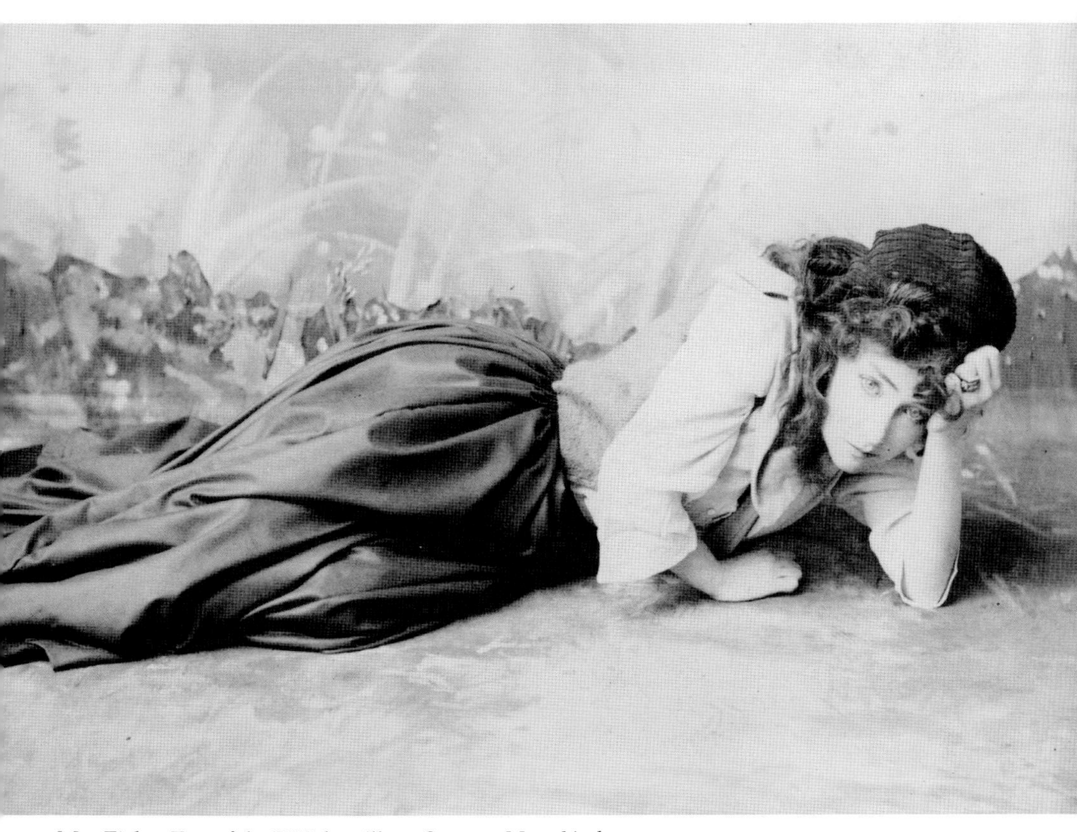

Mrs Fiske, *Tess of the D'Urbervilles* – Sarony, New York

Thomas and Florence at Aldeburgh, 1909

Max Gate

Florence and Thomas at Max Gate 1920
(after six years of marriage)

Martha Sparks

Agnes Grove's dedication to Thomas Hardy

Tryphena Sparks

Gertrude Bugler as Eustacia Vye

Thomas Hardy: man about town

Agnes Grove

Florence Henniker

Right: Thomas Hardy received honorary degrees from both Cambridge University (1912) and Oxford University (1920) – in some small ways, a salve for Jude and his own academic pretensions.

Below: Louise Harding, who Hardy was infatuated with when he was still at school– when he was eighty-seven he wrote 'To Louisa in the Lane' in her memory

Horace Moule

First Night at a Theatre, Alfred Stevens
In the audience are Joseph Conrad, Lily Langtry, Thomas Hardy, Conan Doyle, H G Wells and Ellen Terry. Hardy very often went to London without Emma, writing to tell her how dull it was!

Thomas Hardy looking distinctly uncomfortable with an unknown child; none of the four Hardy siblings had any children

Thomas holding court with two actresses, Christine Silver and Gwen Ffrangcon-Davies 1924

Thomas Hardy's birthplace

he wrote to Emma to say that he was done with *'novel-writing for ever and was going on with architecture henceforward.'* [13] Emma, to our enduring gratitude, replied immediately that her desire was that he should *'adhere to authorship which she felt sure would be his true vocation'*. Reassured and spurred on by her encouragement, Hardy decided to continue to seek out a publisher for *Under the Greenwood Tree* while at the same time sitting down to write his next book *A Pair of Blue Eyes*. But it was a difficult time and one that both scarred him and made him more cautious.

Under the Greenwood Tree was an altogether different book, a pastoral idyll with its portrayal of rural town life and memorable depictions of the countryside. Set around the fictitious village of Mellstock, which included the villages of Higher and Lower Bockhampton, Stinsford and other local houses and hamlets, it was the countryside that Hardy knew best from his childhood. The heroine of the novel was Fancy Day, a young schoolteacher and daughter of the local gamekeeper who was probably based on Tryphena Sparks who was almost certainly in Hardy's mind at the time. The romance of Fancy and Dick runs through the story although it is the Wessex rustics, the musicians and Dick Dewy, the successful suitor and his family that dominate much of the book.

In the novel, Fancy becomes romantically involved with one of the village choir, Dick Dewy with whom she ends up being secretly engaged. Her father is not happy with Dick, however, and when Fancy receives another proposal, this time from the much more prosperous and worldly Vicar Maybold, she accepts. When Maybold meets Dick the following day, Dick reveals his secret engagement with Fancy. Shocked, Maybold sends for Fancy and asks her to say whom she is to marry. Faced with the choice, Fancy ends up marrying Dick and asks the Vicar not to ever tell Dick that she had betrayed him. The Vicar agrees but says to Fancy in return, *'Tell him everything; it is best. He will forgive you'* (Pt. 4, Ch. 7) something which she duly fails to do, even by the story's end. Her unwillingness to admit her disloyalty to Dick or to seek his forgiveness means that the end of the story is not quite as conclusive as it might otherwise be and leaves us with the impression that there may well be trouble ahead for Dick and Fancy.

While Fancy is pretty and flirtatious, and embodies the younger and more enlightened generation of women, there is little substance to her and the love story that follows of Fancy and her three suitors (early on an archetypal wealthy farmer also features) is subsumed by the rich detail of Hardy's writing on the countryside and rustic life, especially the Mellstock Choir. He employs gentle irony and good humour in his writing that makes this the most tranquil and pastoral of his novels and a strong contrast to his previous effort with its strident Gothic strains. Throughout, Jemima's influence can be seen both in the subject matter and particularly on Hardy's writing on nature, on the heath and woodlands and on local customs, knowledge and folklore that she had passed onto him.

Apart from highlighting Fancy's inconstancy, it is tempting to think Hardy uses his characters as mouthpieces during the novel to express some of his own views on women or occasionally, to provide some humour. At one point when the fathers of Fancy and Dick are discussing Fancy's step-mother, Jane Day, Mr Dewy comments *'Tis my belief she's a very good woman at bottom'* to which her husband responded, *'She's terrible deep, then.'* (Pt. 5, Ch. 2) Tomalin feels she is the most entertaining character in the book and certainly she is unique amongst Hardy's women characters.[14]

The pity is that Fancy most certainly isn't particularly 'deep' either, and her fickleness becomes very evident when her head is turned by the offer of marriage to the Reverend Maybold. It is in her flirtations with Dick that we see her as a shallow and capricious, even heartless, young woman leading on the awkward young man who struggles under the onslaught of his hormones and is soon lost to her. Their courtship was amorous: *'If Fancy's lips had been real cherries probably Dick's would have appeared deeply stained observed the landlord of "The Ship"'.* (Pt. 3, Ch. 2) Dick reeled from the full force of love and sensation, first with the experience of physical touch when he and Fancy were washing their hands in a bowl: *'It being the first time in his life that he had touched female fingers under water, Dick duly registered the sensation as rather a nice one'* (Pt. 2, Ch. 7) and later with the knowledge that he was powerless to resist the lures of Fancy. When confronted by the feelings he was experiencing that had placed him in her thrall, he realised how they had rendered him powerless, that he was *' . . . conscious of a cold and sickly thrill throughout him; and all he reasoned was this, that the young creature whose graces had intoxicated him into making the most imprudent decision of his life, was less an angel than a woman.'* (Pt. 4, Ch. 7)

Throughout Hardy's fourteen novels, Hardy has a good deal to say about marriage although it is the timing of the comments on marriage in *Under the Greenwood Tree* written around the time he was weighing up the nature of his own relationship with Emma that make interesting reading. Most are in accord with the novel's general levity although a number are unusually matter of fact and/or pessimistic especially when uttered by his male characters. A perfect example of Hardy's tongue in cheek advice was that given to Dick: *'When you've made up your mind to marry, take the first respectable body that comes to hand – she's as good as any other; they be all alike in groundwork: 'tis only in the flourishes there's a difference.'* (Pt. 2, Ch. 8) Fate also had a hand in marriage just as Thomas felt somewhat powerless in his own situation with Emma and where it was headed. His own views on marriage were evolving, but he invariably saw the institution as something out of a man's control, observing only *'If we be doomed to marry, we marry; if we be doomed to remain single we do.'* (Pt. 2, Ch. 6)

As with Cytherea, Fancy Day is defined by the various behaviours and characteristics Hardy deemed as stereotypically belonging to women and which, to the chagrin of some feminist critics, contributed at least in equal part to the parlous positions in which some of his heroines found themselves. Vanity and pride are paraded once again and even someone as dim as Dick Dewey comes to the realisation that Fancy is more concerned with her own appearance than almost anything else, sagely observing *'What she loves best . . . is her hair and complexion. What she loves next best, her gowns and hats; what she loves next best, myself, perhaps!'* (Pt. 4, Ch. 1)

Throughout Hardy's novels, some of these innately feminine weaknesses as he saw them, are paraded in different guises; but pride, vanity, an unwillingness to compromise or deal pragmatically with situations often cost his women dear. Few heroines escape Hardy's feminine cloak – Tess perhaps and Marty South, but most others are afflicted by female posturing in some form or other.

Some writers have seen a link between Fancy Day and the early, carefree Emma although it is tenuous. [15] Hardy's women after all, are full of the habits and foibles, mannerisms and opinions of women of the time and their strength is their vitality and their relevance (in this, I am at odds with Hubbard who opined that *'there are two kinds of women – God's and Thomas Hardy's').* [16] But the most important woman in Hardy's life at this point was undoubtedly Emma who was busy assisting and encouraging him when he was wracked by self-doubt following his earlier poor reviews and sales and whose practical help in editing, and transcribing proved invaluable to him.

By the time *Under the Greenwood Tree* was published, the draft of Hardy's next novel, *A Pair of Blue Eyes* was almost completed. By this time, he and Emma were courting, mainly by letter and while their correspondence from this period was later burnt by Emma, the decision to set the novel in Cornwall was no doubt inspired by the time they had spent together there.

A Pair of Blue Eyes was published in 1873 and was the first book published under Hardy's own name. Having mined his home area for material for the writing of *Under the Greenwood Tree*, this time he turned his eyes westwards in a book that provides us with a good deal of autobiographical detail in the setting and characters, if not in the storyline. Even though Hardy initially took pains to dissociate any autobiographical element from the novel, after Emma's death he admitted that *'the character of the heroine is somewhat – indeed, rather largely – that of my late wife, and the background of the tale and the place where she lived'* while adding *'But of course the adventures, lovers, &c. are fictitious entirely . . . .'* [17]

The story of Elfride Swancourt, a beautiful and modern young woman caught between two suitors, Henry Smith and Stephen Knight, and unsure whether to follow her heart or her mind, is set against the expectations and conventions of society. In the end, having rejected one and been rejected by the other, Elfride out of desperation marries the elderly Lord Luxellian. To the list of feminine traits we can now add the desire for financial security rising above romantic love, a subject which resurfaces later in Hardy's work.

Of the themes present in the book, there are a number that typify Hardy's writings and go some way towards explaining his social views. His criticism of class is one of the most significant (and the undoing of one of Elfride's suitors, Stephen Smith). Other themes in the novel include the conflict between love and respectability; the hypocrisy of the Victorian moral code (as evident in Elfride's rejection by the respectable Henry Knight); and the unfair and often harsh expectations and mores of society that discriminated against women. Hardy uses his characters to comment variously on the nature of women, their propensity to vacillate and the general helplessness in which they find themselves that often leads to tragic decisions or outcomes (Hardy seems to excel in the novel at thwarting any possibility of a happy ending). He talks about women as a sex, ground down by their situation and circumstances and the fact that they all too meekly *'. . . accept their destiny more readily than men'* although Elfride certainly does not. (Ch. 9) Already, three novels in, it is apparent that being cast as a woman in one of Hardy's novels is a life sentence for if fate does not do for you, then a woman's foibles will.

There are a number of details that link the book to what was happening in Hardy's own life at the time, apart from the setting and while Seymour-Smith warns against making too much of the similarities there are some parallels we can safely draw. After Emma's death, Hardy confirmed that not only had he drawn on the Emma of their early meetings for Elfride's character, but that his friend, Horace Moule was the basis for the character of Stephen's rival, Henry Knight. This last association was the most significant for in September 1873, Moule had taken his own life while at Cambridge, an action that deeply affected Hardy. The triangle of Knight, Smith and Elfride that lies at the heart of the novel is commonly assumed to represent Hardy, Emma and Moule and, not surprisingly, the novel raises a few questions about the relationships, each with each. Moule never met Emma, however, and it is just possible that the parson's daughter Elfride was, in fact, a cover for Tryphena, who was an intimate friend of both Hardy and Moule. To suggest that Hardy was capable of such subtlety and subterfuge may be reading rather too much into the novel, but it could explain something of those years between Hardy's return from London and his marriage, a period that he seemed determined to consign to obscurity.

Thomas had met Emma not long before he started writing and between Elfride and Emma, there are obvious comparisons that can be made, albeit mainly superficial. Both, for instance, are living in a Rectory, both are high-spirited, blue-eyed (although Emma's were really deep grey), outwardly beautiful and fine equestrians. Elfride's first suitor, Stephen like Thomas, is an architect, quiet and retiring by nature – as indeed Emma had found Thomas at the outset. He is passed over for reasons of social rank (Stephen's father was a mason, Hardy's, a builder) and their upbringings were not dissimilar although Stephen's lack of worldliness paled when compared with Hardy's cosmopolitan outlook and metropolitan experience.

While the characters and setting might be familiar, the plot was most definitely not with Elfride's marriage to Lord Luxellian bringing the story to a sad conclusion, leaving Henry Knight (like Angel Clare in *Tess*) remonstrating with himself over the damage wrought by his exaggerated sense of propriety and Stephen, heart-broken at having lost his one chance in love through his timidity and lack of masculinity.

Is it written by Hardy with his own life in mind? Quite possibly so and certainly he would have had it in the mind each day as he sat down to write the novel. It is, of course, possible that all may be coincidence and that we should accept Hardy's view of the active (and usually malignant) role played by fate. But can we stretch our credibility enough to be persuaded to take Hardy's (or is it largely Florence's?) word that there were no parallels at all between the characters in the novel and the lives of the courting couple. I doubt it.

Critics have been ambivalent about Elfride and her fate and the vacillations of her affections towards her suitors, loving four men in quick succession with disastrous results and feeling little sense of disloyalty towards any of them. Yet for all of her indecision and actions, in her defence, Elbert Hubbard, the contemporary American writer who died along with his wife in the sinking of the *Lusitania* in 1915, came to her defence at the time, writing of Elfride *'she is a beautiful creature, a true woman, sinned against by the gods but never sinning.'* [18] Hubbard felt that Hardy saw the circumstances that affected peoples' lives as predestined, fate, determined by the situations in which his heroines, in particular, found themselves. His observation on the reasons for Elfride's inconstancy was that *'she is in love with love not with her lover'*, an observation he felt could be applied to many of Hardy's heroines – and probably a charge that could be levelled at Hardy himself.[19]

Elfride, however, is not a conventional heroine. She is described by Rosemarie Morgan as 'no iconic Victorian maiden' for in her daring she *'puts herself so much at risk, because in her candour she is so self-exposing, because she is strong and weak, brave and fearful, headstrong and vulnerable'*.[20] Faced with her two main suitors, one lacking in masculinity and the other, excessively fastidious, possibly sexually repressed, Elfride does not shrink from telling them so. At one stage, Elfride exhorts Harry *'I almost wish you were of a grosser nature, Harry; in truth I do!'* (Ch. 30) an exhortation that shocks the reader. Her open and forthright manner is at odds with the conventions of the time, especially that part of her that Morgan so aptly describes as *'sexually instigative'*.[21]

More and more, when looking at Hardy's novels, we can identify elements that are equally applicable to his own life. The idea of someone, invariably a woman, or some incident being frozen in the memory to be called up and used in the future, was particularly apposite. So it was in *A Pair of Blue Eyes* when Hardy noted that *'Every woman who makes a permanent impression on a man is usually recalled to his mind's eye as she appeared in one particular scene, which seems ordained to be her special form of manifestation throughout the pages of his memory.'* (Ch. 3) For Hardy never forgot his first meeting with Emma in her brown riding habit, her hair flying loose behind her, and all the other memories from that time that fuelled his poetry in the period immediately after her death.

By now, a pattern was emerging in his plots. Each story seemed to be set around a somewhat complicated love story, often involving a love triangle of two or more suitors from different social backgrounds, laced with a combination of social traits and behaviours and an added dash of Victorian hypocrisy. With three novels behind him and having already given his readers the orthodox Gothic heroine, Cytherea Graye, the anti-romantic and flighty heroine Fancy Day and the altogether more worldly and forward Elfride, Hardy was about to publish the book that was to make his name and with it, give us Bathsheba, one of his best-known heroines.

Far from the Madding Crowd, reputedly based on a story told to him by his cousin, Tryphena Sparks, first appeared as a monthly serial in *Cornhill Magazine* before being published in book form in 1874. It is the story of Bathsheba Everdene and another love triangle, consisting of herself, William Boldwood, an older farmer whose passion she inadvertently awakens and the first of Hardy's Victorian cads, the dashing Sergeant Troy, precursor to later seducers, Fitzpiers and Alec D'Urberville. The hero is Gabriel Oak, a childhood friend of Bathsheba, who sits outside the triangle and was her first love (and set to be her last) before their respective circumstances changed dramatically.

Early in the story, Bathsheba inherited a farm from her late uncle and it is her trials and tribulations that set the backdrop for the story. Rejecting Gabriel when he falls on hard times, Bathsheba employs him as a shepherd, blunders through an awkward relationship with Boldwood, is seduced by the charms of Sergeant Troy who she marries before he absconds. Thinking him dead, she allows herself to be promised to Boldwood again until Troy returns to be killed by Boldwood. With two of the three suitors happily disposed of (Boldwood is generously spared the gallows, but imprisoned for life), Bathsheba goes back to the dependable and ever constant Gabriel Oak at the story's end.

Apart from Bathsheba, two other women in the novel take important roles. The first is one against whom the world seems pitted, Fanny Robin, who Sergeant Troy loved and pledged to marry before both are robbed of the opportunity through circumstance. Alone and pregnant, she is abandoned while Troy, ignorant of her fate, marries Bathsheba. Destitute and alone due to yet another cruel trick of fate, Fanny falls ill whereupon Troy finds her and brings her back to Weatherbury where she dies in childbirth. As the abandoned woman, cast adrift through fate and circumstance yet able to command a man's love and his belated regrets at not acting before tragedy struck, she was to become a familiar character type in Hardy's novels. The other woman who has a significant place is Bathsheba's maid, Liddy. She acts as the confidante to her mistress throughout the novel, a sounding board to her mistress, as well as offering her own unsophisticated but often perceptive advice in return. Through their relationship, we learn a good deal of Bathsheba's character as Liddy watches her mistress mature and mellow.

Published in the year of Thomas and Emma's marriage, Hardy's observations on womanhood and marriage stand alongside the vacillations of Bathsheba who, in the course of little over two years, sees her husband murdered, an erstwhile suitor locked up for life before concluding with a marriage, soaked in homily and reeking of Jane Austen.

The character of Bathsheba, Hardy later attested, was based on his mother's youngest sister and aunt of Tryphena, Martha Sharpe, who young Thomas and Jemima went to stay with for several months at the end of 1849. Within two years, Martha and her husband, John Sharpe had emigrated to Canada much to the disappointment of the extended family and, no doubt, to Thomas in particular. Martha was a glamorous and romantic figure to the young Hardy. When Thomas was young, her physical beauty and charm completely won over her young nephew. She was only forty-three-years -old when she died in childbirth with her tenth child and the exactitude of the entry in his notebook from June 1874 was poignant: *'My Aunt Sharpe died in Canada the Sunday before August 30, 1859 at 4.00pm, at Paris, British North America.'*[22]

When the book was released, critics were quick to comment on Hardy's depiction of Bathsheba, not of her talents and physical presence, but for the shallowness of her emotions, her vanity and her class prejudice. Henry James was particularly scathing writing in *The Nation* of Bathsheba that she was *'inconsequential, wilful and meddlesome'* neither likeable or understandable before widening his sights onto the novel as a whole that *'everything in the book strikes us as factious and insubstantial'*.[23] Other reviews were much more encouraging, however, as were sales which, for the first time as a writer, provided Hardy with an income on which he could now contemplate marriage.

In the first half of the book Bathsheba is, indeed, depicted as rash and impulsive, passing judgement on those about her and affected by her financial independence. Boldwood thinks her beautiful, with her *'black hair, her correct facial curves and profile, and the roundness of her chin and throat'* noting *'the side of her eyelids, eyes and lashes, and the shape of her ear'* before *'he noticed her figure, her skirt, and the very soles of her shoes.'* (Ch. 17)

As if to check whether his observations were accurate, being forty years old and still a bachelor he asked a neighbour, not whether Bathsheba was beautiful but whether she was considered *'handsome'* to which he received a reply in the affirmative that, yes, she was *'a very handsome girl indeed.'* (Ch. 17)

There are other descriptions of her appearance. Further on, we are told of her *'red cheeks and lips contrasting lusciously with the mazy skeins of her shadowy hair'* though it is the word 'handsome' that seems to suit her best. Physical features aside, it is her temperament and the flaws in her character that determine her fate. She is more outspoken than many of Hardy's heroines and less likeable, but by the conclusion of the novel, because of her trials and tribulations, she manages to garner at least some of the reader's sympathies. (Ch. 23)

When reading the novel which was written during the latter part of Emma and Thomas's courtship and published soon after their marriage, some of the phrases and sentences must have made Emma look twice at her husband to be and wonder that he was capable of writing such things. It is likely at this time that Hardy was himself having some doubts over his engagement, especially during the period from their Christmas together in 1873 (Hardy's last visit to Cornwall until after Emma's death) and their eventual marriage in September 1874 and it would not be unreasonable to think that such thoughts would surface in his writing. [24] There is no doubt that Hardy trawled his own experiences in writing the book, often without Emma being aware of the background. The instance of Bathsheba sending the Valentine card to Boldwood when in 1871 he had engaged in a similar duplicity by sending Valentines to both Emma and Tryphena shows how unaffected he was by guilt or embarrassment in using such intimate details in his writing (if we are to believe the account by Gittings).[25] Like Florence, some forty years later reading the elegies to Emma that so upset her, Emma must have wondered at some of the sentiments and observations that Hardy's characters espoused, including Troy's deeply disturbing comment to Bathsheba that *'All romances end at marriage'.* (Ch. 41)

From the outset of the novel where she appears as a rather shallow and self-centred woman, lacking in humility and feeling, Hardy develops her character – leading her by the nose at times – into someone altogether more sensible and likeable. From the outset, she has a strong sense of her own independence and self-importance. She tells Gabriel *'I wouldn't mind being the bride at a wedding if I could be one without having a husband'* then proceeding to tell him that she was *'too independent'* and challenging him, indeed all mankind, by stating, *'I want someone to tame me'* before dismissing his approach in the same sentence *'and you would never be able to, I know.'* (Ch. 4) Her rudeness irritates even her friend and companion Liddy who, when she asks Bathsheba about his suit is told *'he wasn't quite good enough for me'*. In reply, Liddy offers the ironic rejoinder, *'How sweet to be able to disdain, when most of us are glad to say, "Thank you!" I seem to hear it. "No, sir – I'm your better," or "Kiss my foot, sir; my face is for mouths of consequence."'* (Ch. 9)

Apart from the voices of the characters in the text of the novel, we are also offered the detached views of the narrator on aspects of love, that can be interpreted with a modern eye as sexist, belittling women, usually representing marriage as an inevitable, although not always welcome, formality rather than the culmination of the courting of a young couple. As Angela Thirwell writes in her introduction to the folio edition of *Under the Greenwood Tree* apposite to that novel, but applicable to Hardy in general, *'Hardy is fascinated by the process by which romance is transmuted into marriage'*.[26] and the inevitability of courtship leading to a mature and enduring relationship citing Hardy's description of Dick Dewy's parents that in marriage they achieve a *'mysterious closeness to each other, a just perceptible current of intelligence passing from each to each'*. (Pt. 1,Ch. 8) In *Far from the Madding Crowd* however, Hardy offers another, more stark definition of enduring love in relation to Bathsheba and Gabriel Oak. After she has been battered by circumstance and become less sure of herself, more humble and more accepting of her lot, he notes:

'Theirs was that substantial affection which arises . . . when the two who are thrown together begin first by knowing the rougher sides of each other's character, and not the best till further on, the romance growing up in the interstices of a mass of hard prosaic reality where good fellowship and pleasures are subsumed by the trials and tribulations of everyday life, for only then can couples achieve "the only love which is strong as death".' (Ch. 56)

The observations on marriage in the novel offer a further insight into how Hardy was viewing marriage in its imminence, including the rationale the narrator suggests that *'It appears that ordinary men takes wives because possession is not possible without marriage and that ordinary women accept husbands because marriage is not possible without possession.'* (Ch. 20) And yet with the very act of marriage, something changes when women 'possess' their husbands, for, as is suggested, they are not so easily satisfied and that having their husbands and having made them to their liking, they are no longer happy with them; that *'Women are never tired of bewailing man's fickleness in love, but they only seem to snub his constancy'*. (Ch. 24) In the novel, it is the inconstancy of Bathsheba towards Gabriel that best bears this out. At one stage, Matthew opines to Gabriel,*' . . . maids rather like your man of sin'*; certainly, the sexual frisson that we sense in Bathsheba's encounter with Troy and his highly suggestive sword display shows how easily Bathsheba was seduced by his roguish character and how gullible and easily duped she was by his daring her, a susceptibility Hardy suggests that could apply to all women in entering marriage.[27]

In the aftermath of her wedding to Troy and its downward spiral, Bathsheba is sorely chastened, particularly as she felt she was one who had *'never taken kindly to the idea of marriage in the abstract as did the majority of women she saw about her'* and that, therefore it was her fault that she found herself in such a situation. (Ch. 41) It was she that had allowed a man to kiss her and put his arm around her waist, even as she reflected ruefully about what becomes of giving yourself to another and the degradation *'. . . in renouncing the simplicity of a maiden existence to become the humbler part of an indifferent matrimonial whole.'* (Ch. 41)

By way of contrast, the male view of marriage, as expressed in the novel is far more dispassionate, and often deeply cynical. Pennyway's opinion given to Troy, that

'A good wife is good, but the best wife is not so good as no wife at all' is hardly encouraging, but common, it seems, of the patriarchy. (Ch. 52) And there is a strong inference that for those men who do succumb and marry, the problem is to somehow sustain the affection that first led to the very act of commitment. One of the most amusing and discursive comments Hardy makes on marriage in any of his novels comes from a conversation involving Bathsheba's father, Levi Everdene, a gentleman-tailor who, by all accounts, was one of the *'ficklest husbands alive.'*

As recounted by Jan Coogan, a farm labourer and friend of Gabriel, *'The poor fellow were faithful and true enough to her in his wish, but his heart would rove, do what he could.'* Levi's solution was to make his wife remove her *'wedding-ring and calling her by her maiden name as they sat together after the shop was shut, and so 'a would get to fancy she was only his sweetheart, and not married to him at all. And as soon as he could thoroughly fancy he was doing wrong and committing the seventh, 'a got to like her as well as ever, and they lived on a perfect picture of mutel love.'*

Thereafter followed a discussion about the ungodly remedy that Mr Everdene had decided upon for his fickleness which concluded with the judgement of Billy Smallbury who chimed in by noting that *'the man's will was to do right, sure enough, but his heart didn't chime in.'* (Ch. 8)

Many of Hardy's own views on women that would have sat comfortably in contemporary Victorian society, today would be seen as sexist or misogynistic. One suspects that Hardy would feel disappointed with the slow progress society has made and that having removed one ceiling, another glass ceiling remained and that while, ostensibly and in the eye of the law, women had achieved a semblance of equality, the reality was somewhat different.[28]

Finally in the novel, Hardy brings us back to the foibles of women, women who are often chastised for their fickleness. When we read *'Bathsheba's feeling was always to some extent dependent upon her whim, as is the case with many other women'* we see the same charge being laid at the feet of many of Hardy's women, cast as shallow, as prevaricators, women capable of shifting affection as easy as changing outfits, thereby becoming too womanly so that this thing, of being a woman, takes over. (Ch. 56) The same applies when Hardy writes of womanliness as an impediment and that Bathsheba had *'too much womanliness to use her understanding to best advantage'* (Ch. 29) and that, as a consequence, the best decision is not obvious to her because of her sex.

It is little wonder that women are described as *'rum things'* by Liddy to Bathsheba, while in confessing to Gabriel of her marriage to Troy, Bathsheba tells him *'And then, between jealousy and distraction, I married him.'* (Ch. 37) With the amount of self-denigration and confession by women, there is little left for the menfolk or, indeed, the narrator to add. Hence, while the idea of women being victims of their sex is not at all uncommon in Victorian literature, with Hardy we can see a constant dripping of the tap telling us that, despite all the horrible things that happen to his heroines, and all the machinations of fate they have to endure, in some small, but significant way, they are victims of their sex as much as circumstance.

Bathsheba is a memorable character created on the cusp of Emma and Thomas's married life. In the absence of his letters to Emma, and hers to him during the years leading up to their marriage in 1874, we can only guess what was going through his mind as he wrote it. Whatever transpired thereafter, the years in which the book was conceived and written became etched on Hardy's memory and became the mine that he would excavate after Emma's death, returning to again and again in later life.

By 1874, Hardy had produced a wide range of heroines: Cytherea Graye, Fancy Day, Elfride Swancourt and Bathsheba Everdene along with a few other significant women characters (of whom Miss Cytherea Adclyffe and Fanny Robin stand out). While he may have been influenced in some way by the women he knew from his own life, perhaps Emma or one or other of the Sparks family (Tryphena, Martha or Maria), we also learn something about Hardy and his own views on women and their situation in the mid-Victorian era. Broadly, he was sympathetic to their lot, but the overall tenet of the novels was that women often found themselves in trouble because of the weakness of their own sex. In the last of the four novels and his first commercial success, *Far from the Madding Crowd*, Bathsheba appears as the summation of his views. She is presented as a character outwardly stronger and able to stand up to men, and very aware of her social status and her influence, but possessing a greater number of the faults that Hardy was inclined to ascribe to women in general, implying that they were often shown as lacking moral judgment and being too easily swayed or, as in the case with Bathsheba, too vain. It is the relations between the sexes and the institution of marriage, however, that received most attention, as Hardy hinted at what we could expect in future novels.

Chapter 10

Eustacia Vye and the Novels of 1875–1885

The Hand of Ethelberta (1876), The Return of the Native (1878), The Trumpet Major (1880), A Laodicean (1881), Two on a Tower (1882)

'Why is it a woman can see from a distance what a man cannot see close.'

(*The Return of the Native*, Bk. 3, Ch. 6)

After their wedding in September, 1874 Thomas and Emma spent the next ten years moving from place to place without ever establishing a home of their own. Following their honeymoon in Paris, they moved to London, first living in Surbiton, then in Newton Road, Bayswater. In July 1875 they returned to Dorset, to the coastal town of Swanage for what was to be only a brief interlude, ostensibly for Thomas to research some scenes for *The Hand of Ethelberta* although they ended up staying in the seaside town until July 1876. From here, they moved briefly to Yeovil before, at the end of May 1876, travelling once more to Europe, this time visiting the Rhine and Low Countries. Returning to Dorset, they rented a villa by the River Stour in the rural town of Sturminster Newton where they remained from July 1876 until early 1878. It was at Sturminster Newton that Thomas wrote *The Return of the Native* introducing his readers to his most capricious, most other-worldly heroine, Eustacia Vye. This time they spent together at Sturminster Newton was acknowledged to be amongst the happiest of their marriage although it is likely that their childlessness continued to weigh upon them.[1]

In March 1878 they were on the move again, this time to 1 Arundel Terrace, Tooting Close. It was here, over the Christmas of 1880, that Thomas fell ill and was bedridden for several months, during which time he wrote *A Laodicean* with a good deal of assistance from Emma. They returned finally to Dorset in June 1881, first to Dorchester while Thomas's brother, Henry began to build the house that Thomas had designed on a site purchased by Thomas from the Duchy of Cornwall. Then, in the autumn of 1882 they returned once again to Paris. In the first nine years of their marriage, they had lived in seven different houses and made three trips to the continent. Why they lived quite so nomadic a life is not obvious although Hardy's writing and need for new experiences and new contacts was partly responsible. Hardy was restless in his private and personal life, that much we can deduce, and wanted to be in London for increasingly longer periods of time, but such a lifestyle was understandably unsettling for Emma and not what she expected when they first married. Yet there were aspects they enjoyed together, including travelling to the continent, something they continued to do until the late nineties. Certainly, their respective families did not feel that such a lifestyle was conducive to a happy marriage and were relieved when they finally moved into Max Gate in the summer of 1885.

During this period of his life, Thomas wrote a further five books which Tomalin categorized as follows: *'failure (*Ethelberta*), masterpiece (*The Return of the Native*); slight historic novel (*The Trumpet Major*), failure (*A Laodicean*)'* and what she labelled an *'interesting oddity (*Two on a Tower.*)'*[2] By the time they finally settled in Max Gate, with these five books behind him, Hardy was already busy writing *The Mayor of Casterbridge* hoping to build on the success of his most successful novel to date *Far from the Madding Crowd* published some eleven years previously.

Although at first glance the heroines in the novels of 1874 – 1885 appear rather subdued compared to the bombast of Bathsheba, they represent a further development in Hardy's range, evident in the diversity of background of the major heroines Eustacia Vye, Ethelberta Chickerel, Paula Power and Anne Garland. Of the five novels, the two described by Tomalin as 'failures' were the two with women in the title roles: Ethelberta and Paula Power (The Laodicean) and yet despite the poor reception that both novels received, the two heroines still managed to stand out, albeit for different reasons.

The Hand of Ethelberta first appeared in instalments in *Cornhill Magazine*, as had *Far From the Madding Crowd*, before being published in a single volume in April 1876.

From the very start there are strong social themes that can be related back to Hardy's mother, Jemima. The heroine Ethelberta Chickerell, a butler's daughter, starts her life in service in the stately home of Sir Ralph and Lady Petherwin where she achieves the unthinkable by eloping with and duly marrying the couple's only son, who promptly dies on their honeymoon. Lady Petherwin, by now herself a widow, embraces her new daughter in law and adopts her as her own, sending her to an expensive finishing school abroad and having her as a companion while giving her all the privileges of a daughter.

Ethelberta has aspirations of becoming a writer, but finds that she is a victim of her own penmanship (as Hardy had occasionally found himself) when she is disinherited for a book of verse that her benefactor felt dishonoured the memory of her son. Out of favour, Ethelberta decides to go and live in a house in London, her one possession, but decides that she must also hide her lower-class background as she sets out on a path of becoming a writer and storyteller. Like Hardy, the complexities and exclusiveness of class beset her throughout the novel and wrestling with its social strictures, and making the best of her situation (pointedly, armed with a pen) become the major themes of the book.

Ethelberta soon makes her mark in London society and before long has four suitors seeking to win her hand, all with their own merits. The fact that she settles eventually on the much older and disreputable Lord Mountclere is seen as a triumph of mind over emotion as, by so doing, she secures her future and that of her family, for whom she is a generous provider, sharing the opportunities that life had given her.

There is much to admire about Ethelberta. Hardy portrays her as facing the same dichotomy that faced many of his women, being, on the one hand, a caring and generous daughter and sibling, keen to use her social position to look after her own family; and on the other, a necessary opportunist, happy to use the power of her sex to advance herself.

Hardy's attempts to portray a character shouldering the responsibilities of her extended family seem credible, and creditable, despite the wider criticisms made of the novel. Ethelberta is a new type of heroine and her major struggles in the novel, those of dealing with class prejudice and social convention, are issues Hardy was becoming increasingly aware of since his marriage to the class-conscious Emma. But Ethelberta is also astute and pragmatic, despite the criticism she occasionally receives from her siblings and the perfunctory way she is seen responding to her suitors. Tomalin describes her as *'quick witted and ambitious,'* in making the most of her complicated situation, attributes that could not usually be applied to Hardy's heroines. [3]

Critics slammed the book, including his good friend, Edmund Gosse [4] and it was widely agreed to be one of Hardy's weakest novels. Yet more recently several critics have felt that while the novel was both subversive and self-reflective, there was something more at work. Robert Gittings, who initially described the book as *'the most uneven and contradictory of all Hardy's novels'* [5] later modified his view when he came to see the novel more in relation to Hardy himself, drawing comparisons between the intelligent and capable Ethelberta, lifted from her own class by her writing and story-telling, and Hardy himself, also from a working class family but with aspirations to being a writer.

Gittings wrote: *'Almost the first thing we know of her is that, like Hardy, she has written a large number of sonnets putting a woman's point of view, a natural echo of the mass of "She to Him" sonnets written by the young Hardy. Unlike Hardy, but like him in intention, she has these published in a book; it will be remembered that Hardy had intended to print his own sonnets in "The Poor Man and the Lady" . . . .'* [6]

Once he has the bit between his teeth, Gittings draws a number of conclusions: That the 'Hand' of Ethelberta refers to the family name of Hardy's mother, Jemima; that the servants are based on his own extended family including his mother and aunt who both were in service; and that references to class and the fact that the servants are given a voice and participated in the narrative, which was shocking to many Victorian readers, could be seen as a rebuke to Emma's attitudes towards class and even to those of his own family. [7]

Pamela L. Jekel also contended that Ethelberta was Hardy's alter ego, a fictional projection of the author, allowing him to live both in the real world and in the world of his fiction:

'There is much evidence in the book that Hardy used Ethelberta as a vehicle for his own thoughts, his own dilemmas (public and private), and even for his own unconscious anxieties. Ethelberta is Hardy's rebuke, for example, to those critics and would-be biographers who refused to separate the teller from the tale, who could not understand the difference between fiction and thinly veiled confessions.' Further, Jekel asserted *'Lady Petherwin's denouncement of Ethelberta's "scandalous" verse is the first hint we have of Hardy's contempt for such intrusion into the artist's right to anonymity . . . . The public eye, as an entity which ignores art and thrives on gossip, is consistently condemned in the novel.'* [8]

And what of Ethelberta? Early on, the narrator gives us a clue, suggesting that she was *' . . . one of those people who are known, as one may say, by subscription: everybody knows a little till she is astonishingly well known altogether; but nobody knows her entirely.'* (Ch. 9) We learn that she is ambitious, wilful, but always pragmatic. She is also intelligent, a poet and a storyteller, well versed in using language, but like all women in love, she can be rash or indiscreet. No doubt we can read too much into her character. Millgate notes that by portraying a character that uses storytelling as a way of social advancement, Hardy must in some sense, *'have been writing an allegory of his own career'.*[9]

Other reviewers attribute some of her characteristics as belonging to Emma. Sometimes the reader can see what they want to see, but it is wrong to dismiss the character of Ethelberta because of the failings of the novel. She is a heroine in the true Hardy mould, confronted by new and different challenges. She signalled a departure for Hardy from some of his earlier heroines and was seen by Tomalin as being

' . . . a brave attempt to show a modern woman who finds herself outside the conventional structures of society and sets out defiantly to make the most of her situation.'[10]

There are the usual comments on love, marriage and women that we have come to expect from Hardy. He seldom fails to take aim at the institution of marriage although often from different vantage points. In *The Hand of Ethelberta,* Hardy sees marriage as functional, but with very little to do with romantic love and more about compromise, noting at one point,

'Lord Mountclere . . . [had] just pocketed a document [a marriage licence] in which romance, rashness, law, and gospel are so happily made to work together that it may safely be regarded as the neatest compromise which has ever been invented since Adam sinned.' (Ch. 40)

Hardy was in the early throes of his marriage to Emma and it is clear not all was going well. It is very likely that when Hardy wrote *'Ethelberta wished heartily, for his sake, there could be warm friendship between herself and him, as well as all her lovers, without that insistent courtship and marriage question. ...'* (Ch. 35) he is voicing some of his own feelings although Pite's assertion that *'Christopher's choice of Picotee over Ethelberta may be taken as an indication of Hardy 's beginning to regret marrying Emma and not, say, Tryphena'* is possibly a step too far.[11] Throughout his life and writing, we see Hardy commenting less and less favourably on the institution of marriage, describing it as an artificial construct impeding long-lasting relationships and genuine friendship, but rarely as the natural outcome of love.

Class is one of the major themes that run through the novel. At one stage, Ethelberta's brother Sol scolds her for abandoning her childhood principles: *'I never seen such a deserter of your own lot as you be . . .When you were a girl, you wouldn't drop a curtsey to 'em . . .But instead of sticking to such principles, you must needs push up, so as to get girls such as you were once to curtsey to you.'* (Ch. 46)

To which Ethelberta may well have responded that needs must and it is not right to bite the hand that feeds you or to pass up the opportunities for betterment that have fallen your way. She could also have acknowledged that she had had to wrestle with the same demons, of belonging, of attachment and loyalty to her family and fight for her own aspirations and ambitions, primarily to be afforded the space and freedom of being able to write.

Ethelberta is no conventional heroine. Imbued with a strong moral purpose she chooses a marriage of convenience that provides for her family, and also allows her the opportunity to write. One senses she represents the new woman so enamoured by Hardy and presages what was to come in his own life. It is, as narrator, that Hardy shows his admiration of what his heroine represents:

'She stood there, as all women stand who have made themselves remarkable by their originality, or devotion to any singular cause, as a person freed of her hampering and inconvenient sex, and, by virtue of her popularity, unfettered from the conventionalities of manner prescribed by custom for household womankind. The charter to move abroad unchaperoned, which society for good reasons grants only to women of three sorts—the famous, the ministering, and the improper—Ethelberta was in a fair way to make splendid use of. ...' (Ch. 31)

The ways in which women bestow their affections was not, in Hardy's words necessarily linked to the concept of romantic love, but to other more pragmatic considerations. Love, after all, is not a rational pursuit as Hardy obliquely observed when writing *'A lover without indiscretion is no lover at all'*. (Chapter 20) In the matter of relationships, of marriage, it is often the women like Picotee, by nature gentle, unremarkable and self-effacing, who wins the man.

Hardy exploits Ethelberta's relationship with Picotee and the contrast between them throughout the novel. Ethelberta's willfulness and strength of character should have seen her triumph rather than the meek Picotee, but it is the younger sister who ends up marrying Julian and raises the question as to whether the unconventional, the assertive woman is always doomed to disappointment in Hardy's novels. When Tomalin suggests that most of the characters in the novel are notional figures, *'there to make points'*, we can ask, indeed, what points Hardy is making about his women here?[12]

That the subservient Picotee is the better woman? Yet that would be to miss the point, that in many ways, and on her own terms, Ethelberta does triumph. She accepts she cannot win everything, even in marriage, but she can win a security and freedom that gives her peace of mind and sets her apart as one of the most pragmatic, if least romantic, of all of Hardy's heroines.

The Return of the Native, published in 1878, gives us one of Hardy's most fascinating characters in Eustacia Vye. The novel was begun soon after Emma and Thomas had moved back to Dorset in July 1876, where they settled near the River Stour in the market town of Sturminster Newton. It was the beginning one of the more settled periods in their lives and, for the first year at least, one of the happiest. It is in this setting that Hardy sat down to write the novel, which was to prove to be his most significant success before moving into Max Gate in 1885.

The novel is set on Egdon Heath, whose brooding, sentient presence becomes one of the main features of the novel. The story follows the events of one year centred on the character of one of Hardy's contradictory and flawed heroines, Eustacia Vye. The daughter of a Corfu sea captain and raised in Budmouth, she lives with her grandfather on the heath. She is one of Hardy's colourful characters and a perennial outsider. The heath is not her natural environment (which is the bustling town of Budmouth), and she sees it as both alien and threatening. From the outset, we can sense that her time there is limited and her own future far from assured.

From the beginning of the story her feminine wiles soon become apparent. A former lover of Eustacia's, Wildeve, is to be married to the niece of Mrs Yeobright, the gentle and loyal Thomasin which makes Eustacia jealous enough to steal him back. It is only the return of the 'native,' Clym Yeobright from Paris, that distracts her. Before long, Eustacia and Clym marry, settling not far from Thomasin and Wildeve from which point the story unravels. Clym's mother dies through one of those coincidences that Hardy revels in and eventually Eustacia, abandoned by Clym, drowns herself. At the end of the novel, Thomasin remarries and Clym lives as an itinerant preacher, blaming himself for the deaths of both mother and wife.

We have the usual array of Hardyesque, feminine types and traits in the novel. Mrs Yeobright, widely acknowledged to be based on Jemima Hardy, strives to protect her son from making the wrong decisions in life and is there offering her admonitions and advice to her love-struck son. She is the realist, but also the pessimist, just as was his own mother and the strained relationship between her and Clym over Eustacia, and her opposition to their marriage has its parallel in the animosity engendered between Emma and Jemima. It is quite possible Thomas pondered his own mother's warning about marriage when writing the novel. Thomasin, Mrs Yeobright's niece, is the antithesis of Eustacia, with her good nature and sense of propriety finding various parallels in other minor character types (similar to Picotee and foreshadowing many of the attributes of Hardy's beloved heroine, Tess). Invaribly, she – they – are all subject to the follies that Hardy attributed to womankind, even if some of those follies are little more than the misplaced values of loyalty and trust or, a particular vanity as given voice by Thomasin, when she proudly tells her aunt *'I wish all good women were as good as I'*. (Bk. 2, Ch. 2)

Despite its popularity, the book was controversial at the time of publication, most notably for its illicit sexual relationships and for Eustacia's amoral character, her selfishness, inconstancy and unworldly tendencies.

Eustacia is a character unlike any other. On one hand, she has *'the raw material of a divinity'* on the other, the presence of a witch. Her great desire, we are told, is to be *'loved to madness'* and yet it was not for one lover, but for *'the abstraction called passionate love.'* Controversially for the time, she did not eschew the idea of illicit love; rather the opposite for as Hardy, the narrator, noted, by way of explanation: *'Fidelity in love for fidelity's sake had less attraction for her than for most women'* (Bk. 1, Ch. 7), a repetition of the adage from his previous novel, that to be a lover, one had to embrace indiscretion.

Later, during her meeting with Wildeve she expands her views on how she sees love: *'I should hate it to be all smooth. Indeed I think I like you to desert me a little now and then. Love is the dismallest thing where the lover is quite honest.'* (Bk. 1, Ch. 9) The attributes and characteristics as seen by Hardy and peculiar to her sex again litter the book, and this time a few are spoken by men. At one point, Clym turns accusingly to Eustacia and rebukes her: *'You are just like all women. They are ever content to build their lives on any incidental position that offers itself; whilst men would fain make a globe to suit them.'* Other observations are made by their own sex, including Mrs Yeobright's rhetorical question,

'Why is it a woman can see from a distance what a man cannot see close.' (Bk. 3, Ch. 6) Why indeed!

The brooding presence of Egdon Heath foretells much of what goes on in the story and the deaths that occur happen not only because the heath allows them to ás part of its natural cycle, but because it is part of the process of death and renewal. For all her animal passion, Eustacia fears the heath as much as those who live on it fear her. Similarly, she is scared of commitment and the durability of love. She warns Clym of her vicissitudes during one of their surreptitious meetings *' . . . I know that we shall not love like this always. Nothing can ensure the continuance of love. It will evaporate like a spirit, and so I feel full of fears'*. Clym's suggestion that she cure her anxieties by becoming his wife elicits the response *'cynics say that marriage cures the anxiety by curing the love'* (Bk. 3, Ch. 4), a recycling of the sentiment from *Far from the Madding Crowd* that *'all romances end with marriage'*. And so Hardy's catalogue of observations on marriage continued to layer, much to Emma's chagrin and annoyance.

Knowing that Mrs Yeobright was based on Hardy's mother, Jemima, it is therefore surprising amongst Hardy's heroines that we have no obvious provenance for Eustacia. Morgan suggests that a model may have been the highly controversial novelist, George Sand, whom Hardy was reading at the time and who was an influence on his writing.[13] Eustacia is his most outlandish creation, a *'voluptuous, idle woman'* who, according to Mrs Yeobright, is both *'lazy and dissatisfied'*. Like a young child, she wants most what is forbidden her or that she has previously spurned until another has taken it up and it has again become desirable. Even before meeting her, and despite the warnings of those he talked about her with, Clym was fascinated by this woman who he called *'this young witch-lady.'* (Bk. 3, Ch. 2) She is always something more than a woman to Clym and only when she agrees to his terms for marriage, does he allow himself to say *'spoken like a woman.'* (Bk. 3, Ch. 4) It is no wonder critics railed against her immorality and licentiousness. After she was stabbed with a long stocking-needle at church she commented ironically to Clym, *'I didn't know I had such a magic reputation.'* Yet it was not magic that caused the suspicion of the other heath dwellers, but the fact that she made herself alien, someone who confessed that she had *' . . . not much love for her fellow-creatures'*, in fact at times seemed *'to quite hate them'* – as, indeed, she hated the world that had produced them. (Bk. 3, Ch. 3) The fact that she married Clym was not just because she had persuaded herself that she loved him, but also because he offered an escape and that she was *'in desperate need of loving somebody.'* (Bk 2, Ch. 6)

The novel is littered with allusions and comments about women. Thomasin's own narrow moral code holds her back in the same way that Eustacia's licentiousness is punished. Her one aim of escaping from the heath is thwarted by marriage and everything that happens from hereon – her inadvertent part in the death of Clym's mother, the re-igniting of her relationship with Wildeve, and eventually her death, all follow as the inevitable consequences of her destructive personality.

Eustacia's character sits outside of the women of Hardy's immediate experience although the poet, Rosamund Tomson, exhibited some of Eustacia's characteristics.[14] Yet one suspects there is much about Eustacia that would have attracted Hardy. She is a creature of the imagination for whom love is transitory and who cannot conceive of love or marriage as an enduring state of being; in contrast to Thomasin, representative of a woman-type that Hardy exploits, the submissive, monogamous woman, meek and subservient, conventional in her views and behaviour, whose function is, at least in part, to act as a moral touchstone in order to pass judgement on her counterparts. This idea of a woman, freed from social constraints and not overly concerned with convention or marriage is one Hardy is always searching for in his own life, if only in his imagination. Even for Hardy, Eustacia is an extreme character, and her rootlessness and sexual frustrations, as well as her erotic leanings and the lack of having any obvious moral code, were shocking at the time the book was written. We sense early on, that there is no likelihood she will be able to find any peace as, for instance, Bathsheba was able to, and from the outset, we are made aware of her destructive force. Before they were married, Eustacia, knowing only too well her own temperament, tells Clym *'How terrible it would be if a time should come when I could not love you' warning him, some fifty pages later, 'it will end bitterly.'* As it surely does. (Bk. 3, Ch. 4 / Bk. 4, Ch. 2)

Leaving Sturminster Newton in 1878, Thomas and Emma returned to London where he began his 'slight historical novel', *The Trumpet Major*. It is Hardy's only historical novel, set during the time of the Napoleonic Wars. Once again, we are confronted with a heroine (Anne Garland) who is pursued by three suitors, John Loveday, the trumpet major, Bob Loveday, his rather feckless brother who is a sailor and the dissolute Festus Derriman, nephew of the local squire. It was the third of Hardy's novels to date in which plot centred around the heroine, plunging the reader into a romantic mystery by guessing which suitor will prevail.

Our heroine, Anne Garland is a gentle country girl who lives quietly with her widowed mother in straitened circumstances at the Overcombe Millhouse, which belongs to the local miller Loveday, the father of two of Anne's erstwhile suitors. She is one of Hardy's 'good' women, a natural successor to Thomasin, possessing none of the vices (and little of the passion) of a Eustacia or a Bathsheba, but still with a number of the flaws with which Hardy imbues his heroines. She is rather pallid compared with her immediate predecessors, belonging to a distinctive group of women that exist in Thomas Hardy's novels.

Contemporary reviews of the novel were guarded although generally encouraging. Julian Hawthorne in *Spectator* (November, 1880) described Anne as *' . . . personally lovely and attractive; she is, moreover, amiable, innocent, generous and tender-hearted and yet she makes woeful havoc of the heart of a worthy man.'*[15] Other reviewers were not so charitable, pointing out the failings of Anne's character, stating that *'It is true, no doubt, that the heroine is, not to put too fine a point to it, a fool, and the gallant Bob Loveday another; and that the reader cannot help feeling more regard for Matilda of the doubtful reputation than for the correct and ladylike Anne.'*[16]

Anne Garland with her gentle demeanour and pretty appearance is a benign heroine. She has our approval, but seldom our admiration. Often in Hardy, the more delicate and pretty the heroine, the more limited in independence of thought and imagination. Their very passiveness militates against them and affects their ability to make anything more than superficial judgements. Anne is always 'pretty' rather than 'attractive' or 'beautiful' and one senses that it is a pejorative word in Hardy's vocabulary. She is described as tender, womanly and coquette, with her hair a *'row of round brown curls, like swallows' nests under eaves'*, reminiscent of those of Emma that so attracted Thomas to her early on in their courtship (and that are still there in later photographs of Emma although they had begun to look ever so slightly ridiculous). It is not surprising that one contemporary critic described her as *'among Mr Hardy's most perfect and delicate creations.'*[17]

Perfect or not, Anne is drawn to the wholly less admirable and flawed Bob rather than to his selfless and noble brother. For Hardy, it is indicative of the foibles of womankind to be tempted by the attractive knave rather than by the upstanding albeit priggish hero. The reviewer concluded in similar vein, *'We cannot quite forgive her for marrying Bob instead of John; but such failures of perception are customary with Mr Hardy's heroines and Anne's womanly instincts never forsake her.'*[18]

Hardy's novels are propelled by the machinations of 'womanly instincts' that often become impediments to social progress or at the very least dampen the possibility of achieving a happy resolution to the plot or the blossoming of relationships. This dichotomy of character between the simple and innocent and the consequences of choice, needs to be understood. Hawthorne offered his thoughts on Anne's character, arguing, *'She is selfish, as Mr Hardy's heroines are selfish – not wilfully or intellectually, but by dint of her inborn, involuntary, unconscious emotional organism. She recognizes John Loveday's goodness, his self-abnegation, his loveableness, and she can no more justify herself in not loving him than she can in loving his scamp of a brother; nevertheless, and despite all the obstacles of self-respect, gratitude and expediency, she marries Bob, and sends John to die on a Spanish battle-field.'*[19]

Somehow, we can forgive Anne for marrying Bob Loveday even if we fear for her, and can empathise with Hawthorne when he said of Anne and her kindred spirits: *'Their conduct is indefensible, but it is charming. – we love them the better for their tender naughtiness'* and yet in a rebuke to Anne and her ilk, adds the sentence that *'We are appalled to see what harm these gentle, compassionate, sweet-tempered creatures can do . . .'*[20] when drawn by Hardy's malevolent pen.

As in many of Hardy's novels, the most admirable character is the peripheral hero, in this instance, John Loveday, who like Gabriel Oak and, to a lesser extent, Clym Yeobright before him, displays the admirable human qualities of forbearance and moral rectitude. Hardy is sympathetic towards Loveday who remains firmly within his grip in a way that a number of his heroines, notably Eustacia and Arabella seem not to. Critics like Hawthorne highlighted the moral authority of John Loveday, describing him as *' . . . the best character that Mr Hardy has ever drawn. Indeed, there are few figures in all fiction more pathetic, and in a quiet way, heroic, than this simple, loyal, affectionate soldier . . .'*[21] For all that, I suspect more than a few female readers would have sided with Anne's choice rather than the bland and perfect hero and could understand why she is not moved sufficiently to feel love for John Loveday with all his obvious qualities. It is love of the flawed and unreliable man, not reason, that moves her. In this respect, Hardy's women do not behave or think like Jane Eyre or the most dutiful and pragmatic Victorian heroines, held back by convention. Rather, as Havelock Ellis pointed out at the time of the book's publication, *'Mr Hardy's women are creatures, always fascinating, made up of more or less untamed instincts for both love and admiration, who can never help some degree of response when the satisfaction of those instincts lies open to them.'*[22]

Anne balances her feelings of guilt about letting John down with the sure knowledge that she loves his brother, despite – or because of – his flaws and inconstancy. And despite all the doubts and prevarication, she succeeds where other heroines do not, even if her readers do not all forgive her for abandoning our popular hero. Unlike Fancy Day who in *Under the Greenwood Tree* ends up committing to a man she does not love, or Ethelberta whose decision to marry is not for reasons of love, Anne gets what she wants in the end.

Hardy's heroines, even the most demure and passive, are capable of exercising free will, though fate and circumstances often swallow them up. Their quest for love, for some romantic attachment, some erotic frisson drives them on as, one suspects, it does their author. And in this respect at least, quiet, gentle, pretty Anne Garland is little different from the rest of Hardy's heroines.

Hardy's next novel, *A Laodicean*, signalled a significant change in Hardy's fiction, both in setting and subject matter. One of Hardy's three novels of ingenuity (the others being *Desperate Remedies* and *The Hand of Ethelberta*), it owes a debt to the melodramatic writings of Wilkie Collins and Charles Dickens as well as to the new technologies of the time. Despite its nod to modernity (or perhaps because of), it was not well-received, with one contemporary review stating that *'In* A Laodicean *the author showed us very queer people doing very queer things'*[23]

Written in London, and much of it dictated to Emma while Hardy was ill, it is the story of Paula Power, the rich heiress to a railway fortune. As the story begins, Paula is setting out to modernise a castle that her tycoon father won in gambling from Captain de Stancy, whose family it had previously belonged to. To assist her, she employs a young architect, George Somerset, who becomes one of two suitors, the other being Captain de Stancy, whose suit his illegitimate son, William Dare, encourages, seeing it as an opportunity to restore the castle to its rightful owners. What makes the plot particularly modern is the way in which technology is used to cast aspersions on Somerset's character, first by using a 'doctored' photograph to apparently show Somerset drunk and secondly, by sending incriminating telegrams in Somerset's name to an unsuspecting Paula – the antecedents of photoshop and fake news. Unusually for a Hardy novel, the heroine, Paula Power ends up with Somerset, after Dare is exposed, although we sense that she is not altogether happy with her lot.

Paula is 'The Laodicean', a word that has its roots in the Book of Revelations referring to the worshippers at the church in Laodicea who are half-hearted in their faith, neither hot nor cold, but just lukewarm.

The vacillations referred to in the novel are several, obviously between her suitors, with an eye on their social class, but also between tradition and modernity. There is also an obvious autobiographical element to the novel with the young architect meeting his future wife who was his social better and having to resolve the issue of class differences (something Thomas never really managed with Emma). Throughout, Hardy uses the characters and their different backgrounds to illustrate the ambivalence and contrariness of human nature. Whether Pite's assertion that the novel was a tribute to Emma for her devoted support is debatable especially when it is considered that there is no public acknowledgement by Hardy of Emma's contribution in the preface; nor is there any dedication to Emma in the novel or elsewhere. Nevertheless, for a time they were compelled to work closely together on the novel as Thomas recovered from his serious illness, a situation that must have given Emma some satisfaction.[24]

Central to Paula's development as a character is the fulfilment of her sexual needs, before moving her attention onto Somerset, who she continues to provocatively flirt with on and off throughout the novel. Seymour-Smith suggests that at first Paula achieves this by an *'intense, unconsciously lesbian, friendship with Charlotte de Stancy'*[25] who lives at the castle, and they act towards each other, as we are told in the novel *'more like lovers than maid and maid.'* As the Laodicean, however, we are never sure of Paula's feelings; while *'Miss Power is looked up to by little de Stancy'* and allowed to love her 'to her heart's content,' it is never clear whether the same intensity of feeling is reciprocated by Paula, who remains *'as deep as the North Star.'* (Bk. 1, Ch. 5)

Of Paula's appearance, we learn at the outset that she appeared to be between twenty and twenty-three-years-old and exhibited a *'modern type of maidenhood'*, and looked ultra-modern; that she was sophisticated with abundant hair *'of good English brown,'* neither light nor dark, and that *'though it could not be said of her features that this or that was flawless, the nameless charm of them altogether was only another instance of how beautiful a woman can be as a whole without attaining in any one detail to the lines marked out as absolutely correct.'* (Bk. 1, Ch. 2) This same ambivalence is evident throughout the novel. Paula is an enigma. She represents modern woman, albeit a dissenting one and yet Hardy allows her to marry the man she sets her heart upon. But even at the end, with her emotional needs having been met, her feelings vacillate yet again and her last words to George, indeed the very last words of the book, are a damning blow to the young architect. De Stancy's castle has burnt down and even though they had agreed to build a new house to show everyone the modern spirit, Paula is regretful.

'But, George, I wish' – and Paula repressed a sigh.
'Well?'
'I wish my castle wasn't burnt; and I wish you were a de Stancy.'
(Bk. 6, Ch. 5)

It is a cruel comment and cruel too for Paula, for it shapes our perception of her as someone who is superficial, desiring social standing and prestige above her true heart's choice. Ambivalence and inconstancy are major themes of the novel and in *The Laodicean*, they are attributed to all women by association.

Leaving London, Thomas and Emma moved to Wimborne where Thomas indulged his interest in science and astronomy by writing his next novel *Two on a Tower*. The story of the unhappily married Lady Viviette Constantine, who falls in love with an astronomer, Swithin St Cleeve, eight years her junior, caused an uproar at the time by crossing over lines of marriage and class and presenting the couple as star-crossed lovers set against the stellar universe. When the husband dies, it appears that there are no impediments to the lovers' future happiness and security until a legacy prevents this happening. Early reviews were damning, one describing the book as *'bad, — the worst the author has written'* adding *'It is melodramatic without strength, extravagant without object, and objectionable without truth"* and accusing Hardy of presenting a pathological heroine.[26]

Viviette, Lady Constantine, is one of Hardy's most controversial heroines and her character was singled out for particular criticism. The same review wrote of Lady Viviette's passion for Swithin St Cleeve, as *'a study which, in its mingling of passion, religion, and false self-sacrifice, appears to us to approach very near to the repulsive'* adding that while Lady Viviette is *'meant to be nice, she is so self-contradictory as to lack all reality.'*

At the outset of the novel, Lady Viviette does not know whether her husband is dead or alive, yet that does not stop her betraying either his person or memory. Coming across the young astronomer, Swithin St Cleeve she falls in love with him despite the difference in their age. From hereon a strong sexual charge takes over as she woos the young astronomer until eventually yielding in *'all the passion of her first union with him.'*

Her moral dilemma is compounded when she finds out that she is pregnant with his child after he has left to continue his research abroad which persuades her to add another transgression, this time deceit, by marrying a Bishop who acts as the baby's father. After he dies, Viviette and Swithin meet up once more before she also dies in an ending evocative of an experience in Hardy's own life.

When he was a child, Hardy fell in love with his teacher, Augusta Martin, the Lady of the Manor at Kingston Maurward. Removed from the School by his mother, Hardy sought her out when he was an adult, only to be shocked by how she had aged.[27] The scene where Swithin St Cleeve makes the same discovery after Viviette returns is similarly affecting:

'The words died upon her lips, and from very faintness she bent her head. For instead of rushing forward to her he had stood still; and there appeared upon his face a look which there was no mistaking. Yes; he was shocked at her worn and faded aspect. The image he had mentally carried out with him to the Cape he had brought home again as that of the woman he was now to rejoin. But another woman sat before him, and not the original Viviette. Her cheeks had lost for ever that firm contour which had been drawn by the vigorous hand of youth, and the masses of hair that were once darkness visible had become touched here and there by a faint grey haze, like the Via Lactea in a midnight sky.'

It is a sad and touching passage about the superficiality of relationships built on physical beauty – ironic that Hardy, the writer, could observe so acutely what Hardy, the man, could not master. Once again, it is the women in his fiction who are beleaguered, cast down, punished by the passing of time. Hardy, however, does try to make the case for the older women by suggesting that Swithin was too immature to appreciate the inner beauty of Viviette, even knowing he could not call on youth as an excuse for his own infatuations:

'Yet to those who had eyes to understand as well as to see, the chastened pensiveness of her once handsome features revealed more promising material beneath than ever her youth had done. But Swithin was hopelessly her junior. Unhappily for her he had now just arrived at an age

whose canon of faith it is that the silly period of woman's life is her only period of beauty. Viviette saw it all, and knew that Time had at last brought about his revenges. She had tremblingly watched and waited without sleep, ever since Swithin had re-entered Welland, and it was for this.' (Ch. 41)

Viviette's aging distressed Swithin to the extent that he realised he no longer loved her and his unspoken response was sufficient for Viviette to give up on life. It was a tragic end to their love affair, but inevitable in Hardy's world, where punishment was meted out to those who chose to cross social barriers or ignore convention on matters of class, age or background.

Apart from Hardy's own feelings for Augusta Martin, there is a further parallel we can draw by looking at Hardy's feelings towards Emma's own loss of beauty as she noticeably gained weight and severity over the decade, with her hair turning grey and her lameness becoming more pronounced. Like Viviette, she would soon feel what it was like to be looked upon with indifference by her errant husband.

Viviette was one of Hardy's more distinctive heroines, full of ambiguity and confusion, trapped in a social situation quite unlike any of his other women. Despite flouting all the conventions of the age, Hardy stood by her. She was, in Tomalin's view, *'one of the well-loved dream women who kept him company away from the real world.'*[28] Attractive and spontaneous in nature, with all the allure of a desirable woman with her dark eyes, and a warm and affectionate nature, she is the vehicle through which Hardy explores the themes of love through class and age, picking up the central theme of the defunct novel, *The Poor Man and the Lady*. At times Viviette acts badly, as when deceiving the Bishop by inveigling him into marrying her and becoming her baby's father (even though she justified her actions by asking *'what woman has a right to blight a coming life to preserve her own personal integrity?')* Hardy saw that she was punished for her transgression (more to appease the public than conclude the story one suspects), but as Tomalin pointed out *'Hardy had a good time imagining Viviette. He was captivated by her, still more than he had been by the beautiful pagan Eustacia.'*[29]

There are few other parallels that can be drawn with Hardy's life. It has been suggested that Swithin's grandmother who raised him bears some resemblance to Hardy's own grandmother, but the links are mainly superficial.[30] As Viviette moves between love and piety, Seymour-Smith also suggests that her character might well reflect Emma's own tendencies at the time as Emma started to move towards a more rigorous theology that was to increasingly drive a wedge between Emma and Thomas [31], but again, any such links are tenuous at best. Viviette contributed to the ideal of the modern woman that Hardy was building up in his own mind, sexually forward, intelligent, and, of course, attractive, an ideal that he would consciously seek out for companionship over the next decade.

By now, through his several novels, Hardy had created several female types, each with their own personality and drawing on the range of feminine traits he had accumulated. In each of his heroines there was inevitably a mixture of vanity and pride, caprice and humility, naivety and worldliness, and a tendency to place feeling ahead of reason (although as we have seen with Ethelberta, not always so). His women often represent extremes, being either pragmatic and thereby lacking emotion, or else scheming and impulsive, inclined to follow their own feelings, usually in a landscape that works actively upon them, as the heath does with Eustacia. Hardy's world is beginning to change, as he embraces advances in technology and science as well as rationalism into his writing. From here on, however, Hardy sets his sights more firmly on social issues, of religion, marriage and class, often by placing the fate of women at the sharp end of his writing. As Hardy entered the latter years of the nineteenth century, he had already created a number of memorable women even though many of his best-known heroines had yet to make their appearance.

In June 1885, Thomas and Emma were about to end the transient life they had lived for the previous eleven years and to settle into what, for both of them, was to be their first and last home. It had been a difficult time for Emma since they had married with the constant changes of domicile, but now there was the promise of some stability at last. Thomas had established himself as a writer of fiction with a growing reputation at home and abroad and was about to widen his horizons and go on to write his best-known novels. Yet, on the very cusp of moving into Max Gate and the opportunity to put down roots in the heart of Wessex, their personal lives were beginning to fray, leading them to drift further and further apart until their final estrangement.

Chapter 11

Max Gate and Tess: 1886 – 1891 Hardy's Great Love.

The Mayor of Casterbridge (1886), The Woodlanders (1887), Wessex Tales (1888) A Group of Noble Dames (1889) and Tess of the D'Urbervilles (1891)

'Tess is vile and the pretence of sexuality is only equalled by the absence of it, and the abomination of the language by the author's reputation for style.'

Henry James[1]

Thomas and Emma moved into Max Gate in June 1885, and for the first time in his career, Hardy had his own study. Already an acclaimed author having published nine of the fourteen novels he was to complete in his lifetime, he still had more than half of his 'major' works ahead of him.[2]

During the writing of *The Mayor of Casterbridge* Emma and Thomas had been living in Dorchester while waiting for his brother, Henry, to complete the building of Max Gate. Thomas was also widening his social circle in London, which included meeting Edmund Gosse and Mary Jeune for the first time. Early in the year, he had accepted an invitation to Eggesford in mid-Devon, home of Lady Portsmouth, who had offered the house's library as suitable surroundings in which he could write. Leaving Emma at Max Gate, Hardy found himself amongst an '*extraordinarily sympathetic group of women*' including Lady Burghclere, Lady Herbert as well as Lady Portsmouth and all her daughters. The house party that followed, consisting of the '*better halves*' as Lady Portsmouth described the gathered women, saw Hardy in his element, surrounded by female admirers. He recalled in *The Life* that in one discussion the subject turned to love and that Lady Portsmouth's daughter Camilla informed him that '*a woman is never so near as being in love with a man she does not love as immediately he has left her after she has refused him*' – a line that would not look out of place in several of his own novels. It was a delightful time and Hardy later remembered how thoroughly he had enjoyed himself and that he had endeared himself to the family. Afterwards, he related to Emma that '*Lady P. tells me she never knew real anxiety until she had a family of daughters,*' adding that '*she wants us to come to Devonshire and live near them.*'[3]

We don't know Emma's response, but we can guess at her growing disquiet over her husband's new found interest and enjoyment in the company of young women that was becoming more evident, both in those whose company he sought and in his correspondence where it was evident that a female admirer was more likely to get a response than a male. Hardy had always taken great pleasure in collecting photographs of his women friends, including Rosamund Tomson, Florence Henniker and Agnes Grove, and was always keen to add to his portfolio. He was never shy in asking; in October 1885, one female admirer's request for an autograph was met with an unambiguous response:

'Dear Madam,
I send my AUTograph;
You send your PHOTograph' [4]

It was a sign of what lay ahead for Emma. Life was about to change for them both and Hardy, the writer, was starting to indulge his growing reputation in order to court favour with those who he had once criticised – the wealthy, the aristocratic and the well connected.

With nine novels completed, Hardy's writing had extended to include new subject matter and settings though the novels that deviated from the rustic and pastoral world of Wessex, populated by people like his own family and fed by his mother's stories and memories, were seldom as successful. His characters were becoming more varied and complex, their situations more convoluted, their problems less straightforward, and their views less orthodox. As a writer, Hardy was also becoming increasingly forthright on social issues, often testing the tolerance of the censors with his outspoken views, although he had learned to disguise these rather better than in his early novels. He played to his strengths as a writer using methods and situations that worked for him. One formula he employed was that of varying the number of suitors he offered his heroines. *A Pair of Blue Eyes*, for instance, limited itself to one heroine + two suitors (although our heroine married a third); *Under the Greenwood Tree, The Trumpet Major* and *Far from the Madding Crowd* each boasted one heroine + three suitors; *The Hand of Ethelberta* went one better with our heroine (already widowed), attracting four. While other plots do not fit so neatly, either being too layered and convoluted to categorise, (or by having the man as the subject of the chase), Hardy's fictional world was becoming more innately pessimistic, especially in the areas of religion and in the relationships between the sexes.

One measure of his growing assurance as a writer was his use of the love triangle which he had developed since he had employed it in his first novel, *Desperate Remedies* where Cytherea Graye, Edward Springlove and Aeneas Manston were locked in a triangle of circumstance driven by economic rather than emotional needs. In Hardy's next novel (*Under the Greenwood Tree*), with its triangle of Dick Dewey, Fancy Day and Reverend Maybold, the heroine is allowed to make her own choices, although she comes across as both opportunistic (a trait better represented by Lucetta in *The Mayor of Casterbridge*) and deceptive, character flaws that Hardy attributes to their gender and for which he was criticised by feminists. *In A Pair of Blue Eyes* he presents a different triangle, widely accepted as autobiographical, despite Hardy's protestations to the contrary: Stephen, the architect (Hardy by profession and social status if nothing else), Elfride, the Parson's daughter (Emma although possibly Tryphena) and Knight (Horace Moule, Hardy's dear friend who died in 1873). Each played an important role in Hardy's own life during the partially forgotten, yet highly significant years leading up to his first marriage. This novel, Hardy's third also highlighted the issue of class (reflecting the divide between Emma and himself) and the choice between two men, one of whom is more overtly masculine than the other (another element common to the men in Hardy's triangles).

Invariably, in each novel, it is the heroine who suffers most, often because of yet another feminine trait, in this instance, naivety, now added to Hardy's growing catalogue of peculiarly feminine weaknesses. The same pattern repeats itself in the novels that follow where the heroine anchors the other vertices of the obtuse triangle. In *A Laodicean*, we have Captain De Stancy and the meek and mild George Somerset vying for the heroine, Paula Power's hand, yet another feminine trait (an inability to commit and ever be satisfied) for Hardy's ever-growing list.

Yet we should hardly be surprised to see the love triangle sitting squarely at the heart of Hardy's plots for it is the same with his life: Hardy / Emma / Tryphena; Hardy / Moule / Emma (or Tryphena); Hardy / Florence (either) / Emma, and so on.

In the novels leading up to *The Mayor of Casterbridge* Hardy made numerous censures of womankind: in *Far From the Madding Crowd* vanity and inconstancy are at the heart of Bathsheba, as she flits between Troy, Gabriel and Boldwood; in *The Hand of Ethelberta* we witness the pragmatic and loveless choice made by our heroine, when wooed by four unsuitable suitors, in order to get the independence and security she craves; in *The Trumpet Major*, Anne Garland, portrayed as one of Hardy's vacillating heroines, shows remarkably poor judgement in choosing the rogue over the hero; while in *The Return of the Native* with its overt sexual relationships and the unequal triangle of Clym, Damon and Eustacia, we have a deeply flawed heroine, full of caprice and desire in Hardy's darkest expression so far of the vagaries and machinations of women.

The Mayor of Casterbridge which Hardy completed in April 1885 introduced three significant heroines in Susan Henchard, her daughter, Elizabeth-Jane Newson and Lucette Le Seuer (Lucetta Templeman), whose lives and fortunes were inexorably linked with the person of Michael Henchard, the Mayor of Casterbridge, whose contradictory character sits at the heart of the novel.

From the opening chapter when Susan is sold by her husband she is one of Hardy's doormats, a poor, ignorant woman although not without spirit. Nor was she unattractive; indeed, we are told the mobility of her face made her *'pretty, and even handsome,'* but she is vacuous so that when Henchard blames her for his disgrace, by railing *'Tis like Susan to show such idiotic simplicity. Meek – that meekness has done me more harm than the bitterest temper!'* we accept what Hardy tells us, that like the rest of his heroines, none are without some responsibility for what eventually happens to them. (Ch. 2) Contemporary reviews of the novel saw Susan similarly, describing her character as *'so colourless as to be almost imperceptible'* and of little consequence.[5]

While our sympathy for Susan is frustrated by her ignorance and her somewhat obtuse nature, to call her one of Hardy's notional characters would be unfair. She shows spirit in making her new life with Newson and a determination to do her best for Elizabeth-Jane when she fears Newson is dead. She is not above a little deceit herself, whether about the colour of her daughter's hair or by her clandestine attempt to throw Elizabeth-Jane and Donald together, but there is little of Hardy in her or of his direct family.

Elizabeth-Jane, who is likened to Hardy's sister, Mary, also struggles to escape Hardy's heavy hand. When we first meet her, she is described as

'A well-formed young woman about eighteen, completely possessed of that ephemeral precious essence youth, which is itself beauty, irrespective of complexion or contour.' (Ch. 3)

One contemporary critic, however, was less complimentary, describing her as *'excellent, but rather more than a trifle dull'*[6] which is how she comes across in the early chapters, where she is rather vapid and colourless, devoid of personality and determined to resist the temptation to be 'gay'. In an echo of the advice Jemima gave to Thomas about providence, Elizabeth-Jane defends her reticence to herself by saying

'It would be tempting Providence to hurl Mother and me down and afflict us again as He used to' (Ch. 14), a clear reference to Jemima's warning to Hardy.[7]

Soon, however, we notice a change in her demeanour when a box of 'delicately-tinted gloves', a gift from Henchard entices her to add in turn, a bonnet, then a dress and a sunshade until the metamorphosis is complete. With her improved circumstances she becomes an altogether more attractive character and, as we are told, *'With peace of mind came development, and with development beauty.'* (Ch. 14)

As Elizabeth-Jane changes from the meek and subservient daughter, accepting her station and the appearance of a young, demure woman, she begins to exhibit the traits and habits of other 'Hardy women,' including some of their vanities. Her belief in the importance of superficial appearance sees her embrace the latest fashions which succeeds in bringing her to the notice of the young men in the town, including Farfrae, whom she soon finds herself attracted to. From here on, the novel, and Elizabeth-Jane's role in it, moves apace, with the arrival of Lucetta and the usual tying and untying of knots, resolutions and disappointments until we find Elizabeth-Jane, having once been spurned by Farfrae, ending up as his wife.

It is a neat ending for Hardy and reward for Elizabeth Jane who is as Farfrae described her, *'so pleasing, thrifty, and satisfactory.'* But she is also submissive, humourless and full of moral propriety, which renders her powerless in the face of Lucetta's sexuality. It is only Lucetta's death that allows Elizabeth-Jane back into Farfrae's affections. Late in the novel she is described as handsome, while Lucetta is merely 'pretty,' but she is never more than the virtuous young maiden. She views her changing situation with equanimity and feels her future is bound up with fate and circumstances that she can affect not one jot. Her passivity towards Lucetta when she realises that she has been supplanted in Farfrae's affections, makes us compare her once again with Mary Hardy, who was gentle, kind and lovable, but so nondescript that when she died, Thomas, her very own brother, attested that hardly anyone noticed.

One can sense how much more Hardy enjoyed the character of Lucetta Templeman. Gallic, dark and voluptuous, she exuded a sexuality and energy that shaded both Susan and her daughter. Having first been compromised by offering succour to Henchard when he is in Jersey, she later finds herself compromised by the passage of events. Lucetta is not without spirit or a mind of her own and when Henchard invites her to Casterbridge after Susan's death, ostensibly to marry her at an opportune moment, Lucetta soon gets cold feet. Instead, she sets her hat on his business rival, Farfrae (and erstwhile suitor to Elizabeth Jane). Lucetta is not, however, always scrupulous. First, she poses the hypothetical question to Elizabeth Jane, that having committed to one man and then finding one she liked better, could she *'in honour, dismiss the first?'* Elizabeth Jane finds the very idea reprehensible although Lucetta is disinclined to listen.

Soon after, Henchard calls in his charge upon her, telling her that *'. . . it is not by what is in this life, but by what appears, that you are judged',* yet again, she is not persuaded. Unlike Elizabeth Jane, Lucetta is made of sterner stuff, and less concerned with what others think of her. After Henchard has left the room, she gives voice to her right to choose Farfrae, pronouncing *'I won't be a slave to the past. I'll love where I choose.'* She remains loyal to Henchard, however, until she hears of the unforgiveable act he committed in selling his first wife. (Ch. 25)

Such admirable honesty, however, seldom passes Hardy by without having some judgment passed upon it. By the end of the novel, the spirited and honest Lucetta has been punished for her temerity while our traditional, but bland heroine, Elizabeth-Jane has come out on top, demonstrating that Hardy's heroines could not stray far before being put back into their boxes. He also cast aspersions on all of womankind by implying that a woman could so easily shift her affections from one lover to another and that 'loving who she chose' in this instance also implied an economic and social choice, an eye for the main chance, as much as any affair of the heart. Hardy, it seems, was not quite ready to unleash Sue Bridehead.

Elizabeth-Jane's reaction to Lucetta's predicament highlights the yawning gap between the two heroines. Elizabeth Jane, priggish and judgmental, tells Lucetta that to marry another would be morally wrong, knowing the other to be Donald Farfrae when *'it was plain as the town-pump that Donald and Lucetta were incipient lovers'* (Ch. 26)

Hardy noted of his heroine, *'Any suspicion of impropriety was to Elizabeth-Jane like a red rag to a bull. Her craving for correctness of procedure was, indeed, almost vicious.'* (Ch. 30) Despite this, she was not above fighting for Farfrae's affections by taking the moral high ground against her rival.

Hardy used the novel to continue making his case against marriage. In the very first chapter, we learn that Susan and Michael must be husband and wife for *'no other than such relationship would have accounted for the atmosphere of stale familiarity'*. From the outset Susan thinks of her husband as a 'master' in an economic sense, as well as a legal and moral one – and so, when sold, she refers to Newson, with possible irony, as her 'present owner' and behaves dutifully and loyally towards him, without ever confessing to love him. It is a damning indictment of the institution of marriage as a legally binding contract that served to entrap women who had fallen out of love. From the beginning of the auction scene, having delivered his charge against marriage, Hardy goes further in challenging Victorian attitudes to women. By his portrayal of Susan as a chattel, able to be bought and disposed of, and whose happiness and welfare depend on the whims of her husband, Hardy takes aim at the Victorian patriarchy. His views were controversial, even for the times, especially in highlighting the indisputable fact that in marriage women are powerless and vulnerable: *'For my part,'* says one of the townsfolk at the auction, *'I don't see why men who have got wives, and don't want 'em, shouldn't get rid of 'em as these gypsy fellows do their old horses.'* (Ch. 1)

The dangers of marrying too early also received Hardy's attention and he would have been aware from his own extended family, that early marriage had been *'the ruin of good men by bad wives, and, more particularly, the frustration of many a promising youth's high aims and hopes . . . .'* (Ch. 1) Rather more sensitively, he writes of the error of maintaining a dogged fidelity to a cause or image long after it has lapsed, locking people together who have ceased to love each other (and here, perhaps, we can see Hardy thinking of his own situation with Emma).

Even the idea of marriage as the way to absolution is quashed. When Henchard vows to re-marry Susan, *'in a dogged unflinching spirit which did credit to his conscientiousness'* he is hardly likely to win the reader round. (Ch. 13) Always, it seems, marriage is presented as the impediment, the default position, something to get round, an obstructive force that was only seldom liberating. Over the next ten years, Hardy's views on the matter become ever more radical bringing the wrath of his critics, and the anger of his wife, down upon him.

The Mayor of Casterbridge is a grim story in which our strong-willed and flawed hero pays heavily for his transgression. His demise is inevitable as he has no way of saving himself although his contrition goes some way to redeem him in the readers' eyes. The triangles (Henchard/Susan/Lucetta; Lucetta/Henchard; Farfrae; and Elizabeth Jane/Lucetta and Farfrae) fall over each other in the unravelling of the story, each adding to the complexity of the plot. But it is, invariably, the women who pay a greater price, caught up in the inexorable events, never dominating, never shaping proceedings. Instead, as Hubbard commented, *'their lives are ordered for them. They are strange angels in hobbles who stand forever in mortal fear of losing their reputations.'*[8] So they are all in the end humiliated because of Henchard: Susan is abandoned by him; Lucetta is publicly chastised for having favoured him; and Elizabeth Jane, despite ending the novel by default as Farfrae's wife, knows she was always second choice.

Late in the book Lucetta asks – and it is a question that Hardy plays with throughout his novels – *'What happens sometimes when women get themselves in strange positions in the eyes of the world from no fault of their own?'* (Ch. 24) The answer is that they are invariably punished, not only through circumstance, but also because of some underlying weakness or flaw in their character, real or perceived. While Hardy does much to raise important social issues facing women and their entrapment by Victorian attitudes and obsolete laws through placing them in compromising circumstances, he is not always inclined to rescue them.

Throughout much of 1886, Hardy was working on his next novel, *The Woodlanders.* Mostly of the time he was writing at home although he was also travelling regularly to London and the British Museum Library researching background material for his epic poem *The Dynasts* (a task Florence Dugdale was still assisting him with nearly twenty years later). When time allowed, he was mixing with his aristocratic and society lady friends. Both he and Emma went to stay with Lady Portsmouth in Devon where they enjoyed a very pleasant week. In London, more often than not with Emma in attendance, he continued the rounds of his confidantes, making his acute and personal observations and relishing the attention he was shown. In calling on Lady St Helier (or Mrs Jeune as he preferred to call her) he noted that *'She was in a rich, pinky-*

red gown, and looked handsome as we sat by the firelight en tête-à-tête' and, further, that *'she was, curiously enough, an example of Whistler's study in red that I had seen in the morning at the Gallery'.*[9] On the same visit, he attended a crush at Lady Carnarvon's where he was soon in intimate conversation with Lady (Winifred) Burghclere who he noted *'wants me to call my heroine 'Winifred','* adding *' but it is too late to alter it.'*[10]

With unusual precision, implying a certain sense of relief, Hardy recorded in *The Life* that he finished *The Woodlanders* at precisely 8.20pm on February 4, 1887.[11] It was the first novel written entirely at Max Gate and was set in the countryside of Melbury Osmond near where his mother was raised. With no fewer than eight characters having their hopes thwarted and their love repulsed at various stages, it is hard to see it as anything other than a tragedy in the finest Shakespearean tradition. Pinion felt the novel to be a reaffirmation of Hardy's loyalties to his family and background and a warning as to what happens *'when precedence is given to social values which run counter to humbler, but more natural or instinctive ties.'*[12] Tomalin saw the novel as a more sinister parable describing it *like a black version of Far from the Madding Crowd* in which *'all the women are humiliated'.*[13] Certainly, the two most admirable characters, Giles Winterborne and Marty South, are held down by their social position and poverty and are powerless over the fate that befalls them. The heroine, Grace Melbury, is a good woman at heart who suffers from a bad marriage and then is twice cursed by the end, first losing the man she truly loves and then being reunited with her faithless husband. Edred Fitzpiers is the villain of the piece, yet escapes almost unscathed having wreaked havoc upon the local community while other characters either die or are compromised in some way or other. Throughout the novel there is a feeling of the powerlessness of women who are impelled to marry and deal with the emotional pressures placed upon them. Hardy highlights the anomalies in the divorce laws and the iniquity of marriage, but then proceeds to treat his women so cruelly that the message seems to be directed not at the society that persecutes them, but at what happens when women transgress. It is a strange paradox, one suspects, more to make the point.

Hardy continued to pick away at the institution of marriage as he had in previous novels including the *The Mayor of Casterbridge*, where he portrayed it as a root cause of unhappiness and domestic tragedy (while, ironically, promoting the institution as a safe house for his women by offering security and a way to advance themselves). In *The Woodlanders* Hardy went a step further by raising the issue of divorce and showing the cruelty and hardship facing women trapped in violent or unhappy relationships. In his introduction to the New Wessex edition on *The Woodlanders* in 1975, F B Pinion pondered whether *'... Hardy's marriage problems prompted him to direct the story towards the question of divorce' adding that if not, it certainly did in* Jude the Obscure.[14]

It is a surprising assertion. At this stage Emma and Thomas had just moved into Max Gate and while there was no doubt some underlying tension between them, it was several years before any significant breach occurred, around the time of Rosamund Tomson's arrival on the scene. Moreover, over half of the manuscript of *The Woodlanders* is in Emma's own hand, which would indicate that they were working well together. In *The Life*, also, there is little to alarm us, other than Hardy's increasing appetite for female attention and approval; significantly, also, the day after the novel was published, he and Emma set off for a long anticipated trip to Italy. No doubt the fact that Hardy's novels were regularly criticised now for their moral laxity and for challenging aspects of Church and convention disturbed Emma, but not yet to the point of open revolt.

The Woodlanders, Hardy's own favourite novel, has various on-going relationships, the most significant being that of the heroine, Grace Melbury and her two suitors, (Giles Winterbourne and Dr Fitzpiers). The novel's anti-hero, Dr Edred Fitzpiers is linked in relationships with two other women apart from Grace (Suke Damson and Mrs Charmond); while the story's rather staid and decent hero, the stalwart Giles Winterbourne is linked with two women, Grace Melbury, who abandons him for large parts of the book, and Marty South, who is Hardy's most poignant portrayal of unrequited love.

From the start of the novel, we are confronted with issues of class and education and the importance of making a good marriage. In Hardy's novels, marriage is seen as the natural course for the woman and, on the other hand, a trap for the man. Throughout *The Woodlanders* Hardy plays on this contradiction between the feckless Fitzpiers, who would prefer to love without the commitment of marriage and Grace, for whom marriage is necessary to secure her place in society.

Having been childhood sweethearts, Grace had become, in the eyes of her father, too good for Giles. She is reminded of the sacrifices he has made for her that should yield a better husband than Giles, advising her *'Whatever a young woman's niceness she stands for nothing alone. You shall marry well.'* (Ch. 12) It is her father's ambition for Grace to secure a good marriage and her compliance that ultimately destroys her. Like Susan Henchard who is abandoned by her husband and sold as a chattel at the start of *The Mayor of Casterbridge*, Grace is also treated badly, albeit by her father rather than a husband and for quite different reasons, yet the outcome is the same. Grace is made aware by her father of her financial debt to him and how she should look at procuring a husband who can look after her, and while she begs him, *'Don't think of me like that. A mere chattel'* (Ch. 12) she does little to save herself. Unlike Lucetta, unlike Eustacia, Grace lacks the fire to follow her heart or sufficient spirit to defy her father until it is too late. Her character is passive and accepting of her lot, even personal humiliation, before the closing chapters when her love for Giles resurfaces and we see her agitated and desperate. We can feel sympathy for her, as she tries to please all the men in her life, including her father. She is not sexless, and as the story develops, we become aware of her sexual feelings and of those around her. She enjoys being kissed by Giles and wishes Giles would throw propriety aside when she stays with him in the cottage; nor does she have any qualms about joining Fitzpiers in his hotel room. Margaret Elvy[15] cites her directness in exclaiming to Mrs Charmond in the woods *'He's had you!* (Ch. 33), and her admonishment to Fitzpiers *'And I don't see why you should mind my having one lover besides yourself in my life, when you have had so many'* (Ch. 46) as evidence that she was no blushing violet, concluding *'Grace's outspokenness on sexual matters at times rivals the most outspoken voice in all Hardy's fiction, that of Sue Bridehead.'*[16]

Felice Charmond, identified in one contemporary review as *'too much of a third-rate French actress'*[17] is an unusual figure for Hardy even though he was often inclined to include an exotic personality in his cast of characters. She is described as 'a woman of perversities' who liked mystery in her life and whom we learn enjoyed smoking and drinking champagne. Her entreaties to Fitzpiers, even after his marriage, also show her to be without scruples or shame and her treatment of Grace is cruel and thoughtless. Her character shocked contemporary readers and critics, with her seduction of Fitzpiers, her own garish and extravagant tastes, her moral lassitude and her violent death all contributing to Hardy's colourful, if at times, hardly credible creation.

In Marty South, we have a heroine whom Elvy describes as an 'entirely new creation', a poor village girl who was recognised from the first publication of the novel as one of its true voices; a heroine who was *'socially, economically and textually marginalized'*[18] and yet emerges as someone that the reader holds dear. In a contemporary review, Marty *'ascends from the ridiculous in the first chapter, in which she loses her hair, to the sublime in the last chapter, in which she loses her hero, and, standing by his tombstone looks almost like a being who had rejected with indifference the attribute of sex for the loftier quality of abstract humanism.'*[19]

No doubt there were many exemplars for Marty South in Hardy's world including some of Hardy's own family, born into service and accepting what the world threw at them with equanimity and dignity. She is one of many heroines trotted out by those ready to accuse Hardy of misogyny, for her lot is so inexcusably ghastly that there seems no other justification.

Suke Damson is the only other woman who deserves a mention; a woman who is both ignorant and lustful and whose predicament is largely of her own making. Suke is the precursor of the lusty and earthy Arabella in *Jude the Obscure*. While her morals are similarly lax and pliable she lacks the pragmatism of Arabella when it comes to accepting her lot. Her night with Fitzpiers which upset the censors at the time and her temporarily heightened expectations that he might have feelings for her in return only serve to poison her subsequent marriage after which she and her new husband emigrate to New Zealand to start a new life.

The Woodlanders is a novel that attempts to highlight the hypocrisy of society towards women, but its conclusions are not reassuring. There are numerous examples of double standards aired in the novel, along with questioning of marital fidelity and an acceptance of extra-marital sex. Even the wronged Grace deals with her own betrayal in a way that was shocking for the time by inviting Suke and Mrs Charmond, the two other woman who have slept with her husband, Fitzpiers, to enter his bedroom when he is ill with the deeply ironic exhortation, *'Wives all, let's enter together!'* (Ch. 35)

What is condemned in women, however, is seen as acceptable in men. The double standards exhibited by Fitzpiers in accusing Grace of betraying him, even after his own dalliances, portrays an uncomfortable truth. The problem is that, having raised the plight of women, Hardy then finds against them, as if the hardships and cruelty they have to endure is simply their lot in life. Women are mere chattels, there to be used, whether it is the brain of a dead woman or the hair of a live one. As a message of hope or a means of advancing womanhood, the novel was hardly reassuring for its female readers.

Before the publication of Hardy's next novel, *Tess of the D'Urbervilles* in 1889, Hardy produced a collection of short stories loosely based on some of local landed families. It was a move that upset Emma. She saw some of his tales parodying the very people who he had ingratiated himself with and needlessly upsetting the local aristocracy by using inside knowledge to poke fun at them. One of those Hardy upset was the Earl of Ilchester whose residence was Melbury House where his mother, Jemima, had once been in service. The Earl was particularly miffed at the suggestion that one story, 'The First Countess of Wessex', was based on his own family's history. It was a relief for Emma, and one suspects for Hardy also, that the expected furore didn't eventuate. [20] However, yet again Emma felt her husband had shown a disregard for propriety and an insensitivity that reflected badly on them both.

In April 1887, Hardy attended the annual dinner of the Royal Academy in London, criticising those giving speeches in his notebook: The Duke of Cambridge, he felt, could not decide *'whether he had ended his speech or not'*; Lord Salisbury's satire was *'rather too serious,'* Huxley *'began well but ended disastrously'* while the Archbishop was simply *'dreary'*. While Hardy clearly felt at home in the august company, what was more telling, however, was his comment that *'I spoke to a good many; and was apparently unknown to a good many more I knew'* adding *'At these times men do not want to talk to their equals but their superiors.'*[21]

Despite all his aristocratic connections, Hardy was still sensitive to his own humble upbringing and the question of class, a subject that was to resurface so vehemently in *Jude the Obscure*. Some six weeks later, Hardy had not forgotten the slight, noting ironically on 2 June, 1887, that it was *'The forty seventh birthday of Thomas the Unworthy.'*[22] Meanwhile, he was busy adding to his group of confidantes that included Lady Portsmouth, Lady Carnarvon and Lady St Helier, by cultivating other members of London society and attending their crushes and dinners. Inevitably, Hardy ended these evenings caught in a tête-à-tête, usually with a modern woman similar to one he met at a dinner at Walter Pater's whom he described as *'an Amazon, more, an Atalanta, most, a Faustine. Smokes: handsome girl: cruel small mouth; she's of the class of interesting women one would be afraid to marry.'* Soon he was to meet and become infatuated with his own 'modern woman', in the person of Rosamund Tomson.[23]

Tess of the D'Urbervilles saw Hardy at the peak of his powers as a novelist. The story of Tess is as well-known as is the character of Tess, who was Hardy's favorite heroine, and his fictional 'well-beloved.' While she ends the story guilty of a heinous crime, she is always, in the eyes of the readers, and certainly of Hardy himself, innocent. After all, *'Never in her life – she could swear it from the bottom of her soul – had she ever intended to do wrong.'* Tess justified as much to herself when she reflected, *'yet these hard judgments had come. Whatever her sins, they were not sins of intention, but of inadvertence, and why should she have been punished so persistently?'* (Ch. 51) If the reader apportions blame, it is Angel Clare they hold responsible for her plight, even more than Alec d'Urberville, but never Tess herself. Yet it is Tess who Hardy punishes for the rape, being cast as an outsider with her dark secret that dooms her relationship with the priggish Angel Clare and leads to the inevitable conclusion to the story. With Hardy, we now know that it is the heroine who pays the price and even Tess, Hardy's favourite heroine, his pure woman, is no exception.

Hardy began writing the novel in the summer 1889 having returned to Dorchester from attending the London season. Around the time, he jotted down a casual thought that encapsulated the journey that Tess was setting off upon: *'When a married woman who has a lover kills her husband, she does not really wish to kill the husband; she wishes to kill the situation.'*[24]

Tess of the D'Urbervilles was described by one early critic, as *'the greatest plea for woman that was ever written'.*[25] Tess's life may be tragic, but she emerges from her travails as a pure woman who suffers because of the unfairness and machinations of a male-orientated world. One contemporary critic recognised her significance and Hardy's advocacy for her, writing in the *Star* in 1891, *'Thomas Hardy has heretofore been more inclined to champion man the faithful against woman the coquette, but in Tess he very definitely espouses "the cause of woman," and devotes himself to show how often in this world – all, alas, because the best of us is so conventionalized – when men and women break a law the woman pays.'*[26] Hardy's close friend, Edmund Gosse who was later to savage him over *Jude the Obscure* wrote *'Your book is simply magnificent, and wherever I go I hear its praises. Your success has been phenomenal. I have not heard a book so earnestly and honestly praised by word of mouth (and that is the praise that tells) for years.'*[27]

Not all critics were well disposed towards the novel, however. The *Quarterly Review* called it a *'clumsy, sordid tale of boorish brutality and lust'* although its particular vitriol seemed to do the book's sales no harm.

By now Hardy was well settled at Max Gate and enjoying his growing reputation. He was also becoming dissatisfied with aspects of his marriage as we can witness in his correspondence with its references to social engagements and the growing evidence of his fascination with young women. He was clearly enjoying the opportunities he now had to observe and meet young ladies. That year, he had become attracted to an actress, Helen Matthews whose dark eyes and *'arch saucy style of countenance'* were reminiscent of Tryphena and her sisters. Gittings suggested that as he turned forty, more and more *'the imaginative Hardy required nymphs and sylphs, of past memory or present discovery.'*[28] One was Rosamund Tomson who was soon to captivate him, the start of a number of young, and attractive women writers to do so. At the same time, his relationship with Emma was beginning to fray. According to Gittings, the poem, 'She Charged Me' which Hardy wrote around this time and which alluded to Emma finding out about Hardy's Weymouth jaunts with Tryphena many years earlier, highlighted the growing impasse between the two. For whatever reason, Emma began to move towards a more conservative position on issues of faith and morality and was ever more sensitive about Thomas's wandering eye, though this did little to hold back her footloose husband.

Tess offered Hardy the opportunity to create his own idealized heroine who epitomised all he thought good in the opposite sex. *'A Pure woman, faithfully presented'*, the book's subtitle reads although this was not to suggest that Tess was bloodless or lacking in vitality. Rather, as Rosemarie Morgan argued *' . . .from her first recognition of sexual overtures in Alex's fruit-thrusting gestures to her ecstasy in the "Garden" sequence, Tess expresses a fully developed sexual nature as sensitive to the needs of her impassioned lover as to her own auto-erotic powers and desires.'*[29]

The shame of being raped condemns Tess – though ironically not her assailant – in the eyes of her family and of society. It is Tess who carries the guilt for the sexual act that she was subjected to and as the novel unravels the layers of hypocrisy in the law and a religion that discriminates against women, and of sexual inequality, there is no respite or exoneration. Instead, her last few days on the run with Angel Clare are as excoriating as any for the reader, knowing it was his prudishness, hypocrisy and cowardice that cost Tess her life.

In championing Tess, a 'pure woman' Hardy uses his heroine to direct the reader's attention towards the attitudes and institutions of late Victorian England. It is hard not to feel sorry for Tess although contemporary readers were rather more judgemental of her moral lapse. Circumstance and convention overwhelm her, society fails to protect her and from early in the novel, her fate is predestined. Caught up in an inexorable and pitiless narrative, starting with her rape by Alec D'Urberville for which the law gives her no protection, to his murder, her situation is steadily compromised by the censorious voice of social convention and propriety. As we follow Tess through the trials of having a child out of wedlock, the perils of sex outside of marriage, the ostracism of the Church in the absence of any natural justice, we sense Hardy's growing anger at the hypocrisy of it all. Thomas no doubt reflected on the Hardy's time at Sturminster Newton when their maid Jane Philips became pregnant and ran off, only for the baby to die after two days and was not adverse to using the recollection in his novel.

Once again, we are presented with a triangle where it is suggested that both men *'find their self-conception of masculinity endangered by their desire for Tess'*. The two vertices of the erotic triangle, represented by the caddish and assertive Alec and the more effeminate Angel, illustrate what Richard Nemesvari goes on to label *'the anxieties about masculine identity that such triangles create'.*[30] Inevitably, in the face of so much testosterone, Tess is rendered powerless to counter the whims and actions of the two men. Even her saint-like demeanour counts for naught when she is caught by the pinchers of sanctimony and lust, forced into marriage against her better judgement because of the jealousy and hypocrisy of man and the society that protected them.

Of the minor themes running through the novel, the hypocrisy of marriage is given another airing, through the sham marriage of Alec and Tess and the legal, but flawed marriages of, first, Tess and Angel and then Tess and Alec. In each, it is the male who is in control as Alec reminds Tess *'Remember, my lady, I was your master once! I will be your master again. If you are any man's wife you are mine!'* (Ch. 47)

While Tess exhibits almost saint like qualities throughout, the God-fearing Angel Clare becomes the villain and is subjected to Tess's emotional and accusatory charge: *'O why have you treated me so monstrously, Angel! I do not deserve it. I have thought it all over carefully, and I can never, never forgive you! You know that I did not intend to wrong you – why have you so wronged me? You are cruel, cruel indeed! I will try to forget you. It is all injustice I have received at your hands!'* (Ch. 51)

We can see why Hardy thought so highly of his creation. Tess was, in Hardy's mind, *'a complex interaction of passive and active impulses'* who was variously *'complex, diverse, unique: fierce and gentle, regenerative and destructive, trusting and suspicious, philosophical, mystical and sexy.'*[31] She was also an object of erotic fantasy. In his article 'Tesssexuality

– A Victim Culture', Tony Fincham describes how Tess '*. . . emerges as both sex object (the subject of perpetual male abuse/delectation) and sexy woman who, drawn through the floating pollen of the damp garden by the indifferent sounds of Angel's harp, reaches "her plateau of sexual ecstasy . . . with waves of orgasmic dilatation" leading to withdrawal and post-orgasmic "detumescence"*.[32] It was strong stuff for the Victorian readers to handle although, as Morgan asserts, it is likely that they were more focused on her moral purity than her sexuality.[33]

It is an injustice that Tess should suffer so at the hands of the author. Cast as the scapegoat, whatever she does in good faith, inevitably rebounds. Her confession to Angel Clare about her relationship with Alec, told in response to a similar confession by Angel Clare, has dire consequences (and is an echo of Fitzpiers similarly hypocritical attitude towards Grace in *The Woodlanders*). Hardy rails against the sanctimonious nature of the Church, especially over its refusal to give Tess's dead child a Christian burial, and in producing a character such as Angel Clare, but wherever and whatever the recriminations for Tess's situation, it is she that is punished. Even the economic deprivations of her family that forced Tess to return to Alec to try and provide for them are presented as an indictment of society that allows such poverty to exist (albeit exacerbated by her fathers fondness of alcohol). All in all, the novel expects the reader to side with Tess and she succeeds in garnering our sympathy, despite the fact that by the novel's end, she is a murderer.

When the book came out, opinion about Tess was divided. Hardy provided an amusing account of the Duchess of Abercorn who, tired of her guests arguing about Tess's character over the dinner table asked them *"'Do you support her or not?"If they say "No indeed. She deserved hanging. A little harlot!" She puts them in one group. If they say "Poor wronged innocent" and pity her, she puts them in the other group where she is herself.'*[34]

For Hardy, Tess was a character in whom he invested a good deal of himself. Unlike early heroines, to whom 'things happened', Tess had her own moral compass that she lived by. Fate, circumstance and the 'President of the Immortals' ultimately may have decided her fate, (*'once victim, always a victim'* she tells Alec) but she also had a hand in what happened to her. Morgan rightly criticizes the idea of Tess being a passive victim, stating that, in her opinion, *'the combination of sexual vigour and moral rigour . . . makes Tess not just one of the greatest, but also one of the strongest women in the annals of English literature'*.[35] While Hardy no doubt had models in mind, those commonly linked with *Tess* are the usual suspects: Tryphena Sparks; Augusta Way, the mother of Gertrude Bugler who, when she was a milkmaid near Bockhampton at the time he was writing Tess had caught his eye; and the beautiful Agatha Thornycroft, who Hardy described as *'the most beautiful woman in England'* and the person he thought of *'when I wrote Tess'*. It is probable that the character was, at heart, an idealisation, a pure woman (a description that caused considerable debate amongst critics of the book), a model rather than one modelled on another.[36] Of all his heroines, Tess was Hardy's beloved, the character of whom he felt proud, the pure woman, whose life, like his own, was full of sadness and disappointment yet who would never disappoint him.

Chapter 12

The Final Flourish: 1892 – 1897
Sue Bridehead and Arabella

Life's Little Ironies (1894), Jude the Obscure (1895), The Well-Beloved (1897) A Changed Man and other Tales (1913)

'People go on marrying because they can't resist natural forces, although many of them may know perfectly well that they are possibly buying a month's pleasure with a life's discomfort.' Jude the Obscure
(Pt. 5, Ch. 1)

' In . . . The Well- Beloved *the whole mechanism of illusion is laid bare. A man is doomed to pursue for sixty years the Ideal that he believes resides in woman. It leads him from form to form. As he is about to clasp it, it darts away and embodies itself otherwhere and beckons him on again.'*
Pite, R [1]

The success of *Tess of the D'Urbervilles* elevated Hardy to new levels of popularity amongst his readers although his critics were also beginning to gather, concerned at the author's criticism of the Church and the social and moral laxity displayed by some of his characters. Sex outside of marriage, illegitimacy, rape and implicit criticisms of the institution of marriage were now prevalent themes in his writing and were causing increasing disquiet amongst some of his closest friends and family, most notably Emma. She felt that *Tess* was further evidence of Hardy's moral ambiguity which highlighted the impasse between them in matters of faith, love and propriety. Nothing, however, prepared them for the outcry that was to greet the publication of *Jude the Obscure*.

It was a time of considerable change in the Hardys' lives. In 1890 Emma's much-loved mother, also named Emma, had died, followed a year later by her father, John Gifford. The following year, Thomas Hardy senior also died, leaving Jemima the only remaining parent and Emma more exposed than ever at Max Gate. Hardy's flirtations, first with Rosamund Tomson and then, more seriously with Florence Henniker along with his general penchant for young and attractive women had further exposed the cracks in his and Emma's relationship which had deteriorated to such an extent that by the middle of the decade they had taken to separate bedrooms. By the time of the publication of *Jude the Obscure* in 1895, Emma was busy writing her diary along with her damning observations about Thomas, catchily entitled 'What I think of my Husband'. Thomas, meanwhile, was busy conducting his very own personal correspondence with Florence Henniker and, soon after the publication of *Jude the Obscure*, with Agnes Grove as well. Clearly, he was not averse to sharing his own antipathy towards marriage and his advocacy for more liberal sexual attitudes with any attractive women prepared to listen. At times he wrote provocatively and yet, when challenged by Florence Henniker for overstepping the mark, he was quick to retreat to a more theoretical position on issues such as free love or the Anglican Church.

From reading his letters and *The Life*, it is clear that Hardy took what Pite called a *'sexually charged interest in aristocratic and/or literary women'*.[2] His fascination bordered on voyeurism and after *Tess* opened yet more society doors, he pursued his interest in attractive women rather more vigorously, often flirting or just looking at them in a way that was akin to leering. He was more at home in London now, especially when Emma was not in attendance, more confident in his own talents and person (although sensitive about fellow authors who he felt talked down to him). He revelled in his popularity at dinner parties where he was often wheeled out by the hostess as the guest of honour. The change in Hardy's demeanour was soon reflected in his appearance. In 1892, he shaved off his beard and, soon after, had the photograph taken that showed his direct gaze, waxed moustache and natty dress, all signals of the 'new man about town' as *Punch* magazine called him in a popular cartoon of the time. He was moderately prosperous and becoming well known in society circles and more than ready to enjoy the adulation and fruits of his labour. Even the shock caused by his new book seemed to do no harm amongst the circles in which he now frequently moved.

When *Jude the Obscure* – or 'Jude the Obscene' as the *Pall Mall Gazette* called it – was published in 1895, it was met with an out-pouring of criticism that shook even Hardy. The most vitriolic attack came from Margaret Oliphant in *Blackwood's Magazine* in January 1896 who began, *'We rather think the author's object must be, having glorified women by the creation of Tess, to show after all what destructive and ruinous creatures they are, in general circumstances and in every development, whether brutal or refined ...'* and continued in the same vein with the damning comment that *'nothing so coarsely indecent as the whole history of Jude in his relations with his wife Arabella has ever been put into English print'* before concluding *'There may be books more disgusting, more impious as regards human nature, more foul in detail, in those dark corners where the amateurs of filth find garbage to their taste; but not, we repeat, from any master's hand.'*[3]

More personally hurtful to Hardy, however, was the reaction of a number of his friends, none more so than Edmund Gosse who wrote a review of *Jude* that appeared in *Cosmopolis* in 1896: *'The vita sexualis of Sue is the central interest of the book and enough is told about it to fill the specimen tables of a German specialist... She is a poor, maimed, "degenerate", ignorant of herself and of the perversion of her instincts, full of febrile, amiable illusions, ready to dramatize her empty life, and play at loving though she cannot love...'* before finishing with the best-known lines of any review of a Hardy novel by posing the rhetorical question *'What has Providence done to Mr. Hardy that he should rise up in the arable land of Wessex and shake his fist at his creator?'*[4]

Nor did the book fare any better abroad. The *New York World* attacked the book for its immorality and coarseness, with the reviewer, Jeannette Gilder concluding *'when I finished the story I opened the windows and let in the fresh air, and I turned to my bookshelves and I said: "Thank God for Kipling and Stevenson, Barrie and Mrs. Humphrey Ward. Here are four great writers who have never trailed their talents in the dirt."*[5]

In *The Life* several pages are given over to the publication of the novel and Hardy's response, including a defence of what he had written. He tried to dismiss the idea that the novel was an indictment of marriage, as it most clearly was, remarking in a letter to Florence Henniker that it was curious that some papers considered the story *'a sort of manifesto on the marriage question, though it is really one about two persons who, by a hereditary curse of temperament, peculiar to their family, are rendered unfit for marriage . . .*[6] Even twenty-five years later, he was still busy distancing himself from the novel. In a letter transcribed for him by Florence he said of *Jude* that *'there is not a scrap of personal detail in it, it having the least to do with his own life of all his books'* his protestations were immediately interpreted by many as meaning the very opposite.[7]

As to the well-publicised letter to the newspapers from the Bishop of Wakefield stating that he had thrown the novel in the fire in disgust, Hardy only provided a wryly sceptical response that the difficulty *'of burning a thick book even in a good fire, and the infrequency of fires of any sort in summer'* made him question the literal truth of the Bishop's outburst.[8]

Emma, however, was incensed and did not see even a smidgen of humour or encouragement in any of the reviews or comments. Having been kept at arm's length from the manuscript, she was shocked at the attack on the Church that was implicit in the novel, especially as her Uncle Edwin Gifford had been elevated to the position of Archdeacon of London by the time the book was published. Moreover, she was concerned that the relationship between Sue Bridehead and Jude might be seen as a parallel to their own marriage, which in many ways it was, and that the novel might be seen as autobiographical.

Sue Bridehead and Arabella Donn are two of Hardy's most extraordinary and provocative heroines and between them, they tell us a good deal about Hardy's thinking on women and women's issues at the time. Written at a time when his relationship with Emma had largely broken down and while he was in the throes of pursuing Florence Henniker under the apprehension that she might allow him near her, we can glean a good deal of Hardy's opinions and feelings. Hardy took great pains to distance himself from his creations, yet often his guard slipped, allowing us to see more of the omniscient writer beneath and the issues that troubled him. There was even much of Hardy in the character of Jude (notably his upbringing in a Dorset village, his reading list, childlessness and university aspirations), but it is his two heroines that dominate so much of the critical writing and any discussions about the novel.

As the novel begins, we see Jude Fawley, a young villager wishing to become a scholar at Christminster (loosely based on Oxford) when he is seduced by Arabella Donn, a coarse local girl whose unambiguous desires and singular intentions are more than a match for the naïve and sexually ignorant Jude. As someone who was seen by some as the original model for Arabella (although Tryphena was a more likely candidate), Emma seethed at the character's portrayal, indeed at the whole novel. Arguably, there is a part of Emma in Sue's unconventional attitudes at the start of the novel and her adherence to the Church by the end, but also in the physicality and appearance of Arabella, as Morgan comments with her *'carefully coiffured hair (to enhance its abundance); the fullness of figure, which, even in Emma's youth is busty; and the slight coarse facial features.'*[9]

Less flattering than the physical descriptions, however, was Arabella's behavior and the suggestion (which Emma also had levelled at her) that she had duped Jude into marriage. The disdain and superficiality with which marriage is treated throughout the book also caused her much grief and anger. Hardy identified most closely with Sue Bridehead, indeed revelled in her, but he also had a fondness for the earthy, voluptuous Arabella whom he still felt excited about in his eighties.

Arabella is a more extreme version of Eustacia, someone who unashamedly enjoys the company of men and is subject to the same strong desires. Not conventionally handsome, but buxom, with dark eyes, full lips and perfect teeth she is an archetypal sexual predator. Early on she tells her two friends *'I want him to more than care for me; I want him to have me – to marry me! I must have him. I can't do without him. He's the sort of man I long for.'* (Pt. 1, Ch 7)

It is clear that Jude has no chance when facing the onslaught of her sexual wiles. Soon she has entrapped him under the pretence of being pregnant and they marry soon after although it is clear that they are ill suited. Arabella is soon bored with Jude and not being one to dally, leaves for abroad telling Jude in a note that she will not be returning.

Jude, his marriage in tatters (but still legally intact), is left feeling morally destitute, his ambitions and plans ruined. His fragile state of mind is compounded by his Aunt who admonishes him with the words, reminiscent of Jemima's advice to her own children that *'The Fawleys were not made for wedlock.'* (Pt. 1, Ch. 11)

Arabella's reappearance almost halfway through the novel (Pt. 3, Ch. 8) is a shock to Jude and while she soon disappears again, having agreed to a divorce, she is as manipulative, opportunistic and materialistic as ever. Her second disappearance is followed by the revelation that she had a son by Jude (also named Jude) before sending the boy to be looked after by his father.

While Sue and Jude try to build a life together, they are socially ostracized for living in sin. Jude loses his job and in their penury, the young boy Jude murders his half-siblings before killing himself, leaving behind the most famous suicide note in literary history, *'Done because we are too menny.'*

The shock pushes Sue back to the Church and into the arms of Phillotson whom she remarries, as do Jude and Arabella in a weak moment, although both relationships are doomed to fail. There is no reason to feel sorry for Arabella, however, as she certainly doesn't feel sorry for herself, already planning her next move. She is all animal instinct; a wild uninhibited creation set against the intellectual and considered character of Sue Bridehead. In condemning her heartlessness, Dutta concludes that: *'The case against Arabella is not that she successfully exploits her sexuality . . . but that she flouts, without regret, every norm of common human decency. Her treatment of her son and of the dying Jude are equally callous and show that, more than Ethelberta, it is Arabella who has succeeded in completely cutting out her heart.'*[10]

Yet it is Arabella who is the survivor and even as Jude is being buried, she has another man in the wings waiting for her. Her instinctive self-interest and ignorance belies an animal intelligence that, when set against the self-absorption and vacillations of Sue, is almost to be admired.

By contrast, in Sue Bridehead, Hardy created a heroine who gave voice to many of his own frustrations and as he noted in *The Later Life 'Sue is a type of woman who has always had an attraction for me, but the difficulty of drawing the type has kept me from attempting it till now.'*[11] Like Emma, during their years of courtship, Sue appears to be unconventional and free-spirited, struggling against social mores until pride, circumstance and a sense of duty, fuelled by guilt after the children's deaths drives her back into a conventional and loveless marriage and to the Church that she had previously criticised so roundly. In their last moments together, Jude lamented the marital situation they found themselves in, reminding Sue that when they made their pledges *'I was gin-drunk; you were creed drunk,'* adding that *'either form of intoxication takes away the nobler vision.'* (Pt. 6, Ch. 8) Sue's nobler vision, however, is defined by her reserve and her aversion to sex and while she had the benefits of education and was intellectually and morally superior, it was Arabella who coped best with the reality of her life.

Sue presents as the new woman, unconventional, emancipated with an intellect that *'sparkles like diamonds'*. A cousin of Jude's, she is bright, educated and independent. Against the raw physicality of Arabella, she appears a blithe spirit and at one stage Jude addresses her as such: *'you spirit, you disembodied creature, you dear, sweet, tantalizing phantom, hardly flesh at all...'* (Pt. 4, Ch. 5) while later, Philottson remarks of the almost spiritual affinity between Sue and Jude as an 'extraordinary affinity or sympathy' evident in *'their supreme desire . . . to be together'* a state of being he describes as *'Shelleyan.'* (Pt. 4, Ch. 4) Sue's rationalism and anti-Church bias, her willingness to challenge the institution of marriage and her non-conformity, weigh more heavily upon her as the novel progresses. To a greater extent, we see that her views are a projection of Hardy's own views and that, as Morgan asserts *'She becomes, in fact, the objective voice for Hardy's own case, his political views.'*[12] What follows, however, is a stark warning to new women that the time was not propitious for any challenge to the status quo. Over the latter stages of the novel, Sue is crushed by the inexorable forces of conformity, first in the shape of Mr Phillotson to whom she feels the necessity of being responsive *'whenever he wishes'* and also by the institution of marriage that has placed her in a prison of her own making.

Hardy was by now well-aware of the new woman, those free spirits who were being paraded in society, a few daring and unconventional, like Rosamund Tomson, or more often dull and shallow flirts who populated the soirées and dinner parties he attended in London. He observed them, occasionally toyed with them and often criticised them, but always enjoyed them. Sue, however, possessed what many of them did not, and that was a fierce intellect and a curious and quixotic personality that Hardy was to drain the life from during the course of the novel

Hardy's cousin, Tryphena Sparks is generally accepted as the woman alluded to in the preface of the first edition where Hardy wrote, *'The scheme was jotted down in 1890, from notes made in 1887 and onwards, some of the circumstances being suggested by the death of a woman in the former year* – the year Tryphena died in childbirth, aged only thirty-nine years. Tryphena was, like Sue to Jude, raised in the same extended family as Thomas and was of the same flesh and blood and shared an intensity and spirituality similar to that possessed by Sue and Jude that defeated Phillotson. The youngest of six children, Tryphena was independent and free spirited, and while training to be a school-teacher it is likely that she came to know Thomas intimately. It is easy to see the conversation between Jude and Sue after the burial of Aunt Drusilla, as a facsimile of the warning they had received from his mother, Jemima, Tryphena's aunt:

"She was opposed to marriage, from first to last, you say?" murmured Sue.
"Yes. Particularly for members of our family."
Her eyes met his, and remained on him a while.
"We are a rather sad family, don't you think, Jude?"
"She said we made bad husbands and wives. Certainly we make unhappy ones." (Pt. 4, Ch 2)

More clues of who Hardy was thinking about while creating his heroine can be found in the full name that Hardy gave her, Susanna Mary Florence Bridehead. The name Mary is possibly a reference to his sister Mary, of whose teaching practice and time in Salisbury (where he had visited her) he made good use, although it may only have been a nod of sibling affection. Florence almost certainly refers to Florence Henniker who Hardy met while writing the book and it is likely that his infatuation with her is very much on his mind throughout the process, especially the subject of marriage and its unnatural constraints that they are discussing around this time. It is arguable that there are also aspects of Tryphena in both Sue and Arabella, and that as well as being Jude's 'dear cousin', some of Tryphena's person is recognisable in the physical appearance of Arabella. We should, however, be wary of the confusion caused when writers set out to link fictional characters with Hardy's family and friends. There is speculation, for instance, that Hardy based the characters of Jude and Sue on himself and Emma which might appear to contradict the idea of Emma being an influence for Arabella, but not so if Hardy is focusing on the parts rather than the whole.

Andrew Norman argued that: *'Emma felt the same way as Hardy's fictitious character Sue Bridehead, who confessed that the idea of falling in love held a greater attraction for her than the experience of love itself; that Emma, like Sue, derived a perverse pleasure from seeing her admirers break their hearts over her; that Emma felt the same physical revulsion for Hardy that Sue had felt for Phillotson.'*[13] It is not an altogether new or convincing claim, but quite possibly accurate to some degree.

With Florence Henniker, the similarities transcend the book's narrative. From early on in their relationship, Hardy's letters to Florence were personal and familiar, occasionally embarrassingly so, and while he clearly hoped that something might come of their relationship, he came to the realisation that Florence shared with Sue something that condemned her, condemned them both, an *'essential character trait'*, of being *'seemingly emancipated, but actually quite conventional . . .'*[14]

Sue is Hardy's most complex heroine. Jekel says of her, *'She is feminine but not an overtly sexual female. She has little sense of real self-worth or pride, yet she has a strong sense of vanity.'*[15] She does not behave like Hardy's other heroines and her lack of physicality is noted, and talked up by Arabella who suggests *'She don't know what love is – at least what I call love! I can see in her face she don't.'* (Pt. 5, Ch. 5) D H Lawrence described her as the villain of the book, representing *'all that was wrong with modern woman as one of the supreme products of our civilization'*. Nor are recent critics any kinder: Tony Fincham labelled Sue *'an inveterate flirt incapable of sexual fulfilment'*[16] while Rosemary Morgan, went even further, describing her as *'less frigid than refrigerated'*.[17]

The contradictions between her intellect and her physicality pain her so that while she has been championed as a representative of the feminine movement, she is never wholeheartedly so. Rather than being a free spirit she is captive to her own binding convictions.[18]

Hardy, however, like Jude, was enamoured of her, revelling in her charms, her lively intelligence and attractive personality despite the transparency of her insecurity and selfishness. Her flaws do not deter, indeed, form much of the attraction. Again, while Hardy lurks within many of his characters, in some shape or form, there is more of Hardy in Jude than may be first obvious, more than he dared to acknowledge, despite his protestations to the contrary.

When they are at last married, after all the difficulties and detours, Sue's suggestion to Jude that they should have lived in *'mental communion, and no more'* was so scarifying that he reacted by accusing her of lacking a passionate heart and was *'upon the whole, a sort of fay, or sprite – not a woman!'*. (Pt. 6, Ch. 3) Sue was not blind to her faults and was not averse to acknowledging the worm in her. What she saw as her woman's failing, was the desire to attract and captivate and take what she desired, regardless of consequences, not knowing whether love might follow these first, baser feelings. Her confession to Jude offered little reassurance:

'At first I did not love you, Jude; that I own. When I first knew you I merely wanted you to love me. I did not exactly flirt with you; but that inborn craving which undermines some women's morals almost more than unbridled passion – the craving to attract and captivate, regardless of the injury it may do the man – was in me; and when I found I had caught you, I was frightened. And then – I don't know how it was – I couldn't bear to let you go – possibly to Arabella again – and so I got to love you, Jude. But you see, however fondly it ended, it began in the selfish and cruel wish to make your heart ache for me without letting mine ache for you.' (Pt. 6, Ch. 3)

The hurtful realisation that it was jealousy that had initially driven her into his arms was now compounded by the realisation that his unfulfilled longing would never be wholly requited, that there was something undeniably cold in Sue, more than mere sexlessness or distrust of love.

In a letter quoted anonymously in *The Life* but addressed to Edmund Gosse, whose criticism of Jude had severely damaged their relationship, Hardy reiterated that there was nothing perverted or depraved about Sue. Rather, he felt that her sexual instinct was *'unusually weak and fastidious'* and that one of her reasons for fearing the marriage ceremony was that she thought it *'would be breaking faith with Jude to withhold herself at pleasure, or altogether, after it; though while uncontracted she feels at liberty to yield herself as seldom as she chooses. This has tended to keep his passion as hot at the end as at the beginning, and helps to break his heart.'* The reality was, as Hardy was at pains to point out that Jude *'. . . has never really possessed her as freely as he desired.'* [19]

It would not be unusual for readers to speculate over Hardy's own sexuality at this point. The process that begins with an initial infatuation and rush of passion, followed by a gradual falling away possibly because of rejection is familiar to Hardy as it is to a number of his characters. We can also speculate on whether Sue's aversion to sex alludes to Hardy's supposed reluctance to be touched which in turn leaves us to wonder whether it is Sue and not Jude, who best represents their creator.

Marriage once again provides the vehicle for much of the misery in the book. Arabella entraps Jude and their marriage is the impediment that drives all else in the story; Sue's guilt and conscience makes her creed-drunk at the end despite Hardy's argument to the contrary. When rebutting the critics, however, Hardy was at pains to deny this was a central theme of the novel and was bemused by the fact that he was criticised for undermining the Church when he had feared, rather, that he might have seemed *'too High-Churchy at the end of the book where Sue recants.'*[20] As the book is full of references to marriage, it is hard to see Hardy's response as anything other than disingenuous. Also, in Sue Bridehead, he has his most vociferous mouthpiece to attack what he described as *'the gratuitous cause of at least half the misery of the community.'*[21]

Like most of heroines before her, Sue is against the notion of marriage being the inevitable outcome of her sexuality. In the novel, the strands of attack on the institution of marriage are manifold, starting with the hopes and expectations of the couple. After marrying Phillotson, Sue confided to Jude:

'Jude, before I married him I had never thought out fully what marriage meant, even though I knew. It was idiotic of me — there is no excuse. I was old enough, and I thought I was very experienced... I am certain one ought to be allowed to undo what one had done so ignorantly! I daresay it happens to lots of women, only they submit, and I kick... When people of a later age look back upon the barbarous customs and superstitions of the times that we have the unhappiness to live in, what WILL they say!' (Pt. 4, Ch. 2)

As her disquiet grew, Sue became insistent that she should be able to be released from her marriage vows on the grounds that *'If it is only a sordid contract, based on material convenience in house holding, rating, taxing, and the inheritance of land and money by children, making it necessary that the male parent should be known'* then it had no moral authority. (Pt. 4, Ch. 2)

And yet, as Jude and Sue begin their life together in a *'dreamy paradise'* Jude soon realizes that society will not countenance living in sin. Sue, meanwhile, sees marriage as the threat to their very happiness and once, when they set out to marry, at the last minute, she defers, declaring *'let's go home without killing our dream.'*

Sue never relents until the very end about the harm that marriage can bring about and how it could undo all that she and Jude hold dear and that, maybe, the very act will destroy them:

'Do you think that when you must have me with you by law, we shall be so happy as we are now? The men and women of our family are very generous when everything depends upon their good will, but they always kick against compulsion. Don't you dread the attitude that insensibly arises out of legal obligation? Don't you think it is destructive to a passion whose essence is its gratuitousness?' (Pt. 5, Ch. 3)

The implications of marriage for a woman, however, were different than for a man. For a woman, as Sue reminds us, marriage involved becoming a legal chattel, as Grace

Melbury and Sue Henchard had previously found out. Sue was not going to make the same mistake. One of her objections to marriage had been a fear of commitment, believing that love, like life, was transitory, that *'it is culpable to bind yourself to love always as to believe a creed always, and as silly as to vow always to like a particular food or drink.'* (Pt. 4, Ch. 3) Yet by the time Jude returns to the debate later in the story, by trying to persuade her to flee from their respective situations by arguing *'we've both re-married out of our senses. I was made drunk to do it. You were the same'* and then in urging her *'Let us then shake off our mistakes, and run away together!'* – Sue's seesaw morality would not countenance it. (Pt. 6, Ch. 8)

Arabella alone is able to balance the benefits and obligations of marriage. When urging Sue to marry Jude, she reminds her of the economic benefits, that *'Life with a man is more businesslike after it, and money matters work better. And then, you see, if you have rows, and he turns you out of doors, you can get the law to protect you, which you can't otherwise... And if he bolts away from you... you'll have the sticks o'furniture, and won't be looked upon as a thief.'* (Pt. 5, Ch. 2).

Sue, by contrast, places no stead on security, but instead, her spirit broken, she reverts to the Victorian convention of marriage with Phillotson, telling herself *'I shall try to learn to love him by obeying him'*. (Pt. 6, Ch. 4) Yet when Sue leaves Phillotson, Arabella has no compunction in telling the schoolteacher *' I shouldn't have let her go! I should have kept her chained on —her spirit for kicking would have been broke soon enough! There's nothing like bondage and a stone-deaf taskmaster for taming us women. Besides, you've got the laws on your side'*. (Pt. 5, Ch. 8)

Towards the end of the novel, we find Sue consumed with guilt, her spirit broken, her willingness to flout social convention thwarted. She is ready to make peace with the Church and tells Jude her views on marriage had changed: *'I see marriage differently now! .... My babies have been taken from me to show me this! Arabella's child killing mine was a judgment; the right slaying the wrong. What, what shall I do! I am such a vile creature – too worthless to mix with ordinary human beings.'* (Pt. 6, Ch. 3)

For Jude, who was always more inclined to the Church than Sue had ever been and who at one stage had held out hopes of studying for a Doctorate in Divinity, this is the final indignity. He launches a vehement attack not on her but on what the Church had done to her:

'You make me hate Christianity, or mysticism, or Sacerdotalism, or whatever it may be called, if it's that which has caused this deterioration in you. That a woman-poet, a woman-seer, a woman whose soul shone like a diamond – whom all the wise of the world would have been proud of, if they could have known you – should degrade herself like this! I am glad I had nothing to do with Divinity – damn glad – if it's going to ruin you in this way!' (Pt. 3, Ch. 6)

By returning to Phillotson, Hardy depicts Sue's abject surrender as *'the self-sacrifice of the woman on the altar of what she was pleased to call her principles.'* (Pt. 6, Ch. 5) Yet it is clear that the principles are not his, nor even Sue's. Morgan asserts that for Sue, marriage, *'With its contractual emphasis placed solely upon terms, the terms most profitable to the bond-holder, in contrast to the simple exchange of promissory oaths under the old practice of betrothal and simple church ceremonial, matrimony has become, in Sue's eyes, less a mutual undertaking than the legitimization of a "sordid business" granting one individual authority and power over another.'*[22]

As disturbing for the Victorian critic as the attack on marriage as an institution was the assertion that marriage was unnatural for the reason that *'it is foreign to a man's nature to go on loving a person when he is told that he must and shall be a person's lover'*. Rather, love, as with people and their attitudes and views, changes over the course of a lifetime, a view that undoubtedly mirrored Hardy's own – indeed, his correspondence with Florence Henniker shows as much. (Pt. 5, Ch. 1)

He felt that transitory nature of love should not be curtailed or limited and while he was unable or unwilling to escape the conventions of his own life, he could see no wrong in projecting his views through another.

Having introduced the subject of divorce in *The Woodlanders* several years early, Hardy revisited the subject, this time dealing more explicitly with its contradictions. Previously Grace Melbury had been under the misapprehension that by the letter of the Matrimonial Cases Act of 1857 (and the 1878 amendment) the absence of a spouse would be enough for her to seek a dissolution of her marriage, something she later found was not possible – indeed, short of the husband committing a criminal offence or a combination of adultery and desertion for a period of at least two years, women were powerless to extricate themselves from a marriage contract. The irony was that for a man, the course was relatively straightforward. When Phillotson resolves to divorce Sue, on the basis that since she had returned and then refused his request to stay after he said he had forgiven her, it was sufficient grounds for the marriage to be dissolved. (Pt. 4, Ch. 6) How much easier it was for Philottson and how much easier, as Sue remarked to Jude, for such an outcome and for their past impediments, such as Arabella's second marriage, to be undiscovered; at least on that issue there was an advantage in being *'poor obscure people'*. The point Hardy was making about the hypocrisy and unfairness of the divorce laws, however, was not subtle and again in the eyes of some of his more vociferous critics, it placed him ever more firmly in the camp of the anti-marriage league.

Sue and Arabella are two of Hardy's greatest heroines, both admired and reviled by different critics, yet both triumphant creations, depicting the lives of two distinct women, each with her own flaws and foibles and each charged with a social agenda that rattled the Victorian cage. By the time the furore had died down, Hardy had quietly accepted that his subject matter had gone as far as the boundaries of censorship would allow at the time, as well as what was deemed acceptable by his reading public (a position he would have found largely unchanged until after the Lady Chatterley trial in 1963).

Sixteen years after its first appearance Hardy was still feeling bruised by the attacks on his person and his novels. In the preface to the 1912 edition, he wrote, *'I have been charged since 1895 with a large responsibility in this country for the present "shop-soiled"condition of the marriage theme'*, reiterating his previously held view that *'a marriage should be dissolvable as soon as it becomes a cruelty to either of the parties'*. Refuting his critics, including the *'screaming of the poor lady in* Blackwood's, Mrs Oliphant, whose scathing review at the time had led the charge against him, Hardy concluded by quoting an 'experienced reviewer' from Germany who had written to him. In her view, '*Sue Bridehead, the heroine, was the first delineation in fiction of the woman who was coming into notice in her thousands every year – the woman of the feminist movement – the slight, pale 'bachelor' girl – the intellectualized, emancipated bundle of nerves the modern conditions were producing, mainly in the cities as yet; who does not recognise the necessity for most of her sex to follow marriage as a profession, and boast themselves as superior people because they are licensed to be loved on the premises.*'[23]

There was one last flurry from the novelist's pen and a disquieting one at that. In 1897, Hardy's final novel, *The Well-Beloved* sub-titled 'A Sketch of Temperament', first serialized in 1892 was finally published in a single volume, albeit in a much-altered form. Since its publication, the novel has polarised critics and readers alike, being greatly admired by Proust while described as *'sheer rubbish'*, by D H Lawrence.[24] It is part-satire, part-history, part-biography, part parody, the story of a transient being (and who cannot smile at Hardy's comparison of Pierston's shifting of affection from one beloved to another like 'moving house'?)

Its plot is deceptively simple, being the story of the sculptor, Jocelyn Pierston, who at the start of the novel falls in love with Avice Caro, his boyhood sweetheart. The book, which focuses on three critical periods in his life,[25] each twenty years apart, sees Pierston fall in love, successively, with Avice's daughter, Ann Avice and, finally, her grand-daughter, another Avice, but each relationship fails before he ends up marrying a previous flame, the once beautiful Marcia Bencomb, who he no longer loves (and is no longer beautiful), but who offers him, at least, friendship and companionship. Pierston is the last in a line of Hardy's characters whose expectations are such that they will accept nothing less than a pure woman – a sequence that started with Henry Knight in *A Pair of Blue Eyes* who abandons his love when he finds out she has been kissed, or Angel Clare abandoning Tess when he felt her to have been besmirched by having been raped. As usual with Hardy there are a number of subsidiary themes criss-crossing the story, notably the cost of pursuing Platonic beauty, but essentially the story is his own, and one by his own admission, that had been many years in its germination.

Pierston's rather sad life story can be seen as a reflection of Hardy's own search that continued throughout his life. Pierston is the central axis to the plot while the women (the three Avices and Marcia) are little more than notional characters whom Pierston embraces then lets go in his quest to find a platonic ideal of perfect female beauty.

Seeing how Hardy's heroines are fleshed out in *Jude* and how sketchily they are developed here, the reader could feel a little let down although all of the women are capable of holding their own in the face of Pierston's quest. By writing of the effect that ageing has on love and desire, Hardy gives us a particularly male viewpoint whereby men can age, but women cannot, for according to Pierston/Hardy women are always defined by their physical beauty. Pierston, therefore, ignores the fact that he, too has aged (although, subconsciously, of course he realises it), yet is still unwilling to forgo the image of young ethereal beauty that he has always imagined would be his one day. He is prepared to compromise, to accept (intellectually at least) he cannot be so fussy now he is older and acknowledges as much when wooing (stalking?) the middle Avice, a process so uncomfortable that our hero comes across as rather creepy. Yet what Pierston (Hardy) is searching for, this intangible and unattainable 'thing', doesn't exist as he acknowledges early on (although it takes the whole novel for the point to be conclusively made): *'To his Well-Beloved he had always been faithful; but she had had many embodiments. Each individuality known as Lucy, Jane, Flora, Evangeline, or whatnot, had been merely a transient condition of her. He did not recognize this as an excuse or as a defence, but as a fact simply. Essentially she was perhaps of no tangible substance; a spirit, a dream, a frenzy, a conception, an aroma, an epitomized sex, a light of the eye, a parting of the lips. God only knew what she really was; Pierston did not. She was indescribable.'* (Pt. 1, Ch. 2)

In the novel, the institution (and omnipotence) of marriage gets its usual withering blast, starting from their first private conversation when Pierston blurts out to Avice *'Will you have me as your husband?'* as recompense for his awkwardness at their first meeting when, in the one truly innocent moment in the novel, Avice Caro greets Pierston when he returns to the Isle of Slingers by running up and kissing him. Yet a mere eighteen pages later there he is asking another (Marcia) *'Will you come and marry me?'*, as if the act of marriage was not a serious consideration at all.

How easy to get married, how hard to become unmarried is the conundrum that underlies many of Hardy's novels although in *The Well-Beloved* the problem is rather turned on its head by Pierston who is both searching for and yet is fearful of, marriage. Throughout, Pierston is Hardy, the seeker of the ideal woman and no more so than in his acute observations on beauty that, at times, border on voyeurism. When we read

'The study of beauty was his only joy for years onward. In the streets he would observe a face, or a fraction of a face, which seemed to express to a hair's-breadth in mutable flesh what he was at that moment wishing to express in durable shape. He would dodge and follow the owner like a detective; in omnibus, in cab, in steamboat, through crowds, into shops, churches, theatres, public houses, and slums — mostly, when at close quarters, to be disappointed for his pains.' (Pt. 1, Ch. 9)

– we are reminded of the incident recorded in *The Life* when Hardy was aged nearly fifty years and spied a girl in an omnibus and noted she *'had one of those faces of marvellous beauty'* before concluding with a series of questions, *'Where do these women come from? Who marries them? Who knows them?'*[26]

What is most disturbing in the plot is not just that Pierston seeks out the same youthful ideal over three generations, but also that they are from the same family: mother, daughter and granddaughter. When we look at Hardy's own life, however, age differences never seemed to bother him unduly. He, too, had a similar experience when he was only nine or ten and became a favourite of his teacher, the local Lady of the Manor, Augusta Martin, who was nearly forty and who sat him on her lap and bestowed kisses upon him. In *The Life* we are told that Hardy's feelings for her were *'almost that of a lover'* and even as Jemima removed Thomas from the school, he had made a pledge he would never desert her and kept his *'lover-like promise of fidelity'* until he met up with her again some years later and was repelled by how old she seemed.[27]

When we dig a little deeper we can see a number of women that appear in Hardy's life who bewitch him. Staying within the family, Thomas spent considerable time early on with his cousins, where age seemed not to be an impediment. Rebecca was eleven years older than Thomas, Emma, nine years older, Martha, six years older while Tryphena was eleven years younger. Certainly, when Tryphena was just a girl, Thomas had been so enamoured of Martha, the prettiest of the sisters, that according to Millgate, the mothers were aroused to *'active opposition'*.[28] The suspicion that her older sister, Rebecca may have been Tryphena's mother, or in one of Deacon and Coleman's more outlandish claims, that Jemima was Rebecca's mother, would not have helped matters.[29]

Emma was the same age as Thomas, but hereafter, his women friends are notably younger than him. Rosamund Tomson, who Hardy first met in 1889 was only twenty-six years old, twenty-three years younger than Thomas; Florence Henniker who Hardy first met in 1893, was thirty-three years old, twenty years younger than Hardy; Agnes Grove was twenty-three years younger than Hardy; and Florence Dugdale, who he first met in 1905 and who he was to marry nine years later, was thirty-nine years younger than her future husband. All are significant age gaps, but clearly Hardy saw nothing incongruous about his interest in younger women and even went one generation further than Pierston in his eighties when he become completely infatuated with Gertrude Bugler who was forty-seven years younger than him.

Of the heroines, we first meet Avice Caro, a 'nice girl', charming and well mannered, *'one of the class with whom the risks of matrimony approximate most nearly to zero'*. Before they started courting, Pierston had already asked himself the question, as to whether he saw his Well-Beloved in her, when by chance he met Marcia Bencomb. Noting her fine figure and striking face and walking with her awhile, he soon became conscious of a change that he explained by saying *'The Well-Beloved was moving house – had gone over to the wearer of this attire. In the course of ten minutes he adored her. And how about little Avice Caro? He did not think of her as before.'* (Pt. 1, Ch. 5) Avice, as we find out later from her daughter, was grievously hurt by Pierston's treatment of her and the callousness of his rejection later haunted him too. But within a few short pages, Avice is forgotten as Pierston sees his beloved, wondrously transformed and embodied in Marcia who now fills *'every fibre and curve of this woman's form.'* (Pt. 1, Ch. 6)

Pierston's obsession with his idea of the well-beloved continues to bedevil him and as he procrastinates, believing that perhaps he should not marry, Marcia abandons him while Avice marries her cousin. Twenty years later, we go through the same ritual although the second Avice Caro is less cultivated, less feminine, her mother's inferior in soul and understanding and while she has the same sweet smile and voice, Pierston sees her mother in her while accepting he cannot be as particular as he once was. Despite the lure of another, Mrs Pine-Avon, he decides on Avice as his 'well-beloved' Avice, however, is not easily seduced and had never considered him a suitor at all. Having spent several days alone with him in his London apartment, she was shocked to find he was thinking of her that way. In an ensuing heart-to-heart, Pierston is brought up short by several revelations: that Avice deemed him too old, that she too had been looking for her own beloved and had loved 'fifteen a'ready' in the process; and even before they met, she had married, and before the end of part two had given birth to a daughter (the third Avice, this time with the surname Pierston).[30]

The third heroine is this same baby daughter, Avice, now aged twenty who Pierston meets when he returns to the Isle of Slingers. Although he is now sixty years old, he soon makes her acquaintance, and before long confides in her mother, Avice Pierston, that he would be 'willing to marry her' despite the obvious age difference. Avice the third, however, has other ideas, and so the novel rambles to a disappointing end with Avice finding a younger husband and Marcia re-remerging, nursing Jocelyn through an illness and then marrying him.

So what does it all mean? In terms of Hardy's women, we have no new heroines as such although Avice the second and Avice the third show spirit and enterprise despite very little development as characters. Marcia has rather more spirit and enterprise, but all are essentially foils to Pierston's machinations and imaginings.

When we look at the cavalcade of Hardy's heroines, the journey from *Desperate Remedies* and Cytherea Graye really finishes with Sue Bridehead and Arabella Donn. By contrast with these heroines, the women of *The Well-Beloved* are shadowy creatures. They exist for Pierston/Hardy who set out to unravel the obsessive mindset that haunts them both. While the three Avices offer little extra to what we know about Hardy's depiction of women and his attitudes towards them, the novel is primarily not about them, but about Hardy. John Fowles felt the story was written to assuage a private guilt related in part to his childlessness and to answer Hardy's *'life-long need, self-parodied, in* The Well-Beloved*, to avoid consummation.'*[31] Despite the women in the novel being bit players in a wider universe, they tell us a great deal about the author and corroborate many of his views on love and relationships that we can glean from his own unsatisfactory life. Unlike Pierston, who abandoned his pursuit of his ideal of beauty, Hardy did not. First, he married a woman nearly forty years younger than himself and then, when well into his eighties, sought out an even younger embodiment of Tess to admire from afar. Sometimes with Hardy the reality becomes more compelling than the fiction, and in *The Well-Beloved* as John Fowles observed, we are given, *'the closest conducted tour we shall ever have of the psychic process behind Hardy's written product. No biography will ever take us so deep.'*[32]

Chapter 13

Hardy and Women: Where Fact meets Fiction

Youth, old age will overtake you
Unawares: he's laying his snares
By day and night, he grips you tight,

Old age will mock you, shock you!
'Youth' from 'Alleys', Emma Hardy April, 1912

After the furore over *Jude the Obscure* had died down, Hardy returned to *The Well-Beloved*, reworking the novel from its serialized form of five years earlier before finally publishing it in 1897. It was to signal the end of Hardy's career as a novelist as he decided, for a variety of reasons that the genre now longer accorded him the freedom to write as he wished. His own disenchantment was no doubt fuelled by the criticism he had received for *Jude* coming on the back of negative comments about *Tess*, but he also wanted to concentrate on his poetry which he felt was the superior literary form. Later he was to write that *'I never wanted to write prose novels at all'* a claim which doesn't stand up to close scrutiny on a number of fronts, but certainly by 1900 he had turned his attention away from the novel never to return.[1] He had always been inclined to see his critics and reviewers as adversarial, set to catch him out and was possibly suffering from depression after *Jude*. What is undeniable was that he did not take criticism well and was over-sensitive and prickly at times when faced with the slights of his critics, as he saw them, and carefully stored them up.

This sensitivity was with him from the very start. Despite a moderately warm reception for his first novel, *Desperate Remedies*, it was the critique in the *Spectator* that he always remembered, picking him up on daring to suggest that an unmarried woman owning an estate could have an illegitimate child and labelling the book *'a desperate remedy for an emaciated purse'*. Even many years later it was recorded in *The Life* that *'the bitterness of that moment was never forgotten; at the time he wished that he were dead.'*[2]

If anything, Hardy became more sensitive with fame and had reacted badly to the outcry that greeted *Tess* and especially the debate that ensued about whether it was right that his heroine was labelled in the words of his sub-title as 'a pure woman'. Reviews in several contemporary journals were critical of the novel, which both upset him and made him defensive. One review in the *Quarterly* drew the response from him that it was *'a mere manufacture, to suit the prejudices of its fossilized subscribers'*.[3] The review in the *Saturday Post* which he described as *'. . . devised with almost fiendish ingenuity so as to contain a sort of half-truth in every sentence, while remaining a lie'* cut even deeper. Angry and feeling betrayed, he wrote to friends to try and find out who had written it and even suggested he should resign from the Savile Club on the grounds that their journalists often met there.[4] Feeling battered, he waited apprehensively for the expected attack from the *Spectator*, which, as he commented to Edmund Gosse *' . . . will be compelled to slate the novel. Reviews, must, after all, remember their circulations.'*[5]

Other comments elicited more angry asides although Hardy placed credence on the opinions of his friends who rallied around and offered him moral support. [6] He was also capable of mounting a spirited self defence, noting that he had gathered *'from numerous communications from mothers (who tell me they are putting "Tess" into their daughters' hands to safeguard their future) & from other women of society who say that my courage has done the whole sex a service (!)'*[7]

What the reviews, and Hardy's reaction to them, makes clear is his sensitivity to criticism, but also his susceptibility to depression. In 1889 he wrote to John Addington Symonds, ostensibly about his novels, but more accurately, about himself:

'All comedy is tragedy, if only you look deep enough into it. A question which used to trouble me was whether we ought to write sad stories, considering how much sadness there is in the world already. But of late I have come to the conclusion that, the first step towards cure of, or even relief from, any disease being to understand it, the study of tragedy in fiction may possibly here & there be the means of showing how to escape the worst forms of it, at least, in real life.'[8]

This deeper malaise explains a good deal of Hardy in his latter life and his own self-pity. In 1910, after a life full of achievement and honours, he wrote to Florence to ask the question *'was there ever so sad a life as mine?'*[9] It is not surprising that she responded with a measure of hurt and indignation.

The last decade of the nineteenth century was a time of significant upheaval in Thomas's life as he entered upon a series of infatuations and relationships with other women, angering and humiliating Emma and destabilizing their marriage. Losses of three of their parents and Emma's subsequent alienation from Thomas's family all contributed to the growing tension and while there was never a fear of them parting (Hardy would not countenance divorce), their relationship was irreparably damaged. Both made an effort, sharing books, cats, even an enthusiasm for cycling, but life was often stressful. The publication of *Jude the Obscure* had been a considerable source of friction and resulted in a significant breach between them, with Emma, lamenting how far her errant husband had drifted from her own religious and social views. Never once had Hardy publicly acknowledged the help Emma had given him, particularly early in his career. Now, when he had the opportunity to make amends by accepting the knighthood he was offered by Asquith in 1908, he deferred and the moment was lost. It is quite possible that the very fact that Emma would have revelled in the title of 'Lady Emma', was the very reason that Thomas did not accept the honour. As it was, Emma had to be satisfied with the sobriquet 'Lady Emma' instead bestowed by the residents in Dorchester because of her aloof manner in and about the town.

On the surface, she and Thomas muddled along, railing against the Boer War and sharing their views and thoughts on vivisection and suffrage and even Florence Dugdale, when Emma finally got to meet her. What was less apparent to outsiders, however, was that Emma had retreated to her attic bedroom, where she was to stay for the rest of her life writing furiously about his betrayal of her.

Hardy spent much of the last decade of the nineteenth century in an emotional hiatus. Rosamund Tomson had aroused him and his infatuation with her beauty and unconventional lifestyle both upset and angered Emma. Florence Henniker, poised and articulate and a published writer, posed an altogether greater threat although the relationship soon shifted from desire and imagining to friendship as Thomas came to realise that Florence's unconventional and easy manner, like that of Sue Bridehead, belied a more conventional person beneath her breezy exterior and that her innate conservatism included an adherence to the Church. And then there was Agnes Grove, who briefly turned his giddy head before Florence Dugdale insinuated herself into his life and stayed there.

On the back of his literary reputation, Thomas was starting to build up a significant coterie of admirers and followers from amongst the many society friends he had met at the many soirées, crushes and dinner parties he had attended and whose paths he had crossed and had stopped long enough for Thomas to engage them.

The Well-Beloved may have been seen as a failure, described by one critic as the *'most trivial of his novels'*[10], but as Jane Thomas convincingly argues, it was also an *'intensely personal novel'* [11] and as such, a suitable crossover from one genre to another. Hereafter, Hardy opted for the more gentle subterfuge of poetry, which continued to be his preferred medium for the last thirty years of his life. His output was prolific totalling 947 published poems in eight collections, including the epic poem *The Dynasts* and the wonderful elegies he wrote following Emma's death, recognised as some of the greatest elegiac poetry in the English language. Not surprisingly, women are a subject of much of Hardy's poetry, usually women he had known and for whom he retained some nostalgic yearning. Desire and affection run through his pen, but even more is regret, regret for moments lost and opportunities that had been denied him.

Poetry had always been Hardy's default position whenever he wanted to say something more personal or oblique. It seemed that it was easier for Thomas to write a poem about someone he took a liking to than to hold a conversation, and there are numerous poems inspired by women he had met in passing. Even a brief encounter was capable of eliciting a poem that could make any lady blush disconcerted at the very thought that he could see them in such a way. Often, his poetry was by way of memoir, of travelling back to his early years to resurrect memories of people and places he had known half a century or more before.

For Hardy, poetry was the fortress from where he could fire out burning arrows or play cupid, spill his heart or air his wild imaginings without ever feeling that he needed to apologise for his meanderings. While some of his poems are deliberately obscure, others such as 'Thoughts of Phena', which upset an increasingly disillusioned Emma, or the *Poems of 1912 – 1913* that so upset Florence, were not.

Florence eventually accepted the distinction between Hardy's real life and his literary life. Discussing the poem 'Wessex Heights' that alluded to Thomas's friendship with Florence Henniker, Lady Hoare had argued that one should not make the poet responsible for what each poem said – to which Florence, surprisingly, agreed. Her answer was that she had learnt to be detached, and that she could now indeed make the distinction and say *'But the poet wrote that.'*[12]

Fiction writing was Hardy's therapy as much as his stock-in-trade. While he may have blamed the hostility generated by *Jude the Obscure* from both his critics and elements of his readership for persuading him to move genres, he would have known the degree to which he was likely to provoke his critics and the establishment. Yet he seemed hell-bent on doing so. What we can conclude from his fiction is that we really don't get to know Hardy. He made obfuscation his modus operandi, in his fiction and in his life. When we read in his ghosted memoir that *'He (Hardy) constitutionally shrank from the business of social advancement, caring for life as an emotion rather than for life as a science of climbing'* we have to smile, knowing that London and the approval of the aristocracy and the well-heeled meant a great deal to him.[13]

It is in Hardy's opinions on women that he is at his most transparent. During the last decade of the nineteenth century he was busy making critical observations of the opposite sex. His early letters to Florence Henniker revealed a flirtatious side to him, often embarrassing in their presumption although Florence invariably handled such missives tactfully. After their meeting in 1893, Hardy was revealing more of himself to Florence Henniker in personal and often flirtatious letters, talking about the 'despicable flirts' and society women as well as his own feelings. His renewed social confidence is evident in other exchanges. He sends a photo to an admirer, Lina Milman, then challenges *'Here it is. Now where is yours that you promised me in return?'*[14] Two weeks later he is at it again, reminding her *'That photograph is to be sent, remember (though no photographer is likely to do justice to you).'*[15]

In reading comments on women from the collected letters, and despite all his possible protestations, his observations on young and pretty women regularly made up the subject matter of his correspondence. Added to this interest was Hardy's penchant of collecting photographs of all the beautiful or desirable women he met in his life, an interest that could strike the reader as obsessive, even though it was not so unusual for the time. Inevitably it takes us back to the question of whether it was the reality or perception of women that drove him. Certainly, his collection can only have served as a reminder to Emma and Florence of their own inadequacies. Hardy's obsession with the photographic image was of course, evident in his novels: the importance of Avice's photograph in *The Well-Beloved* or Jude first seeing his cousin Sue in a photograph in their Aunt's house. We can also recall both Jude and Phillotson kissing photographs of Sue and wonder whether this was something Hardy did too. We can only assume that after Hardy's death, Florence took little time to burn what have been by then a very considerable and well-thumbed collection.[16]

By 1890, his letters are full of the great and the good, the aristocrats and hostesses he was being wined and dined by and the great families he was familiar with. Constant name-dropping in his letters show he clearly revelled in their company and especially the company of attractive women, as when he wrote of sitting at a luncheon between 'a pair of beauties' sizing each up: *'Mrs A G – with her large violet eyes, was the more seductive: Mrs R C – the more vivacious . . . more venust and warm-blooded.'*[17] By now, usually he went out in London without Emma, who either had stayed at Max Gate or was persuaded by Hardy that she wouldn't enjoy herself, and invariably he found himself in the company of women. In 1893, when he visited his friend Lady Londonderry (who along with Lady Portsmouth and Mrs Jeune was one of Hardy's most successful conduits into London Society) he noted of her *'A beautiful woman still and very glad to see me, which beautiful women are not always'* before relating that *'The Duchess of Manchester (Consuelo) called while I was there and Lady Jeune. All four of us talked of the marriage laws, a conversation which they started, not I; also of the difficulties of separation, of terminable marriages where there are children and of the nervous strain of living with a man when you know he can throw you over at any moment.'*[18]

During one week in 1894, he recalled in *The Life*, he had invitations from Lady Carnarvon, Agnes Grove, Lady Malmesbury and some other distinguished houses he had to turn down. At one dinner he talked at length to *'a woman very rich and very pretty'* (Marcia, Lady Yarborough) who he captured as the lady of the 'Pretty Pink Frock'. Coming home from one evening party in the same week, he recalled getting on the top of a bus: *'No sooner was I up there than the rain began again. A girl who had scrambled up after me asked for the shelter of my umbrella and I gave it – and she startled me by holding on tight to my arm and bestowing on me many kisses for the trivial kindness.'*[19] Everywhere there are references to women, *'much uncovered in the neck and heavily jewelled, their glazed and lamp-blacked eyes wandering.'*[20] As were his, constantly.

Despite his often bumptious behaviour, Hardy never really felt at home in London society, apart from when he was with his trusted confidantes. In 1890, he and Emma attended a crush at the Jeunes and later wrote he had met *'. . . Mrs T and her great eyes in a corner of the room, as if washed up by the surging crowd'* before observing *'the most beautiful woman present . . . But these women! If put into rough wrappers in a turnip field, where would their beauty be?'*[21] The next year, after visiting a teacher training college for schoolmistresses, he went on in the same vein, observing *'How far nobler in its aspirations is the life here than the life of those I met at the crush two nights back!'*[22] But despite the superficial attraction, despite whatever issues of social class and resentment he had about education and background, Hardy couldn't help ingratiating himself with those he had often talked and written about so disparagingly.

Through his fictional characters we can find out a great deal of what Hardy knew and thought about women and women's issues. He had seen his own sisters and cousins starting life in working class households and from his first meeting with Emma had been on the defensive about his own humble background. He felt the lack of a university education was, in the eyes of many, a disadvantage while he sensed that a number of writers looked down their noses at him, as a writer of rural and rustic subject matter only. Many of his heroines were drawn from women he had known and there is no doubt that characteristics of the most important women in his life up until the publication of *Jude the Obscure* – his mother, sisters, cousins and an occasional outsider like Florence Henniker – run through his heroines like seams of coal. In the same way in later life, he saw people in relation to his characters (when he met Lady Cynthia Graham in late 1893 he noted *'in appearance she is something like my idea of Tess')* while Gertrude Bugler was, famously, to take on the mantle of Tess in Hardy's mind in later life.[23] Hardy became close to his heroines and was protective of them, often referring to them as real persons, writing to one admirer of the novel *'I am so truly glad that Tess the Woman has won your affections. I, too, lost my heart to her as I went on with her history . . .'*[24]

While Tess remained the one woman that Hardy held most dear, like many of his heroines, she was harshly treated by circumstance, and by society's iniquitous conventions. Hardy is labelled by some of his critics as a misogynist for bringing down so much unhappiness and pain upon his characters. In their view, the process that Hardy followed was that he created ideal women – such as Tess – as well as flawed characters such as Eustacia and then destroyed them. The ones who got off lightly were always the less-adventurous and the bland, Thomasina and Elizabeth Jane, or the 'bogus heroines,' Anne Garland and Fancy Day. Invariably, the question we return to is what impelled Hardy to create such complex and flawed heroines who often let themselves down while, at the same time, he was trying to make a case for the plight of women in the eyes of the law?[25]

This distinction between poet and husband, between writer and man, sits at the heart of Hardy and his women. It is always tempting to draw parallels between the women Hardy knew and their links with the heroines he created, but it is also true that he sought out the types of women he had written about, a real-life Tess, especially after 1889 when his on-off relationship with Emma became more fragile and tenuous.

He felt that he was never emotionally faithful to Emma and when he wrote *'I am more than ever convinced that persons are successively several persons, according as each special strand in their characters is brought uppermost by circumstances'*[26] he was merely intent on presenting another defence of his own aberrant behaviour.

By the time Hardy had finished with *Jude*, he had created a number of memorable heroines, many of whom he used as vehicles to express his views on a range of social and political issues. Not many escaped from his novels without some scarring and a number did not escape at all. From a trawling of his novels gathering up most of the significant women, we arrive at the following:

Dead: Tess, Felice Charmond, Susan Henchard, Lucetta Templeman, Viviette, Eustacia Vye, Avice I and II, Mrs Yeobright

Unhappily married or in compromised marriages:
Grace Melbury, Avice III, Anne Garland *(unsuitable man)*
Suke Damson, Fancy Day *(past secrets)*
Sue Bridehead, Marcia Bencomb *(loveless marriage)*
Ethelberta Chickerell, Elfride Swancourt *(expedient marriages to older men)*
Paula Power *(ambivalent in love)*

Happily married: Elizabeth Jane Newson *(although a second chosen)*, Cytherea Graye, Bathsheba *(eventually)*

Other: Arabella Donn *(constantly between marriages)*, Marty South *(unrequited love)*, Thomasin Yeobright *(remarried to Diggory Venn as an alternative ending)*

From their number, Hardy managed to cover an array of specific social issues including incest, illegitimacy, divorce, co-habitation outside of marriage, lesbianism, suffrage, as well as offering a perspective on the cruelties of social convention and the legal position of women at the time. Jane Thomas contended that *'Hardy recognized women's physical, mental and emotional susceptibility to convention, and their consequent capitulation in the face of apparently overwhelming social pressures'*[27] and that he was an unstinting advocate for woman against those who countenanced interference and bigotry. He used stereotypes, most notably the bland women (such as Thomasin, Grace and the shadowy Mrs Yeobright) who are the passive recipients of whatever Hardy chooses to throw at them – the Victorian concept of the angel in the house. Set against them are the protagonists, the temptresses or radical women, full of passion and spirit, or with tainted pasts. They are the ones who challenge conventions such as marriage and are inevitably punished for their temerity (Felice, Eustacia and Arabella are amongst a much longer list of examples). It is through the mouthpieces of this cavalcade of heroines that Hardy took aim at some of the sacred cows of Victorian life, beginning with marriage.

Hardy's views on marriage have been well-documented from the first mutterings in *Desperate Remedies* to the open opposition of Sue in *Jude the Obscure*. In *The Well-Beloved* he launched a last, oblique attack on marriage which was also his darkest comment on the subject. When Pierston tells Marcia before they married *'I have no love to give, you know, Marcia, but such friendship as I am capable of is yours till the end'*, he manages to reduce marriage to merely fulfilling a social need, rounding off *'other people's histories'* in *'the best machine-made conventional manner'* without any talk of love. (Pt. 3, Ch. 8)

Divorce is also one of Hardy's targets and a central theme in *The Woodlanders* and *Jude the Obscure* where the law is manipulated, ridiculed and ignored. By raising the issue, Hardy highlighted the iniquitous situation married women could find themselves in, but despite a private members' bill in 1923 that made it easier for women to petition for divorce for adultery and a change in the law in 1937 to include drunkenness, insanity and desertion as grounds for ending a marriage, it was not until 1969 when the Divorce Reform Act allowed for a two-year period of separation that Hardy would have felt that some sort of justice had been achieved.

Hardy's views regarding suffrage were less progressive than the social commentary of his novels would suggest. In 1892, he wrote a letter to Alice Grenfell thanking *'the committee of the Women's Progressive Society for their proposal to elect me as Vice-President, but I must unfortunately decline it being that I have not as yet been converted to a belief in the desirability of the society's first object'* (the first object being women's suffrage).[28] Not long after, however, he did become a convert and it is very likely that it was the result of him succumbing to the lures of a pretty woman, Agnes Grove whom he met in 1895. She was a strong advocate for women's suffrage having made her name writing on the subject and soon convinced Hardy of the worthiness of the cause. It was also helpful in his relationship with Emma when he supported her by becoming a supporter of the movement. In 1907 both took part in a march in London organised by the National Union of Suffrage Societies, in the company of many other reformists and writers, including George Bernard Shaw. As well as counting such feminists as Marie Stopes amongst his correspondents, Hardy was also undergoing a significant change in his own affections, shifting from Florence (Henniker) to Florence (Dugdale) in the decade following the publication of *Jude the Obscure*. Both were to become significant influences on him during the remainder of Emma's life and beyond.

Amongst the many charges levelled at Hardy, was one of voyeurism. As a novelist, Hardy would no doubt protest that his observational skills and jottings were his bread and butter, yet there are times when his observations on the women he met at crushes or dinner parties seemed to be unusually intrusive. There are still some scenes (those that escaped the censor's pencil) that can still make the reader uneasy, for instance, the stalking of the second Avice in *The Well-Beloved*; and Captain de Stancy observing Paula Power in her pink costume through a hole in the wall of the gymnasium in *A Laodicean*. His preternatural interest in the female form even extended to the dead female form as we know from his sexually charged description of the hanging of Martha Browne witnessed when he was an adolescent (*'and how her tight black gown set off her shape as she wheeled half-round and back'*).[29]

Hardy was not someone women felt mistrustful of despite his proclivities and, indeed, as with Lady Portsmouth's daughters, who very much enjoyed his company, he was a popular house guest. It was felt that he had an intuitive understanding of women and imbued his heroines with the sensibilities and sensitivities that other women were able to identify with even though his depiction of them, warts and all, could have the effect of dividing.

Hardy's references and allusions to various subjects he raises in his novels, such as extra-marital sex, divorce and incest raised the hackles of his Victorian readers, but also educated them in the most pressing social issues of the time. In the same way, the struggles of his heroines against convention and the patriarchy have aroused the wrath of feminists, although they are the group with whom Hardy would have most identified. Despite all the charges levelled against him, of representing the patriarchy, of presenting characters who were flawed and amoral, the charge that is leveled against Hardy of being a misogynist, seems strangely misplaced. Hardy would undoubtedly have argued that he was, rather, a feminist and on balance, his writing supports this view. In a response to a letter he received following the publication of *The Return of the Native* Hardy was at pains to defend his portrayal of Bathsheba by stating *'I have no great liking for the perfect woman of fiction,'* before providing the defensive caveat that *'I must add that no satire on the sex is intended in any case by the imperfections of my heroines.'*[30]

In her book *Ambivalence in Hardy* Dutta quotes several writers who berated Hardy, for his attitude towards women. Samuel Chew in his book *Thomas Hardy* published in 1921, wrote *'On the whole . . . Hardy's attitude towards women is unfavourable; his opinion of them is bitter. They have many good qualities of heart, but they are fickle and vain, insincere . . . and seductive'* noting a page further on that *'Daudet classified Hardy as a woman-hater, like Ibsen, and found in Hardy's rejection of Woman as a redemptive force the roots of his pessimism.'*[31] By imbuing his characters with a sexuality and physicality largely unknown in Victorian heroines and by restraining himself from making any overt moral or idealistic judgement on the way they conducted themselves, he defied the puritanical views of the age as well as upsetting the censor and the sensibilities of many of his readers. But in the process of tying his heroines into a world determined by fate and convention, by patriarchy and outmoded laws and attitudes, Hardy was surely making a case for them to be set free.

What we see after Hardy stopped writing novels is a blurring between fact and fiction. For many years, critics and readers speculated about the women who may have influenced Hardy's heroines even though views varied wildly with critics – for instance whether Emma was an influence on the characters of Sue or Arabella – or both. Several of his characters took on a life of their own and in the years after *Jude the Obscure* forward, we can see evidence of Hardy searching for the ideal that he had created or an amalgam, a pure Tess, perhaps with Eustacia's energy and Sue's intellect.

In the same way Hardy looked to escape himself – at one stage Millgate suggests that he wanted to model his own life on that of Horace Moule – and looked to women to facilitate his own escape.[32] Morgan cites as evidence for Hardy's *'love of gifted, imaginative, strong women'* his enduring friendship with Florence Henniker (once the fires of the summer of 1893 had blown out) and his admiration of George Sand. As his coterie of admirers grew, he took solace from the time he spent apart from Emma, living in his own world, where his heroines also had their place amongst his family and friends. [33] Later as he moved into old age with Florence by his side, his heroines, both real and imaginary, travelled with him, undimmed in memory and frozen in age and beauty so he could call upon them when he was in need of succour.

Conclusion

Misogynist, Fantasist, Romantic, Feminist: Just who was Thomas Hardy?

'I think he really needs affection and tenderness more than anyone I know – for life has dealt him some cruel blows. I remember, some years ago, he said to me most pathetically:- "I do not ask for much – I only want a little affection."'

Florence Hardy [1]

Who was Thomas Hardy and what, exactly, were the cruel blows life had dealt him other than an unfortunate first marriage? What made him feel that his was the 'saddest of lives?' And what led him on a pathway of obfuscation, of secrecy, hiding the details of his personal life to an extraordinary degree in a series of bonfires that raged from after the death of the first Mrs Hardy in 1912 until the death of the second Mrs Hardy a quarter of a century later?

At one stage early in *The Life* he conjectured *'Who will I be with in five years time?'* (it may not have reassured him in retrospect that the answer would have been Emma), and throughout his life he was pining for the ideal woman without really knowing what he would do if he found her. Without taking too much of what his characters say to heart, there is every reason to suspect that Hardy feared the impermanence of love. *'Nothing can ensure the continuance of love. It will evaporate like a spirit'* he wrote in *The Return of the Native*, and later, defined true love not as a positive, but as a threat, *'I love you to oppressiveness.'*

Everything he wrote suggested that he believed that marriage was not the culmination of love, but the opposite, not only capable of suffocating the impulse, but likely to do so. The ardent lover cannot stay ardent and when love goes through its metamorphosis, as it must, then it dulls. Hardy was no believer in constancy and when he wrote in *Desperate Remedies* that *'The love of an inconstant man is ten times more ardent than that of a faithful man'*, we should trust that he is speaking from the heart. For Hardy is nothing if not complicated, especially in his ambivalence towards women.

Hardy's own life was populated with strong women, particularly his mother who cast a shadow over his whole life. Early on he had been subject to the doting of Augusta Martin and the liveliness of the three Sparks cousins, Rebecca, Martha, and Tryphena. After his marriage to Emma which failed to provide him with the female companionship he needed, he made a number of friendships with attractive, intelligent and liberated women, often of a literary bent, but apart from the enduring friendship with Florence Henniker, none provided him with the succour and affection he sought. Florence Dugdale's appearance in 1905 led to seven years of emotional tumult for Hardy but even she, a devoted admirer, he managed to alienate by writing his wonderful and touching elegies to his previous wife, who he had neglected and spurned for much of their marriage, and then by falling in love with another when in his eighties. Hardy's second marriage, like his first, was, at best, companionable and by marrying a woman (Florence Dugdale) who was forty years younger than him Hardy was himself imitating Pierston's quest to overcome the challenge of ageing, in a rather pitiful example of life imitating art.

There are so many things we just don't know about Hardy. The subject of this book excludes other possibilities, including the speculation that Hardy had a physical and emotional relationship with Horace Moule, which would not have been unusual for the times. We still know so little about Hardy in the decade before he married Emma, largely because of Hardy's purge of many of the sources of information that would have cast him in an unfavourable light. It is not the place of this book to make assumptions about Hardy's sexuality, but nor should we assume that he had no other sexual experiences or that he was chaste when he met Emma, for both assumptions would be naïve. Academic scholarship might not provide the answers and it may be painstaking joining of dots between fact and fiction that takes us closer to him. His biographers are either ambivalent or silent on such matters and the admission by one redoubtable writer on Hardy that he would not feel able to write anything critical on Hardy, such was his admiration for the man and his work, highlights the difficulty we have in getting under Hardy's skin.

Whatever relationships he had in the years leading up to his marriage (and his later attempts to recreate the same fertile ground), his mind kept going back to women he had met earlier in his life and who he called up in his poetry. Of all the women he knew and who knew him, none influenced him more than his mother and possibly the idealization of his own creation, Tess, his pure woman. Who was the well-beloved? John Fowles thought that *'Before he married Emma, ' . . . she appeared to him as his Well-Beloved. However, gradually his fascination waned and he looked for the feminine ideal in other women. A series of beautiful women including Mary Scott-Sidons, Helen Matthews, Rosamund Tomson, Florence Henniker, Helen Patterson Allingham, Lady Agnes Grove, Gertrude Bugler, and Florence Dugdale, respectively, could have become the reincarnations of the Well-Beloved'* – to which list we could no doubt add others such as Agatha Thornycroft or even someone from his formative years.[2]

Hardy's place as a writer of women's issues has seen him criticised for his pessimism and for subjecting his heroines to the most brutal of lives in which they are made subject to the interference of men and the conventions of a society that was heavily weighted against them. Dutta in her study of Hardy's attitude to women began her book with a critics' debate that set out the various positions in regards Hardy and feminisim before concluding that it would be *'historically suspect'* for us to contemplate a feminist Hardy.[3] And yet there is much in Hardy's writing that endorsed and furthered the cause of women in the same way that Dickens' had done for the poor.

When Hardy wrote in a vein that seemed hostile to women – for instance, that a woman would marry any man, however wretched, simply so as not to be alone, (*Desperate Remedies* Pt. 16, Ch. 4), it is little wonder that, in the eyes of contemporary and subsequent feminist critics, he was implicated in the *'same misogynistic, patriarchal attitudes as his male contemporaries.'*[4] What is obvious is that he did his heroines few favours and the hopelessness of their condition added to the impression that there was little that was redemptive in Hardy's writing for womankind. Nor was there much evidence of his feminism in his treatment of his wives, showing little sympathy for Emma during her illness and even less for Florence when she required surgery for a possible cancerous tumour.

Yet despite his abiding pessimism, it was Hardy who raised so many of the issues that continue to affect women today. In this respect, he was in tune with the 'the woman question' that had gathered momentum in the second half of the nineteenth century with its *'demands for access to education and the professions suffrage, the right to divorce and liberation from other forms of injustice and discrimination'*, issues which still have resonance today.[5]

At the same time that Hardy was writing *Tess*, the French artist Jean-Leon Gérôme was painting one of his most celebrated paintings, 'Pygmalion and Galatea.' The painting depicts Ovid's legend of Pygmalion, in which the young sculptor was carving a statue of Galatea, depicted as his ideal woman, embodying beauty, grace and virtue. Pygmalion's creation was so exquisite that the sculptor fell in love with his own creation, embracing the cold stone and kissing its idealised form. In the painting, Gérôme captures the moment that Galatea is brought to life by Venus and, as Gérôme paints her, is half-stone and half-human.

There is much of the Pygmalion in Hardy. Having created Tess as his ideal woman and faithfully presented her as a Pure Woman, Hardy embarks on his own love affair with one of his own creations. He takes pleasure in listing the actresses lining up wanting to play the part of Tess and sees in Gertrude Bugler, his last great infatuation, the embodiment of Tess.[6] Little wonder that Emma and Florence stood so little chance of becoming his 'well-beloved.'

Amongst the many things we don't know for sure about Thomas Hardy was what stirred his heart. Why he was so unhappy for much of his life, pitting himself against the windmills of class, education, society and beauty. Tomalin asked the same question then attempted to answer her own question: *'Neither Hardy nor anyone else has explained where his black view of life came from. I have suggested that something in his constitution made him extraordinarily sensitive to humiliations, griefs and disappointment and that the wounds never healed but went on hurting him throughout his life.'*[7] It may also have come from some event, some relationship, some painful occurrence in his life that triggered feelings of remorse or guilt. What seems clear is whatever demon was in his breast, it was planted there before he married Emma, and was likely the result of some scarifying incident of a personal nature – perhaps the death of his dear friend, Horace Moule in 1873, with whom he was particularly close over these years or some early emotional trauma.

We sometimes forget how far Hardy travelled, from his humble beginnings at Bockhampton to the soirées and dining rooms of society London and what he gave up on the way in his quest to be recognised and acknowledged as a great writer. He was most at home with the women in his life – his own immediate family and his two wives, his many women friends and his heroines – yet few, if any, professed to really know him. He lived much of his life in his head and what he saw and imagined, and what he wrote about, often bore scant resemblance to the mundanity of his own life. He wrote on the plight of women and fought their fight in their Victorian settings, but even today, one suspects, such complex characters as Eustacia and Sue would find it difficult to cope. Hardy was elusive, emotional and pathologically secretive and while he enjoyed the company of women and professed to understand many of the hardships they had to endure, he struggled in his own relationships with them. Despite the thousands of words that have been written about him and his substantial body of work, he was, and remains, an enigma. Fitting then, that the last word should be the transparent lines from *The Well-Beloved* that we began with:

'Nobody would ever know the truth about him; what it was he had sought that had so eluded, tantalised and escaped him; what it was that had led him such a dance.'

That we may never know.

Footnotes

Abbreviations of correspondents:

FA F Adams
WB Walter Besant
HB Howard Bliss
EC Edward Clodd
SC Sydney Cockerell
FD Florence Dugdale (pre-February 1914)
GD George Douglas (Sir)
AG Alice Greenhill
EG Elspeth Grahame
AH (Lady) Alda Hoare
EH Emma Hardy
FH Florence Hardy (post February, 1914
JH Jemima Hardy
MJ Mary Jeune, Baroness St Helier
MH Mary Hawe
JSL J Stanley Little
TEL T E Lawrence
LM Louise MacCarthy
LM Lina Milman
KM Katharine Macquoid
RO Rebekah Owen
HP Hester Pinney (Lady)
JCP John Cowper Powys
JAS John Addington Symonds
MS Dr Marie Stopes
SS Siegfried Sassoon
LY Lousie Yearsley

The Early Life of Thomas Hardy, 1840 – 1891 and *The Later Years of Thomas Hardy, 1892 – 1928* are the two books that make up the single edition *The Life of Thomas Hardy* (Florence Hardy) used in writing this book. In the footnotes, identification is made separately as either *The Early Life* or *The Later Years*.

Introduction

(1) Rosalind Miles 'The Women of Wessex' pp 25-26 in Anne Smith *The Novels of Thomas Hardy* Vision Press, 1979
(2) *The Early Life*, p.288
(3) Gittings, R *Younger Thomas Hardy*, p.167
(4) Norman, A *Thomas Hardy Behind the Mask* referring to George Egerton's book Keynotes, p.98
(5) Millgate, M (ed) *Letters of Emma and Florence Hardy*, FH to LH, 7.4 14, p.97
(6) Millgate, M (ed) *Letters of Emma and Florence Hardy*, EH to MH, 1.11.1894, p.6
(7) Havelock Ellis in *Thomas Hardy: The Critical Heritage* ed R J Cox p.133
(8) Hubbard, Elbert 'Thomas Hardy's Women' in *Preachments: Elbert Hubbard's Selected Writings*, Part Four, (facsimile) Kessinger Publishing 2010 p.305
(9) *The Later Years*, p.196

Chapter 1

(1) *The Return of the Native* Chapter 4
(2) Kay-Robinson, Denys *The First Mrs Thomas Hardy*, p.23-24
(3) Thomas Hardy's Notebooks, p.32
(4) *The Early Life*, p.9
(5) *The Early Life*, p.24
(6) *The Early Life*, p.134
(7) *The Early Life*, p.25
(8) Tomalin, C *Thomas Hardy The Time-Torn Man* p.27
(9) *The Early Life*, p.21
(10) Gittings, R *Young Thomas Hardy* p.46
(11) *The Early Life*, p.27
(12) Herbert, Michael 'Hardy and Lawrence – and their mothers.' *The Thomas Hardy Journal*, Autumn, 2006, Vol XXII, p.127
(13) *Letters of Emma and Florence Hardy*, EH to EG 20.8.1899, pp.15-16
(14) Millgate, M *Thomas Hardy A Biography* p.21
(15) Gittings, R *Young Thomas Hardy* p.166
(16) Gittings, R *Young Thomas Hardy* pp.98-99

(17) *The Later Years*, p.11
(18) Gittings, R *The Older Hardy* p.432
(19) *The Later Years*, p.106
(20) *Collected Letters*, Volume 1 TH to JH, 1.4.87, p.163
(21) *The Later Years*, p.10
(22) *The Later Years*, p.11
(23) Gittings, *The Younger Hardy*, p.248
(24) Flower, Newman *Just as it Happened*, p.94

Chapter 2

(1) 'Conjecture,' *Thomas Hardy: The Complete Poems*
(2) Tomalin, C *Thomas Hardy The Time-Torn Man* p.59
(3) Millgate, Michael and Mottram, Stephen *Sisters: Mary and Kate Hardy as Teachers*, p.6
(4) *The Later Years*, p.220
(5) Tomalin, C *Thomas Hardy The Time-Torn Man* p.93
(6) Millgate, Michael and Stephen Mottram, p.11
(7) Ibid
(8) Winslow, Donald J *Thomas Hardy's Sister Kate* p.3
(9) Tomalin, C *Thomas Hardy The Time-Torn Man*, p.334
(10) Ibid p.287
(11) Diary entry 23 December 1925 cited in *The Later Years of Thomas Hardy*, p.245
(12) Tomalin, C *Thomas Hardy The Time-Torn Man* pp.264-265
(13) *The Later Years of Thomas Hardy* p. 170
(14) 'Conjecture' *Thomas Hardy: The Complete Poems*, p. 477
(15) Gittings, R *Young Thomas Hardy* p.291
(16) Brown, Joanna Cullen (ed) *Figures in a Wessex Landscape: Thomas Hardy's Picture of English Country Life* p.30
(17) Winslow, *Thomas Hardy's Sister Kate* p.23
(18) Ibid p.19
(19) Ibid p.13
(20) Ibid p.13
(21) Gittings R *The Older Hardy*, p.644. The source of Gittings quotes is John Antell, a local friend of the family who was one of those who gathered at Talbothays after the ceremony.

Chapter 3

(1) Millgate, Michael (ed), *The Letters of Emma and Florence Hardy*', FH to EC 3.12 1913 p.88
(2) Millgate, Michael (ed), *The Letters of Emma and Florence Hardy*' FH to EC, 3.12.1913 p.86
(3) Tomalin, C *Thomas Hardy The Time-Torn Man*, pp.137-138
(4) Millgate, Michael (ed), *The Letters of Emma and Florence Hardy* FH to HB, 10.01.1931 p.312
(5) *The Early Life*, pp.92-93
(6) Emma went on in the same flowing style with the rest of her description of the setting in ' . . . this very remote spot, with a beautiful sea-coast, and the wild Atlantic Ocean rolling in with its magnificent waves and spray, its white gulls, and black choughs and grey puffins, its cliffs and rocks and gorgeous sunsettings, sparkling redness in a track widening from the horizon to the shore.' Ibid, p.90-91
(7) Ibid p.94
(8) Ibid p.103
(9) Millgate, M 'Some Early Hardy's Scholars and Collectors' in *Thomas Hardy Texts and Contexts* p.194
(10) Ibid, p.95
(11) *The Early Life*, pp.132-133
(12) *Emma Hardy's Diaries*, p.40 (cited in *The First Mrs Hardy*, p.87)
(13) Tomalin, C *Thomas Hardy The Time-Torn Man*, p.153
(14) Ibid, p.147
(15) *The Early Years*, p.153 (also cited in Tomalin, p.148)
(16) Norman, A *Thomas Hardy Bockhampton and Beyond*, pp.106–116
(17) Tomalin, C *Thomas Hardy The Time-Torn Man*, p.178

(18) Millgate, Michael (ed), *The Letters of Emma and Florence Hardy*, EH to TH July, 1874 p.3
(19) *The Early Life*, p.151
(20) Purdy, R L and Millgate, M *Collected Letters*, Volume One, TH to EH, 16.05.1885 p.131
(21) Purdy, R L and Millgate M *Collected Letters*, Volume One TH to EH, 16 May, 1885 p.133
(22) Tomalin, C *Thomas Hardy The Time-Torn Man*, p.241
(23) Weber, C J *'Dearest Emmie'* pp.62
(24) Ibid p.66
(25) Tomalin, C *Thomas Hardy The Time-Torn Man*, p.240 citing Gertrude Atherton's 'Adventures of a Novelist,' p.258, in 'Interviews and Recollections,' p.26
(26) Fanny Stevenson to S. Colvin and D. Norton Williams, 1885, both cited in Tomalin p.239
(27) Ibid
(28) Tomalin, C *Thomas Hardy The Time-Torn Man*, p.240 citing 'Interviews and Recollections', p.41
(29) Millgate, Michael (ed), *The Letters of Emma and Florence Hardy*, EH to EG 20.08.1899 pp.15-16
(30) Millgate, M (ed), *The Letters of Emma and Florence Hardy*, EH to LM 3 November, 1903 p.26
(31) Millgate, M (ed), *The Letters of Emma and Florence Hardy*, EH to AH 6.05.1908 p.48
(32) Purdy, R L and Millgate, M *Collected Letters*, Volume One TH to EH, 24.01.1891, p.227
(33) Purdy, R L and Millgate, M *Collected Letters*, Volume One TH to EH, 11 – 18.04.1885 p.230-232
(34) *The Early Life*, p.32
(35) Weber, C J *'Dearest Emmie' Thomas Hardy's Letters to his First Wife* p.45
(36) Millgate, M (ed), *The Letters of Emma and Florence Hardy*, EH to LM, 6.05.1908 p.40
(37) Tomalin, C *Thomas Hardy The Time-Torn Man*, p.289 citing Jacques Blanche 'Mes Modèles' (1928), p.84
(38) A C Benson, the famously woman-fearing Cambridge academic, and the oft-quoted entry he made on Emma in his diary not long before her death.
(39) Llewelyn Powys, 'Recollections of Thomas Hardy'
(40) Seymour-Smith, p.610
(41) *The Early Life*, pp. 296-297
(42) Fincham, Anthony 'Emma Hardy: The (Mad) Woman in the Attic? *The Thomas Hardy Journal*, Autumn, 2006, Vol XXII, p.115
(43) Millgate, Michael (ed), *The Letters of Emma and Florence Hardy* FD to EC 07.03.13 p.78
(44) Millgate, Michael (ed), *The Letters of Emma and Florence Hardy* EH to EC 16.01.1913 p.76
(45) Singleton, Jon 'Spaces, Alleys, and other Lacunae: Emma Hardy's Late writings Restored' *The Thomas Hardy Journal*, Autumn, 2015, Vol XXXI pp.48-62
(46) *The Later Years*, pp.153-154

Chapter 4

(1) Millgate, Michael (ed), *The Letters of Emma and Florence Hardy* FH to TEL 05.03.28 p.275
(2) Millgate, Michael (ed), *The Letters of Emma and Florence Hardy* FH to RO 1.12.14, pp.101-102
(3) Millgate, Michael (ed), *The Letters of Emma and Florence Hardy* FD to EC 30.01.1913, p.77
(4) Gittings, R and Manton, Jo *The Second Mrs Hardy*, p.4
(5) Millgate, Michael (ed), *The Letters of Emma and Florence Hardy*, FD to EH, 15.07.1910
(6) Millgate, Michael (ed), *The Letters of Emma and Florence Hardy* FD to EH 30.09.1910 (Hardy had noted to Edward Clodd that the *Inspirer* was a novel about a wife who inspired her husband's novels).
(7) Millgate, Michael (ed), *The Letters of Emma and Florence Hardy* FD to EC 11.11.10 p.66

(8) Ibid
(9) Millgate, Michael (ed), *The Letters of Emma and Florence Hardy* FD to EC 19.11.10, p.68
(10) Ibid
(11) Millgate, Michael (ed), *The Letters of Emma and Florence Hardy* FD to EH 13.01.11, p.72
(12) Millgate, Michael (ed), *The Letters of Emma and Florence Hardy* FD to EC 11.12.11 p.73
(13) Millgate, Michael (ed), *The Letters of Emma and Florence Hardy* FD to EC 07.03.13 p.79
(14) Llewelyn Powys, 'Recollections of Thomas Hardy' (unpaginated)
(15) Norman, Andrew *Behind the Mask*, p.170
(16) Millgate, Michael (ed), *The Letters of Emma and Florence Hardy* FH to MS 14.09.23 p.203
(17) Millgate, Michael (ed), *The Letters of Emma and Florence Hardy* FH to SC 26.11.1922 p.193
(18) Millgate, Michael (ed), *The Letters of Emma and Florence Hardy* FD to EC 07.03.1913 p.78
(19) Millgate, Michael (ed), *The Letters of Emma and Florence Hardy* FD to EC 03.12.1913 p.86
(20) Millgate, Michael (ed), *The Letters of Emma and Florence Hardy* FH to SC 13.02.1914 p.93
(21) Millgate, Michael (ed), *The Letters of Emma and Florence Hardy* FH to AH 22.07.14 pp.98–99
(22) Millgate, Michael (ed), *The Letters of Emma and Florence Hardy* FH to AH 06.12.14 p.104
(23) Ibid
(24) Millgate, Michael (ed), *The Letters of Emma and Florence Hardy* FD to EC 30.01.13 p.77
(25) Millgate, Michael (ed), *The Letters of Emma and Florence Hardy* FH to RO 18.01.16 p.114
(26) Millgate, Michael (ed), *The Letters of Emma and Florence Hardy* FH to RO 13.12.17 p.136
(27) Millgate, Michael (ed), *The Letters of Emma and Florence Hardy* FH to SC 07.12.18 p.139
(28) Millgate, Michael (ed), *The Letters of Emma and Florence Hardy* FH to EC 03.12.13 p.86
(29) Millgate, Michael (ed), *The Letters of Emma and Florence Hardy* FH to SC 23.07.17 p.132
(30) Millgate, Michael (ed), *The Letters of Emma and Florence Hardy* FH to SC 07.12.18 p.139
(31) Millgate, Michael (ed), *The Letters of Emma and Florence Hardy* FH to SC 30.01.19 p.155
(32) Millgate, Michael (ed), *The Letters of Emma and Florence Hardy* FH to SC 03.01.21 p.179
(33) Millgate, Michael (ed), *The Letters of Emma and Florence Hardy* FH to SC 17.12.22 p.194
(34) Ibid
(35) Millgate, Michael (ed), *The Letters of Emma and Florence Hardy* FH to MS 10.08.27 p.203
(36) Millgate, Michael (ed), *The Letters of Emma and Florence Hardy* FH to SS 24.02.28 p.273
(37) Gittings, R and Manton Jo *The Second Mrs Hardy*, p.109
(38) Millgate, Michael (ed), *The Letters of Emma and Florence Hardy* FH to JCP 15.08.29 p.299
(39) Ibid
(40) Gittings, R and Manton, Jo *The Second Mrs Hardy*, p.116
(41) Millgate, Michael (ed), *The Letters of Emma and Florence Hardy* FH to HB 1934
(42) Millgate, Michael (ed), *The Letters of Emma and Florence Hardy* FH to FA 20.12.36 p.341
(43) Ibid
(44) Millgate, Michael (ed), *The Letters of Emma and Florence Hardy* FD to EC 03.12.13 p.88
(45) Millgate, M (ed), *The Letters of Emma and Florence Hardy* FH to SC 02.04.1922 p.182
(46) *Thomas Hardy The Time-Torn Man* p.301
(47) Seymour-Smith, M *Hardy*, p. 692
(48) Millgate, M (ed), *The Letters of Emma and Florence Hardy* FH to SS 30 June, 1922, p.xxii
(49) Seymour-Smith, *Hardy* , pp.767-794

(50) *The Thomas Hardy Journal* Vol XX, No 3 October, 2004 Chairman's Notes, pp.10-11

Chapter 5

(1) *The Early Life*, p.292
(2) *The Early Life*, p.33
(3) Millgate, M 'Some Early Hardy's Scholars and Collectors' in *Thomas Hardy Texts and Contexts* p.194. In the same article, Florence Hardy is quoted as having talked with Henry Reed about her husband's relationships with Horace Moule and that Hardy's affection for him were 'impossible to overestimate'.
(4) Seymour-Smith, *Hardy* p.32
(5) Brown, Joanna Cullen (ed) *Figures in a Wessex Landscape: Thomas Hardy's Picture of English Country Life*, p.34
(6) Millgate, M *Thomas Hardy A Biography*, p.100
(7) Millgate, Michael and Mottram, Stephen 'Eliza Bright Nicholls: New Source, Old Problems' *The Thomas Hardy Journal*, Autumn, 2010, Vol XXVI, p.33
(8) Ibid p.31
(9) Tomalin, C *Thomas Hardy The Time-Torn Man*, p.94
(10) Ibid p.94
(11) Gittings R, *Young Thomas Hardy* p.229
(12) Gittings R, *Young Thomas Hardy* p.248
(13) Ibid p.248
(14) Tomalin, C *Thomas Hardy The Time-Torn Man*, p.150
(15) Deacon, Lois and Coleman, Terry *Providence and Mr Hardy* pp.22, 170-174
(16) Deacon, L *'The Chosen' by Thomas Hardy: Five Women in Blend – an Identification*
(17) Gittings *Young Thomas Hardy*, p.313
(18) Gittings *Young Thomas Hardy*, p.315
(19) Gittings *Young Thomas Hardy*, p.241
(20) Millgate, M *Thomas Hardy A Biography*, p.106
(21) Millgate, M *Thomas Hardy A Biography*, Ibid
(22) Millgate, M *Thomas Hardy A Biography*, p.84
(23) Seymour-Smith, *Hardy* pp.92-98
(24) Hillyard, N *Introduction to 'About Tryphena.'*
(25) Larkin, P, from a review of Gittings, R *Young Thomas Hardy.*
(26) Tomalin, C *Thomas Hardy The Time-Torn Man*, p.281
(27) Preface to *Jude the Obscure*, Ibid, p.248
(28) Hillyard, Nicholas *About Tryphena* 2007 XXXVI

Chapter 6

(1) Tomalin, C *Thomas Hardy The Time-Torn Man*, p.241. Tomalin, however, is mistaken in suggesting Rosamund left Arthur Tomson for a third husband. Despite her long relationship with H B Marriott Watson, including having a child with him, they never married.
(2) 'An Old Likeness' (Recalling R.T.) *Collected Poems* 631 , p.669
(3) Purdy and Millgate *Collected Letters*, Volume 2, TH to FH, 16.7.93
(4) Millgate, M *Thomas Hardy A Biography*, p.298
(5) Millgate, Michael (ed), *The Letters of Emma and Florence Hardy* FH to AH, 9 December, 1914.
(6) Tomalin, C *Thomas Hardy The Time-Torn Man*, p.246 noted that 'Hardy knew many aristocratic women, but he had never met one so congenial, so delightful, so intelligently responsive and intuitive.'
(7) *The Later Years*, p.18
(8) *The Later Years*, p.19
(9) Dalziel, Pamela *Thomas Hardy: The Excluded and Collaborative Stories* (Oxford: Clarendon Press, 1992), 260
(10) Purdy, R and Millgate, M *Collected Letters of Thomas Hardy*, Vol 2, TH to FH,

3.6.93 p.10 (n. b. Pearl Cragie wrote under the pseudonym, John Oliver Hobbes)
(11) Ibid p.14
(12) Ibid TH to FH 20.6.93 pp16-17
(13) Purdy, RL and Millgate, M (ed), Collected Letters of Thomas Hardy, Volume Two, p.18
(14) Hardy, Evelyn and Pinion, FB *One Rare, Fair Woman*, TH to FH, July 13, 1893, p.13
(15) Gittings, R *The Older Hardy* pp.464-465
(16) *Collected Letters of Thomas Hardy*, Vol 2, TH to FH, 17 August, 1893, p.28
(17) Ibid TH to FH p.33
(18) Ibid TH to FH p.23
(19) Purdy, RL and Millgate, M (ed), *Collected Letters of Thomas Hardy* Vol 2 TH to FH 18. 12 93, p.44 (ORFW, p.39)
(20) Hardy, Evelyn and Pinion, FB (ed), *One Rare, Fair Woman*, TH to FH 4.8.95 p.41
(21) Ibid TH to FH 1.6.96 p.52
(22) Ibid TH to FH (undated) p.64
(23) Ibid TH to FH 1.1.99 p.75
(24) Ibid TH to FH 23.8.99 p.82
(25) Ibid TH to FH 25.2.00 p.92
(26) Ibid TH to FH 19.12.1910 p.143
(27) 'In 1896, Hardy told his friend, Edward Clodd that Mrs Henniker had been his 'model' for Sue; his second wife Florence told Professor Purdy that Sue Bridehead was 'in part drawn from Mrs Henniker.' Pinion, F *Hardy the Writer: Surveys and Assessments*, p.156
(28) 'A Broken Appointment' first published in 1901 in the collection, *Poems of the Past and the Present.*
(29) Tomalin, C *Thomas Hardy The Time-Torn Man*, Footnote 7 p.427 that states 'Florence Henniker kept a bundle of manuscript poems given to her by Hardy, which have sadly disappeared.'
(30) Seymour-Smith, *Hardy*, p.403
(31) *The Later Years*, p.230
(32) *Letters of Emma and Florence Hardy*, FH to LY, 10.4.23 pp,126–127
(33) *Letters of Emma and Florence Hardy,* FH to SC 28.5.23, p.200
Interesting, considering how close Florence felt they were, there are no extant letters from one to the other. Perhaps this was Thomas's exclusive territory.

Chapter 7

(1) Hawkins, Desmond *Concerning Agnes: Thomas Hardy's Good Little Pupil*, p.92
(2) Local newspaper account of the evening as noted in *The Latter Years of Thomas Hardy*, p.37
(3) Hawkins, Desmond Concerning Agnes: Thomas Hardy's Good Little Pupil p.95
(4) Purdy, RL and Millgate, M (ed), *Collected Letters of Thomas Hardy*, Volume 2, p.87
(5) *The Latter Years*, p. 53
(6) Hawkins, Desmond, *Concerning Agnes: Thomas Hardy's Good Little Pupil*, p.28
(7) Ibid p.29
(8) Ibid p.30
(9) Ibid p.96
(10) Purdy, RL and Millgate M (ed), *Collected Letters of Thomas Hardy* Volume 2, TH to AG, 3.11.95, p.91
(11) Ibid TH to FH, 10.11.95 p.94
(12) Ibid TH to FH 12.8.95 p.84
(13) Hawkins, Desmond *Concerning Agnes: Thomas Hardy's Good Little Pupil*, p.77-78
(14) Ibid pp.64 and 75
(15) Purdy, RL and Millgate, M (ed), *Collected Letters of Thomas Hardy* Volume 2, TH to AG, 3.11.95, p.91
(16) Ibid TH to AG, 7.11.95 p.92
(17) Ibid TH to AG, 24.4.96 p.117
(18) Ibid TH to AG, 25.8.96 p.128
(19) Ibid TH to AG, 15.11.96 p.137
(20) Ibid TH to AG, 20.9.99 p.230
(21) Ibid TH to AG, 16.2.00 p.247
(22) Ibid TH to MJ, 12.7.97 p.171
(23) Hawkins, Desmond *Concerning Agnes: Thomas Hardy's Good Little Pupil*, p.122
(24) Ibid p.124
(25) Ibid p.125
(26) Ibid pp.125-126

(27) Purdy, RL and Millgate, M (ed), *Collected Letters of Thomas Hardy*, Vol 3, TH to AG, p.354. Cited in Dutta, S p.158
(28) Purdy, RL and Millgate, M (ed), *Collected Letters of Thomas Hardy*, Vol 2, TH to AG 6.12.96 p.140 Early in their relationship, Hardy had remarked in a letter to Agnes, 'what an energetic scribe you are becoming!'
(29) Hawkins, Desmond *Concerning Agnes: Thomas Hardy's Good Little Pupil*, p.138

Chapter 8

(1) Millgate, M *Thomas Hardy A Biography*, p.293
(2) Gittings, *The Older Hardy*, p.622
(3) Ibid
(4) Millgate, Michael (ed), *The Letters of Emma and Florence Hardy*, FH to LY, 30.12.20 p.172
(5) Millgate, Michael (ed), *The Letters of Emma and Florence Hardy*, FH to SC, 26.12.20 p.171
(6) Gittings, R *The Older Hardy* p.623 (Tomalin refers to the same letter although the wording differs, if not the meaning: 'As you must know this (calling unannounced) is a most extraordinary thing to do. In the first place, all invitations to Max Gate naturally come from me . . . and again it is not usual in our station of life for any lady to call upon a gentleman. It is simply "not done". P. 353 citing Florence Hardy to Gertrude Bugler, 13 June 1922 in possession of Gertrude Bugler)
(7) Tomalin, C *Thomas Hardy The Time-Torn Man*, p.353 and Letters of Emma and Florence Hardy (FH to SC 26.11.22, p.193
(8) Bugler, G 'Personal Recollection of Thomas Hardy' (unpaginated)
(9) Tomalin, C *Thomas Hardy The Time-Torn Man*. According to Tomalin, Cockerell's attendance was the result of a request from an emotional Florence for him to be at the meeting because of the gossip she imagined was circulating about Thomas's obsession with her p.354.
(10) Bugler, G 'Personal Recollection of Thomas Hardy' (unpaginated)
(11) Bugler, G 'Personal Recollection of Thomas Hardy' (unpaginated)
(12) Blunt, W *Cockerell* p.216
(13) Tomalin, C *Thomas Hardy The Time-Torn Man*, p.352-356
(14) Ibid p.355
(15) Bugler, G *Personal Reminiscences*
(16) Millgate, M *Thomas Hardy A Biography* p.556
(17) Ibid
(18) Ibid
(19) Blunt, W *Cockerell*, p.215
(20) This is at odds with the entry in Hardy's diary which noted '12 F's birthday. Mrs Gertrude Bugler lunched. Cockerell left' (although this may have been written retrospectively). Cited in Seymour, p.843
(21) Norman, A *Thomas Hardy : Behind the Mask* p.194 (this was the quote about Mary referred to in chapter two that 'She came into the world . . . and went out . . . and the world is just the same . . . not a ripple on the surface left' to which Norman added that it unkindly glossed over Mary's skill as a portrait painter who painted excellent portraits of several members of the family – apart from all else she achieved, professionally as a head teacher.)
(22) Hardy, FE *The Life of Thomas Hardy*, p.222
(23) Ibid p.236
(24) Ibid p.237
(25) Ibid p.240
(26) Millgate, Michael (ed), *Letters of Emma and Florence Hardy*, FH to EC, 8.8.25 p.226
(27) Seymour *Hardy* p.846
(28) Nicholson 'Winter'
(29) Wilkins, Damien 'Max Gate'
(30) Tomalin, C *Thomas Hardy The Time-Torn Man*, p.356 re. *The Personal Notebooks of Thomas Hardy*, ed Richard H Taylor, 1978, p.92. The translation of the whole passage that Hardy copied down reads; 'Few people understand the subjective nature of love and the way it creates another being, different from the actual person bearing

the same name, and endowed with characteristics for the most part imagined by the lover . . . Desire arises, satisfies itself and disappears – that's all there is to it. So the young person you marry is not the person you fell in love with.'

(31) Tomalin, C *Thomas Hardy The Time-Torn Man*, p.356
(32) Blunt *Cockerell* pp222-223
(33) Norman, A *Thomas Hardy: Behind the Mask*, p.188

Chapter 9

(1) It is estimated to be worth around close to £2000 today
(2) Included among these authors were Lewis Carroll, who paid the expenses of publishing *Alice's Adventures in Wonderland* and most of his subsequent work. Mark Twain, George Bernard Shaw, Edgar Allan Poe, Rudyard Kipling, Henry David Thoreau and Walt Whitman.
(3) Two years later, Tinsley refused to sell back the rights for £300
(4) *The Early Years* p.110
(5) Ibid p.111
(6) 'A great statesman thinks several times, and acts; a young lady acts, and thinks several times.' *Desperate Remedies* Ch. 8, Pt. 5
(7) 'Don't love too blindly: blindly you will love if you love at all, but a little care is still possible to a well-disciplined heart. May that heart be yours as it was not mine. Cultivate the art of renunciation.' *Desperate Remedies*, Ch. 1 Pt. 4
(8) Morgan, R 'Women and Sexuality in the novels of Thomas Hardy' p.5
(9) Ibid p.4
(10) Tomalin, C *Thomas Hardy The Time-Torn Man*, p.97
(11) Sylvia, Richard p.105-106
(12) Elvy, *Sexing Hardy Thomas Hardy and Feminism* p.34
(13) *The Early Years*, p.114
(14) Tomalin, C *Thomas Hardy The Time -Torn Man*, p.101
(15) Seymour-Smith, Hardy, p.139
(16) Hubbard, E *Thomas Hardy's Women* p.305
(17) Purdy, RL and Millgate, M (ed), *Collected Letters of Thomas Hardy*, Volume 4, p. 288 cited in Dutta, S, p.209
(18) Hubbard, E *Thomas Hardy's Women* p.302
(19) Ibid p.302
(20) Morgan, R *Women and Sexuality in the novels of Thomas Hardy* p.8
(21) Ibid
(22) *Thomas Hardy Notebooks*, p.48 (although Seymour-Smith reminds us (p.423) of George Douglas's comment of Emma that ' she has the makings of a Bathsheba, with restricted opportunities.'
(23) Cox, XVII and Dutta, p.2
(24) Tomalin, C *Thomas Hardy The Time-Torn Man*, p.137-139
(25) *The Younger Hardy*, pp.211-212
(26) Thirwell, *Introduction to Under the Greenwood Tree*, p.xv
(27) *Far from the Madding Crowd* chapter 28 and Elvy, M p.80. Some of the interpretations of what Elvy describes as 'the famous phallic sword-weilding scene between Troy and Bathsheba are particularly Freudian, Elvy writes 'Hardy's narrator makes it clear that Troy's sword display corresponds to sexual intercourse; as in pornography, the narrator concentrates on Bathsheba's bodily responses to Troy's phallic thrusts.' Other interpretations are no less suggestive, but rather more prosaic.
(28) Apart from legal status, a lot has not changed and that would disappoint Hardy. Goldie Hawn summed up the present position of women when she wrote 'We've cracked our heads on the glass ceiling, and I know that I've got bumps all over the top of my head. But, you know, things change very slowly. It's really hard to be a ballsy, tough woman, and be liked by everybody, and not carry some sort of reputation or baggage before you even walk in the room. I think it's changed a bit. But it's still tough.' – Goldie Hawn interview in the *DT*, 6 May, 2017.

Chapter 10

(1) *The Early Years*, p.147
(2) Tomalin, C *Thomas Hardy The Time-Torn Man*, p.147
(3) Tomalin, C *Thomas Hardy The Time-Torn Man*, p.184
(4) Gosse was even more critical when he reviewed *Jude the Obscure* leading to a much more serious falling out between the two writers.
(5) Gittings, R *Young Thomas Hardy* p.289
(6) Gittings, R *Young Thomas Hardy* p.290
(7) Gittings, R *Young Thomas Hardy* p.292 'Ethelberta's socially unmentionable relatives ... turn out to be a fascinating amalgam of Hardy's own.'
(8) Jekel, P *Thomas Hardy's Heroines* p.75-76
(9) Millgate, M *Thomas Hardy A Biography*, p.174
(10) Tomalin, C *Thomas Hardy The Time-Torn Man*, p.148
(11) Pite *Thomas Hardy: The Guarded Life* p.228
(12) Tomalin, C *Thomas Hardy The Time-Torn Man* p.148
(13) Morgan, R *Women and Sexuality in the novels of Thomas Hardy* p.156
(14) Rosamund Tomson married, first a wealthy Australian, George Armytage with whom she had two daughters. When the youngest was two years old, she left Armytage and eloped with the artist, Arthur Tomson with whom she lived for several years. After divorcing him she lived with the novelist H B Marriott until her early death. They never married.
(15) Julian Hawthorne in *Spectator*, in *Thomas Hardy: The Critical Heritage* ed R J Cox p.75
(16) Review of *The Trumpet Major* in *Athenaeum* from November 1880. From *Thomas Hardy: The Critical Heritage* ed R J Cox p.72
(17) Havelock Ellis, p.131
(18) Ibid p.131
(19) Julian Hawthorne in *Spectator*, in *Thomas Hardy: The Critical Heritage* ed R J Cox , p.76
(20) Ibid p.76
(21) Review in *Athenaeum*, in *Thomas Hardy: The Critical Heritage* ed R J Cox p.72
(22) Havelock Ellis, *Thomas Hardy: The Critical Heritage* ed R J Cox p.133 in Cox, ed
(23) Unsigned Review, 1881, in Cox, ed *Thomas Hardy: The Critical Heritage* p.109
(24) Pite, *Thomas Hardy: The Guarded Life* p.259
(25) Seymour-Smith, *Hardy* p.270-271
(26) Harry Quilter's review in the *Spectator* November, 1883
(27) As recalled in the poem 'The Dream Follower' F B Pinion, 'The Ranging Vision' in *Thomas Hardy after Fifty Years*, ed Lance St John Butler, Macmillan, 1977, p.10)
(28) *Thomas Hardy The Time-Torn Man*, p.197
(29) *Thomas Hardy The Time-Torn Man*, p.196
(30) *Thomas Hardy The Time-Torn Man*, p.193
(31) Seymour-Smith, *Hardy* pp.288-289

Chapter 11

(1) Henry James cited in Thomas Hardy Notebooks.
(2) In 1912, Hardy divided his novels into three categories: the 'major' novels he grouped together as the Novels of Character and Environment: *Under the Greenwood Tree*, (1872), *Far from the Madding Crowd*, (1874), *The Return of the Native* (1878) *The Mayor of Casterbridge* (1886) *The Woodlander'* (1887), *Tess of the D'Urbervilles*, (1891) and *Jude the Obscure*, (1896) with the 'minor' novels being divided into two categories: The Novels of Ingenuity *Desperate Remedies*, (1871), *The Hand of Ethelberta* (1876) and *A Laodicean* (1881); and Romances and Fantasies: *A Pair of Blue Eyes*,(1873), *The Well-Beloved*, (1897), *The Trumpet Major*, (1880) and *Two on a Tower* (1882) plus the collection, *A Group of Noble Dames* (1889).
(3) *The Early Life*, p.222
(4) Purdy, RL and Millgate, M (ed),

Collected Letters of Thomas Hardy, Volume 1. TH to unnamed correspondent 19.10.85 p.136
(5) From an unsigned review of the novel in the *Saturday Review*, 29 May, 1886 in *Critical Heritage*, p.135.
(6) Ibid
(7) The entry refers to Hardy's entry in his notebook which read 'Mother's notion (and also mine) – that a figure stands in our van with arm uplifted, to knock us back from any pleasant prospect we indulge in as probable.'
(8) Hubbard, E *Thomas Hardy's Women* p.302
(9) *The Early Life* p.241
(10) *The Early Life* p.242
(11) *The Early Life* p.243
(12) Pinion, F B *Thomas Hardy: His Life and Friends* p.204
(13) *Thomas Hardy The Time-Torn Man*, p.219
(14) Pinion, F B introduction to the new Wessex edition of *The Woodlanders*, p.17
(15) Elvy, M *Sexing Hardy: Thomas Hardy and Feminism*, p.106
(16) Ibid, p.106
(17) William Wallace, Academy review of *The Woodlanders*, 9 April, 1887 from *Hardy: The Critical Heritage*, p.166
(18) Elvy, M *Sexing Hardy: Thomas Hardy and Feminism* p.102
(19) William Wallace, Academy review of *The Woodlanders*, 9 April, 1887 from *Hardy: The Critical Heritage*, p.154
(20) Millgate, p.317
(21) *The Early Life*, p.261
(22) *The Early Life*, p.262
(23) *The Early Life*, p.278
(24) *The Early Life*, p.289
(25) T O'Connor cited in Dutta, S *Ambivalence in Hardy*, p.6
(26) Richard le Gallienne's 1891 comment in *The Star*, p.6 Dutta
(27) Thwaite, Ann 'My Dear Gosse': The Friendship between Edmuund Gosse and Thomas Hardy' *The Thomas Hardy Journal* Vol XX No. 3 October 2004 p.47
(28) Gittings, R *The Older Hardy* p.401
(29) Morgan, R *Women and Sexuality in the novels of Thomas Hardy* p.85
(30) Nemesvari, Richard 'The Thing Must be Male, we suppose': Erotic Triangles and masculine Identity in *Tess of the D'Urbervilles* and Melville's *Billy Budd* in Mallet, P *Hardy: Texts and Context*, pp.87–109
(31) Morgan, R *Women and Sexuality in the novels of Thomas Hardy* p.98
(32) Fincham, T 'Tessexuality – A Victim Culture', *The Thomas Hardy Journal*, Autumn, 2007, Vol XXIII, p.126 with reference to Morgan, R, p.88
(33) Morgan, R *Women and Sexuality in the novels of Thomas Hardy* p.83
(34) *The Later Years*, p.6
(35) Morgan R, *Women and Sexuality in the novels of Thomas Hardy* p.85
(36) Pite, R *Thomas Hardy The Guarded Life*, p.329

Chapter 12

(1) Hubbard, E *Thomas Hardy's Women* p.303
(2) Pite, R *Thomas Hardy: The Guarded Life* p.327
(3) The Anti-Marriage League article of 1896 by Margaret Oliphant in *Blackwood Magazine* attacked Jude fiercely – Dutta, S p.4
(4) Dutta, S p.5 quoting Edmund Gosse's view of Sue Bridehead and of the novel itself
(5) *The Later Years*, p.50
(6) TH to FH, 10 November, 1895, Collected letters, p.94
(7) *The Later Years*, p.196
(8) *The Life*, p.48 in the preface of the 1912 edition of *Jude the Obscure*, Hardy mentions the incident of the book being burnt by the Bishop, adding 'probably in his despair at not being able to burn me.'
(9) Morgan, R *The Student Guide to Hardy*, pp.126–127
(10) Dutta, S *Ambivalence in Hardy: A Study of his Attitude Towards Women* p.153
(11) *The Later Years*, p.42
(12) Morgan, R *Women and Sexuality in the novels of Thomas Hardy* p.123

(13) Norman, A *Thomas Hardy: Behind the Mask* p.
(14) Dutta, S *Ambivalence in Hardy: A Study of his Attitude Towards Women* p.153
(15) Jekel, Pamela L *Thomas Hardy's Heroines: a chorus of priorities* p.142
(16) Fincham, Tony 'Tessexuality – A Victim', *The Thomas Hardy Journal* Vol XXIII, Autumn, 2007, p.134
(17) Morgan, R *Women and Sexuality in the Novels of Thomas Hardy* p.152
(18) see 'Sue Bridehead: A Representative of the Feminine Movement', Mohammad, Shazia Ghulam and Khalis, Abdus Salam from *The Journal of Humanities and Social Sciences*
(19) *The Later Years*, p.42
(20) *The Later Years*, pp.42-43
(21) Stubbs, P *Women and Fiction: Feminism and the Novel 1800–1920* p.60
(22) Morgan, R *Women and Sexuality in the novels of Thomas Hardy* p.126
(23) Thomas Hardy, Postscript to the Preface of the first edition of *Jude the Obscure*, April, 1912
(24) Lawrence, D H *Studies of Thomas Hardy and Other Essays*, ed Bruce Steele, Cambridge University Press, p.93
(25) 'A Young Man of Twenty', 'A Young Man of Forty', and 'A Young Man of Sixty'
(26) *The Early Years*, p.288
(27) *The Early Years*, pp.24-25
(28) Millgate, M *Thomas Hardy A Biography*, p.59
(29) Deacon and Coleman, *Providence and Mr Hardy* pp.204-205
(30) This was the result of Avice having married a namesake of Jocelyn, Isaac Pierston, which draws her tantalizingly closer in name, though not in love
(31) Fowles, John 'Hardy and the Hag', in *Thomas Hardy after Fifty Years* Lance St John Butler (ed) p.30
(32) Ibid p.34

Chapter 13

(1) Weber, Carl J *Thomas Hardy: His Life and Literary Career*, p.64
(2) *The Early Years*, p.110-111
(3) Purdy, RL and Millgate, M (ed), *Collected Letters of Thomas Hardy*, Vol 1 TH to JSL 22 4 92 p.265
(4) Purdy, R L and Millgate, M (ed), *Collected Letters of Thomas Hardy*, Vol 1, TH to WB, 17.01.92 p.252
(5) Purdy, RL and Millgate M, (ed), *Collected Letters of Thomas Hardy*, Vol 1, TH to EG 20.1.92, p.255 In the event, the main thrust of their attack was on the godlessness of Tess.
(6) Hardy in a letter to Edward Clodd lamented that one critic 'had a heart instead of a hollow place where his heart ought to be.' Purdy, RL and Millgate, M (ed), *Collected Letters of Thomas Hardy*, TH to EC, Vol 1. 4. 2 92, p.257
(7) Purdy, RL and Millgate, M (ed), *Collected Letters of Thomas Hardy*, TH to EG 20.1.92, p.255
(8) Ibid, TH to JAS 14.04.1889 p.190
(9) Millgate, M (ed), *The Letters of Emma and Florence Hardy* FD to ED 11. 11.1910
(10) Guerard, Albert J *Thomas Hardy: The Novels and Stories* Harvard University Press, Cambridge, Mass, 1949 p.68
(11) Thomas, Jane *Thomas Hardy and Desire: Conceptions of the Self* Palgrave Macmillan, 2013.
(12) Millgate, M (ed), *The Letters of Emma and Florence Hardy* FH to AH, 09.12.1914 p.105
(13) *The Early Life*, p.70
(14) Ibid, TH to LM, 4. 9. 93 p.28
(15) Ibid, TH to LM, 18. 9. 93, p.33
(16) 'Phantom Photographs: The Camera's Pursuit and disruption of consciousness in *Jude the Obscure* pp.72–84 *The Thomas Hardy Journal*, Autumn, 2006, Vol XXII,
(17) *The Early Years*, p.311
(18) *The Later Years*, pp.22- 23
(19) *The Later Years*, pp.31-32
(20) *The Early Years*, p.295
(21) *The Early Years*, p.293
(22) *The Early Years*, p.308
(23) *The Later Years*, p.26
(24) Purdy, RL and Millgate, M (ed), *Collected Letters of Thomas Hardy* Vol 1, p.249 TH to GD 30.12.1891

(25) Rimmer, Mary 'History and the Bogus Heroine: Gender and Genre in *The Trumpet-Major The Thomas Hardy Journal*, Autumn, 2010, Vol XXVII Autumn, 2012, pp.70-80
(26) *The Early Years*, p.301
(27) Thomas, J, *Thomas Hardy and and Desire: Conceptions of the Self* p.48
(28) Purdy, R L and Millgate, M (ed), *Collected Letters of Thomas Hardy* TH to AG, 23 April, 1892 p.266
(29) Millgate, M *Thomas Hardy A Biography*, p.63
(30) Purdy, R L and Millgate, M (ed), *Collected Letters of Thomas Hardy* Vol I, TH to KM 17.11.1874
(31) Dutta, S *Ambivalence in Hardy: A Study of his Attitude Towards Women* pp.33–36
(32) Millgate, M *Thomas Hardy A Biography*, p.68
(33) Morgan, R *Women and Sexuality in the Novels of Thomas Hardy*, p.156

Conclusion

(1) Millgate, M (ed), *The Letters of Emma and Florence Hardy*, FH to LH 22.7.14 p.98-99
(2) Diniejko, A 'A Quest for the Eternal Feminine Ideal in *The Well-Beloved*' p.1
(3) Dutta, S, *Ambivalence in Hardy: A Study of his Attitude Towards Women* p.21
(4) *The Hardy Society Journal* Spring, 2006, Vol 2, No. 1 'Whatever happened to "Good Little Thomas Hardy?"' pp.21-29
(5) Al-Ajmi, Nada 'Women in Thomas Hardy's "On the Western Circuit" ' *The Hardy Society Journal*, Summer, 2006, Vol 2, no. 2 pp.44-51
(6) *The Later Years*, p.33
(7) *Thomas Hardy The Time-Torn Man*, p.223. On the following page Tomalin recounts the letter Hardy sent to Rider Haggard on the death of his ten year old son, offering his sympathy before making the extraordinary statement that ' . . . to be candid, I think the death of a child is never really to be regretted when one reflects on what he has escaped.' Purdy, RL and Millgate, M (ed), *Collected Letters of Thomas Hardy* Volume 1, p.135

Selected Bibliography

Al-Ajmi, Nada 'Women in Thomas Hardy's "On the Western Circuit"' *The Hardy Society Journal*, Vol 2, No 2 pp.44-51

Blunt, W *Cockerell*, Hamish Hamilton, London, 1964

Boylan, Rebecca Warburton 'Phantom Photographs: The Camera's Pursuit and Disruption of Consciousness in *Jude the Obscure' Thomas Hardy Journal*, Vol. XXII Autumn, 2006, pp.72-84

Brown, Joanna Cullen (ed) *Figures in a Wessex Landscape: Thomas Hardy's Picture of English Country Life,* W H Allen, 1987

Bugler, Gertrude 'Personal Recollections of Thomas Hardy' *The Dorset Natural History and Archaeological Society*, The Friary Press, 1962

Bulaila, Aziz '*Desperate Remedies:* Not Just a Minor Novel.' *The Thomas Hardy Journal 14* (1998): 65-74

Cox, R G ed *Thomas Hardy: The Critical Heritage*, Routledge, New York, 1979

Dalziel, Pamela *Thomas Hardy: The Excluded and Collaborative Stories*, Clarendon Press, 1992

Dalziel, Pamela 'Whatever Happened to Elizabeth Jane? Revisiting Gender in *The Mayor of Casterbridge*, in Mallett, Thomas *Hardy: Texts and Contexts*, pp.64-86

Daleski, HM *Thomas Hardy and Paradoxes of Love*, University of Missouri Press, 1997

Deacon, L *'The Chosen' by Thomas Hardy' Five Women in Blend – An Identification* Toucan Press, St Peter Port, Guernsey 1966

Deacon, Lois and Coleman, Terry *Providence and Mr Hardy*, Hutchinson, London 1966

De Casseres, Benjamin 'Thomas Hardy's Women', *The Bookman*, October, 1902 pp.131-133

Diniejko, A 'A Quest for the Eternal Feminine Ideal in *The Well-Beloved* by Thomas Hardy' Victorian web October, 2015

Doheny, John R 'The Characterisation of Jude and Sue: the Myth and the Reality' in Mallett, P *Thomas Hardy: Texts and Contexts* pp.110-132

Dorn, Maria '"I won't be a Slave to the Past – I'll love where I choose": Gender and Time Paradigms in *The Mayor of Casterbridge*', *The Thomas Hardy Journal*, Vol XXVII Autumn, 2012, pp.114-126

Dutta, S *Ambivalence in Hardy: A Study of his Attitude Towards Women*, Palgrave Macmillan, 2000

Elvy, Margaret *Sexing Hardy: Thomas Hardy and Feminism* Crescent Moon Publishing, 2nd edition, 2007

Fang, L Q, & Jiang, W Q 'Thomas Hardy's Feminist Consciousness in *Jude the Obscure' Studies in Literature and Language*, 2015

Fincham, Tony 'Tessexuality – A Victim', *The Thomas Hardy Journal*, Autumn, 2007, Vol XXIII, pp.126-136

Flower, Sir Newman *Just as it Happened,* Cassell, London, 1950

Gibson, James (ed) *Thomas Hardy: Interviews and Recollections,* Macmillan, 1999

Gittings, Robert *Young Thomas Hardy,* Penguin Books, 1978

Gittings, Robert *The Older Hardy,* Penguin, 1980

Gosse, Edmund 'Mr Hardy's New Novel', *Cosmopolis*, 1 January 1896

Guerard, Albert J *Thomas Hardy: The Novels and Stories,* Harvard University Press, 1949

Hardy, Emma *Alleys,* April, 1912

Hardy, Evelyn (ed and notes) *Thomas Hardy's Notebooks* (and some Letters from Julia Augusta Martin), The Hogarth Press, 1955

Hardy, Evelyn and Pinion F B, (ed) *One Rare Fair Woman Thomas Hardy's Letter to Florence Henniker, 1893 – 1922*

Hardy, Florence *The Early Life of Thomas Hardy, 1840 – 1891,* Macmillan, 1928

Hardy, Florence *The Later Years of Thomas Hardy, 1892 – 1928*, Macmillan, 1930

Hardy, Thomas Poems and Novels

Hardy, Thomas and Gibson, James (ed) *Thomas Hardy The Complete Poems*, Palgrave Macmillan, 2001

Hawkins, Desmond *Concerning Agnes Thomas Hardy's 'Good Little Pupil',* Alan Sutton, 1982

Herbert, Michael 'Hardy and Lawrence and their Mothers', *The Thomas Hardy Journal*, Vol. XXII, Autumn, 2006, p.127

Hillyard, Nicholas *About Tryphena*, 2007 (private publication)

Hubbard, Elbert *Thomas Hardy's Women* – Pamphlet (extracted from the book *Preachments: Elbert Hubbard's Selected Writings Part 4*)

Jekel, Pamela L *Thomas Hardy's Heroines: a chorus of priorities* Thomas Hardy's Heroines, Whitston Publishing, 1986

Kay-Robinson, Denys *The First Mrs Thomas Hardy,* Macmillan, 1979

Larkin, Philip Review of 'The Young Hardy by R. Gittings ' published in *The New Statesman*, 18.04.75

Lawrence, D H *Studies of Thomas Hardy and Other Essays*, ed Bruce Steele, Cambridge University Press

Mallett, Phillip (ed) *Thomas Hardy: Texts and Contexts,* Palgrave Macmillan, 2002

Mallett, Phillip V and Draper, Ronald P (ed) *A Spacious Vision: Essays on Hardy*, The Patten Press, Newmill, 1994

Millgate, Michael *Thomas Hardy A Biography,* Oxford University Press, 1985

Millgate, Michael (ed) *Letters of Emma and Florence Hardy*, Clarendon Press, Oxford, 1996

Millgate, Michael and Mottram, Stephen 'Sisters: Mary and Kate Hardy as Teachers' *The Thomas Hardy Journal*, Volume XXV, Autumn 2009

Millgate, Michael and Mottram, Stephen 'Eliza Nicholls: New Source, Old Problems' *The Thomas Hardy Journal*, Volume XXVI, Autumn 2010

Millgate, M 'Some Early Hardy Scholars and Collectors' in *Thomas Hardy Texts and Contexts* p.194

Mohammad, Shazia Ghulum and Abdus, Salam Khalis 'Sue Bridehead: A Representative of the Feminist Movement' *The Journal of Humanities and Social Sciences,* August 2013

Morgan, Rosemarie 'Mothering the Text: Hardy's Maternal Abode' in Mallett and Draper, pp.33-48

Morgan, Rosemarie *Women and Sexuality in the novels of Thomas Hardy* Routledge 1988

Morgan, Rosemarie (ed) *Student Companion to Thomas Hardy*, Greenwood Press, 2006

Mottram, Stephen 'Hardy, Emma and the Giffords, a Reappraisal' *The Hardy Society Journal* Volume 8, No 1, Spring 2012

Newman, Flower *Just as it Happened,* Cassell, London, 1951

Nicholson, Christopher *Winter,* Fourth Estate, 2014

Norman, Andrew *Thomas Hardy: Behind the Mask* The History Press, 2011

Norman, Andrew *Thomas Hardy Bockhampton and Beyond*, Halsgrove, 2017

Oliphant, Margaret 'The Anti-Marriage League', *Blackwood's Magazine*, January 1896

Pinion, F B *Thomas Hardy: His Life and Friends*, Macmillan, 1992

Pinion, F B *Hardy the Writer: Surveys and Assessments,* Palgrave Macmillan, 1990

Pite, Ralph *Thomas Hardy: The Guarded Life,* Picador, London, 2006

Powys, Llewelyn *Recollections of Thomas Hardy* (unpaginated)

Purdy, Richard (October 1944). 'Thomas Hardy And Florence Henniker: The Writing Of "The Spectre Of The Real"' *Colby Library Quarterly*, series 1, no.8: 122–6

Purdy, Richard Little and Millgate, Michael (ed) *The Collected Letters of Thomas Hardy* Volume I – VII, Clarendon Press, Oxford, 1978–1988

Rimmer, Mary 'History and the Bogus Heroine: Gender and Genre in *The Trumpet-Major' The Thomas Hardy Journal*, Autumn, 2010, Vol XXVII Autumn, 2012, pp.70-80

Roberts, Patrick 'Patterns of Relationship in *Desperate Remedies*.' *The Thomas Hardy Journal* 8, 1992, pp.50-57

Sasaki, Toru 'Viewer and Victim in *Desperate Remedies*: Links Between Hardy's Life and His Fiction.' *The Thomas Hardy Journal* 10, 1994, pp.77-86.

St John Butler, Lance (ed) *Thomas Hardy after Fifty Years,* Macmillan, 1977

Seymour-Smith, Martin *Hardy,* Bloomsbury, 1994

Smith, Anne *The Novels of Thomas Hardy,* Vision Press, 1979

Singleton, Jon 'Spaces, Alleys, and other Lacunae: Emma Hardy's Late writings Restored' *The Thomas Hardy Journal,* Autumn, 2015, Vol XXXI pp 48-62

Stubbs, P *Women and Fiction: Feminism and the Novel 1800-1920,* The Harvester Press, 1979

Sylvia, Richard 'Thomas Hardy's *Desperate Remedies*: "All my sin has been because I love you so."' *Colby Quarterly,* Volume 35, Issue 2, June, 1999

Taylor, Richard *The Neglected Hardy: Thomas Hardy's Lesser Novels,* London, Macmillan, 1982.

Teller, Joseph R 'Bathsheba as Hardy's Palimpsest: The Effacement and revision of Feminine Identity in *Far From the Madding Crowd' Thomas Hardy Journal,* Volume XXIII, Autumn, 2007, pp.98-116

Thomas, Jane *Thomas Hardy and Desire: Conceptions of the Self,* Palgrave Macmillan, 2013

Thwaite, Ann 'My Dear Gosse: The Friendship between Edmund Gosse and Thomas Hardy', *The Thomas Hardy Journal* Vol. XX No. 3 October 2004, p.47

Thorpe, Michael 'His Volume 2: Defending Florence Hardy' *The Hardy Society Journal,* Volume 4, Number 2, Summer, 2008

Tomalin, Claire *Thomas Hardy: The Time-Torn Man,* Penguin, 2007

Weber, Carl J *Hardy of Wessex: His Life and Career,* Routledge, 1945

Weber, Carl J (edited) *'Dearest Emmie' Thomas Hardy's Letters to his First Wife,* Macmillan, London, 1963

Wilkins, Damien *Max Gate,* Victoria University Press, Wellington, 2013

Winslow, Donald J *Thomas Hardy's Sister Kate* ed F.B. Pinion Monograph No.2, *The Thomas Hardy* Society Ltd, 1982

Index

Women Referenced in the Poems

JH = Jemima Hardy
MH = Mary Hardy
EB = Eliza Brown
LH = Louise Harding
EN = Eliza Nicholls
JN = Jane Nicholls
TS = Tryphena Sparks
HP = Helen Paterson (Allingham)
FH = Florence Henniker
AG = Agnes Grove
FD = Florence Dugdale / Hardy
EG = Emma Gifford